Daytripping & Dining

in Southern New England

An eclectic guide to 50 special places and restaurants

Betsy Wittemann and Nancy Webster

Imprint Publications Inc.
20 Isham Road
West Hartford, Conn. 06107

Readers should bear in mind that prices, especially in restaurants, change seasonally and with inflation. Prices quoted in this book were correct at presstime. They are offered as a relative guide, rather than an absolute.

Copyright © 1978 by Betsy Wittemann and Nancy Webster

Library of Congress Catalog No. 78-57197

Published in the United States of America
All rights reserved.
First Edition.

Contents

MASSACHUSETTS

1 Arrowhead, Pittsfield..1
Alice's at Avaloch, Lenox 4

2 Bartholomew's Cobble, Ashley Falls 8
Stagecoach Hill Inn, Sheffield...................................11

3 Historic Deerfield, Deerfield.....................................14
Deerfield Inn, Deerfield..18

4 Laughing Brook, Hampden.......................................21
Salem Cross Inn, West Brookfield............................24

5 Higgins Armory, Worcester......................................27
The Victorian, Whitinsville.......................................30

6 Garden in the Woods, Framingham..........................33
Longfellow's Wayside Inn, Sudbury..........................35

7 Fruitlands Museums, Harvard..................................38
Chez Claude, Acton 41

8 Cape Ann, Rockport and Gloucester.........................44
Old Farm Inn, Pigeon Cove......................................48

9 Isabella Stewart Gardner Museum, Boston 50
Cafe Budapest, Boston...53

10 Museum of the American China Trade, Milton..........56
Joyce Chen, Cambridge..60

11 Yesteryears Museum, Sandwich 63
La Cipollina, Yarmouthport......................................67

RHODE ISLAND

12 Old Slater Mill, Pawtucket.......................................70
Rue de l'Espoir, Providence......................................73

13 Green Animals, Portsmouth.....................................76
The Black Pearl, Newport..79

14 Block Island 82
Custy's, North Kingstown 85

CONNECTICUT

15 Mystic Seaport, Mystic 88
     Harborview, Stonington 92

16 Gillette Castle, Hadlyme 95
     Copper Beech Inn, Ivoryton 98

17 Roseland Cottage, Woodstock 102
     Cumbie's, South Woodstock 106

18 Mark Twain Memorial, Hartford 109
     The Signature, Hartford 113

19 Thimble Islands, Stony Creek 117
     The Little Stone House, Guilford 121

20 Whitlock Farm, Bethany 124
     Poor Lads, New Haven 127

21 Barnum Museum, Bridgeport 130
     Ocean Sea Grill, Bridgeport 134

22 American Indian Archaeological Institute, Washington 136
     Hopkins Inn, New Preston 139

23 Aldrich Museum of Contemporary Art, Ridgefield 142
     Stonehenge, Ridgefield 144

NEARBY NEW YORK

24 Hammond Museum, North Salem 148
     Auberge Maxim, North Salem 151

25 Museum of Cartoon Art, Port Chester 154
     Greenstreet, Greenwich, Conn. 157

Introduction

A Southern New England sampler — of sights to see and tastes to savor. That's this book, for people who like to discover interesting spots to visit and places to eat.

Southern New England is the place for daytrips and dining. Marvelous scenic destinations, relatively short distances and outstanding restaurants encourage people to take to the high road for more than the popular Sunday afternoon drive.

Daytrippers and diners are not necessarily the same people — on the same day. But whether you want to take off for a drive to an especially interesting attraction or to find a restaurant where you can linger over your favorite foods, or both, this book is for you.

It's a book for weekday and Sunday drivers, for families with children, for retirees with time to mosey, for urbanites who want to get out of the city and exurbanites who want to go back, and for travelers who are just passing through (we're sorry for them) but who don't want to miss some of the fine treats the three southern New England states have to offer.

The book works like this: Each of the 25 sections details an interesting place to visit (from a unique doll museum on Cape Cod to beautiful Old Deerfield, from Mark Twain's house in Hartford to a boat cruise through the Thimble Islands). Paired with each attraction is a special restaurant in the vicinity (from Joyce Chen's creation in Cambridge to revered Stonehenge, from a clam shack near Gloucester to Alice's at Avaloch). Each section also includes alternate suggestions, nearly 200 in all, every one worth a visit.

The day trips, written by Betsy Wittemann, are indicated by this symbol ; the restaurants, reviewed by Nancy Webster, are indicated by .

You might just want to go off on the day trip and visit the site about which you've read. Or you might just want to make the trip to have dinner at the restaurant. And it's quite possible to do both on the same day.

Whatever way you want to work it, this book will work for you. It will tell you about places that are favorites of the authors for one reason or another, unusual attractions that are well worth a visit and restaurants about which you'll likely rave.

No other book does what this book does. No other book makes it so easy for you to make a day away a day to remember. So come along with us — and sample these very special places in Southern New England.

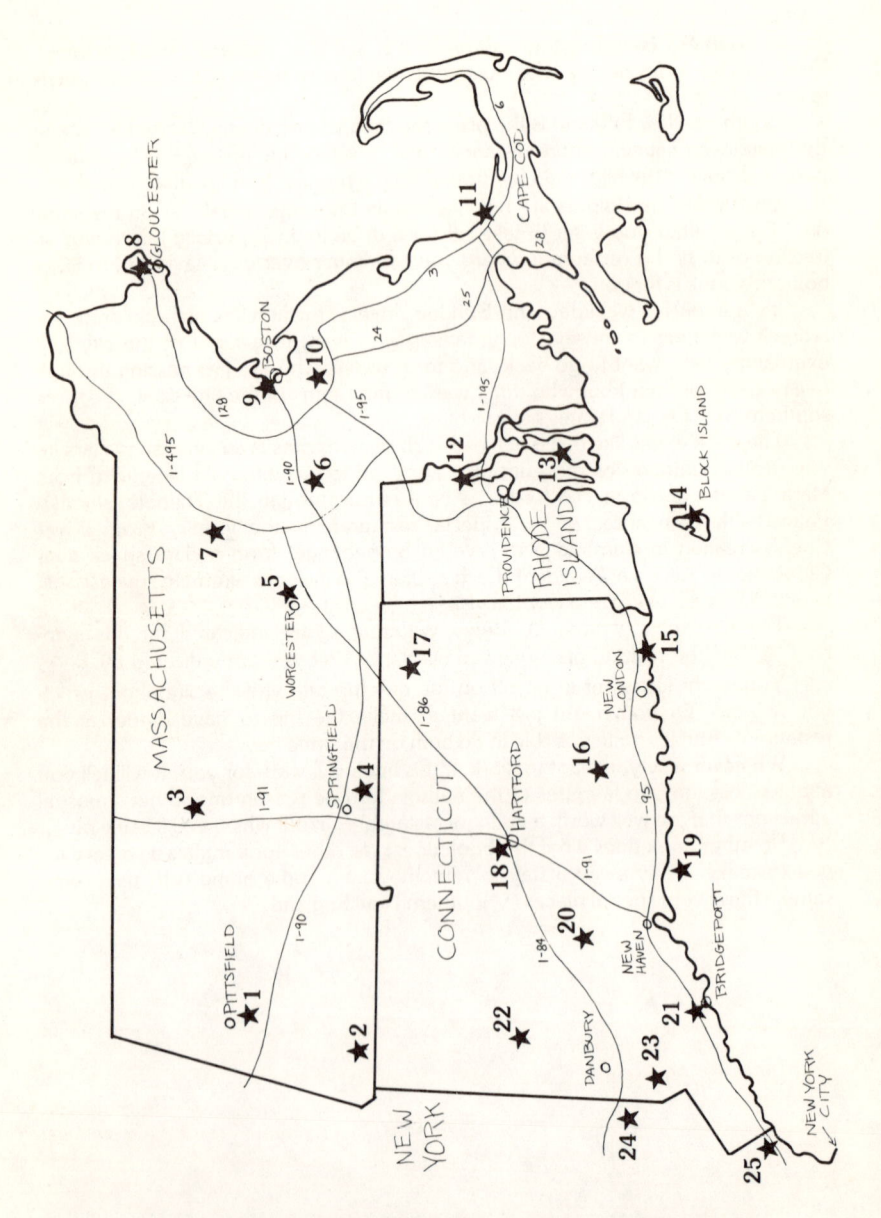

DAYTRIPPING AND DINING
in Southern New England

Daytrip 1

Where Melville Wrote *Moby Dick*
Arrowhead/Pittsfield, Mass.

There are literary sites and literary sites. Just because Hemingway sat in a chair, or Fitzgerald in a bar, does not, in and of itself, mean a thing. If the former penned chapters of *For Whom the Bell Tolls* from that chair, however, or the latter did most of his work on *Gatsby* in the bar, the picture changes.

Arrowhead, Herman Melville's beloved home in the Berkshires of Massachusetts, is a literary site, and a hallowed one at that.

At first it seems a bit surprising. One expects to find Melville writing from an island in the South Seas, or at the very least from a place with a view of the sea.

But up in Pittsfield, far from the scent of sea air, with a view of a mountain instead of an ocean, Melville wrote *Moby Dick*. He wrote it — and rewrote huge portions of it — in a house now 200 years old that he named for the many Indian arrowheads he found on the property. The mountain to the north, in direct line with his second floor study window (when the low clouds so common in those hills have not obscured it) is Greylock, which has, in the wake of Melville's success, been likened to the hump of a whale.

You can decide for yourself when you visit the house, which is remarkably as

1

it was when the author and his family lived there from 1850-63, and which has been opened to the public just recently after having been for years a private home.

Thanks to the Berkshire County Historical Society, which bit the bullet and purchased Arrowhead in 1975, Melville fans, scholars, readers and even "old house" buffs have the opportunity to visit the magnificent old home in one of western New England's loveliest areas.

Melville saw it that way, too. He had strong connections with the Berkshires from the time when he was a little boy, and was sent by his family to spend summers with an uncle at his Pittsfield farm. (That large home, "Broadhall," is now the Country Club of Pittsfield and can be viewed from Route 7).

Melville even taught in the Pittsfield area for a year before he went to sea on the voyages that were to provide the fuel for his most famous works, not just the adventure of the white whale, but for "Typee," "Omoo," and "Billy Budd." And so it wasn't really remarkable that he returned as a young married man in his 30s, already a father, to settle in the hills he had grown to love, and where he thought he could find the right atmosphere for his serious writing.

When he moved into Arrowhead in 1850, it is said he had a good part of the *Moby Dick* manuscript already in hand. But that very first summer, Melville went on a picnic which was to prove an important turning point in his life, and that of his book.

At the picnic he was introduced to the young Nathaniel Hawthorne, who was living in nearby Lenox, and who was already an author of some reputation, as was Melville. The two hit it off immediately and in subsequent weeks and months would often roam the western hills together, or spend long hours in Melville's barn, smoking pipes in the hayloft and talking.

They talked philosophy among other things, and it was Hawthorne who influenced Melville into changing the tone of *Moby Dick* from being just another sea adventure to one with greater psychological and symbolic implications. Critics today hail the book as one of the finest ever written by an American, or indeed in the English language.

The red barn where Hawthorne and Melville spent so many hours in deep philosophical discussion, and where Melville, the "gentleman farmer," milked his cows and fed his horses before he went to his "real" work each day, is also standing and may be visited. The society uses it to mount changing exhibits.

But the house with its magnificent grounds, which housed generations of Melvilles until as recently as 1927, is the real draw. It stands in an impressive state of preservation, much as the author and his family knew it, and where changes had been made, the historical society under the leadership of its young and enthusiastic director, Kathleen L. Brady, is doing its best to return to the original. The piazza along the north side, which was the subject of one of Melville's short stories, was rebuilt just last year.

Another favorite part of the house was the massive central chimney, 12 feet square, which provides for the many fireplaces. Melville loved the whole house, but especially that chimney, and he wrote an amusing short piece about it, "I and My Chimney," in which he told of a running battle he and his wife were having over it. According to the story, Elizabeth Shaw Melville wanted to have the chimney removed so she could have a gracious hallway running from the front door to the back of the house. Melville tells how he daunted her every move.

The author's brother, Allan Melville, who took over the house when Herman's family left in 1863, had quotations from the story inscribed on the exceptionally large fireplace of the keeping room of the old house, which was used as a dining room by the Melvilles. The quotes are still there, quite readable, and you

Location: 780 Holmes Rd., Pittsfield, just south of the city, east off Route 7.

Open: June 1 to October 31. Monday through Saturday, 10 a.m. to 5 p.m.; Sundays, 1 to 5.

Admission: $1 adults; 50 cents students through university age.

Telephone: (413) 442-1793.

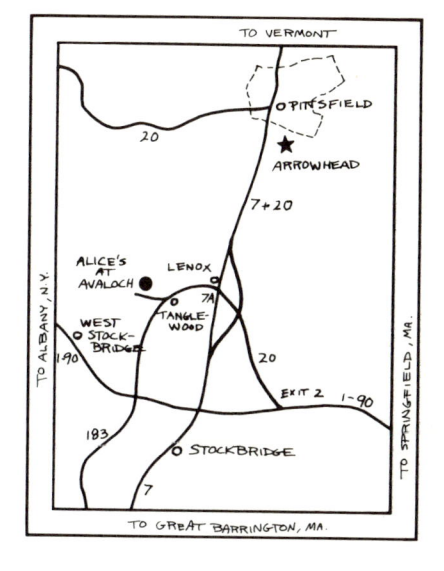

will see them when you start your guided tour (included with the price of admission.)

In this room, too, are the only Melville family pieces owned so far by the historical society. There are a tiny toy chest which had been Frances Melville's (the author's daughter) and some fine pieces of Chinese dinnerware. Genealogical charts of the family, family portraits and photographs mounted on the walls will help you to put things into perspective.

While the society has no other family pieces with which to furnish the home, it has chosen to do so with some fine Berkshire county pieces and collectors or furniture enthusiasts will enjoy that aspect of the trip. Don't miss the Chippendale chairs in the north parlor, which is set up as a dining room today.

For admirers of Melville, the second-floor study is the jewel of the house. A simple but pleasant room, it offered Melville the view of Greylock which he found so inspiring before him, and a warming fire at his back. There, with only a candle to light his work and a quill pen in hand, he wrote compulsively, so engrossed that his wife often had to bang loudly at the door several times before she roused him for a meal.

A candle, a quill pen and an inkstand rest today on a table in the center of the room as Melville might have had them. Nearby, in a bookcase to the left of the north window, are copies of all of Melville's works. Seeing them, the visitor is newly impressed with how prolific the man was.

The sheer quantity of Melville's work is even more remarkable when you consider that he did very little after *Moby Dick*.

Stung by the lukewarm reviews the book received by contemporary critics, and even more deeply hurt by the scathing criticism given his subsequent, deeply psychological work, *Pierre*, Melville all but gave up writing, returned to New York, and went to work in a customs house.

Melville's genius wasn't appreciated until long after he was dead, and then a regular Melville mania erupted, fired by the publication of Raymond Weaver's biography, *Herman Melville: Mariner and Mystic*, in 1921.

For some results of that mania, don't leave Pittsfield before visiting the

3

Melville room at the Berkshire Athenaeum, the public library, at 1 Wendell Avenue in Pittsfield's center. In the Herman Melville Memorial Room are many items you may have expected to see in the author's home and didn't.

The room, established in 1953 by Dr. Henry A. Murray of Harvard, contains furniture and framed pictures from Melville's home. The secretary from his New York apartment, on which he is said to have penned "Billy Budd," which was published posthumously, is among the items. There are also manuscript correspondence of Melville and other family members, first editions of his books, and a case of personal items, such as a pipe he bought on a trip to Europe or a coin touched with lava flow from Mt. Vesuvius.

Dennis J. Lesieur, the amiable local history librarian who opens the room to visitors and Melville scholars, points out that among the most valuable items from a research point of view are the books from Melville's own library, many of them fully annotated by the author. The room is open from 9 a.m. to 5 p.m. Monday through Saturday.

Also in the Area

Hancock Shaker Village, Hancock, Mass. (413) 443-0188. A few miles west of Pittsfield on Route 20 is this beautifully restored Shaker settlement dating from 1790. The famous Shaker round stone barn is open to the public as are most of the other buildings, which total 18 in all. A five-story brick dwelling house with 1830 kitchen in basement is of particular interest; also shops where Shakers made chairs, brooms, baskets, and the like. The herb garden is lovely. A fine, small shop sells Shaker items, and Shaker chairs and tables furnish the small but adequate snack bar. Picnicking is also possible. Annual Shaker Kitchen Festival in August with tastings of Shaker foods is very popular. Melville was known to have visited the Shaker village. Open June 1 to October 31, seven days a week, 9:30 a.m. to 4:30 p.m. Admission: $3 adults; $2.50 students and senior citizens; $1 children.

Tanglewood, (413) 637-1600. The Summer home of the Boston Symphony Orchestra in nearby Lenox offers weekend concerts in July and August. If you don't have reserved seats, spreading a blanket on the grass is a popular Sunday afternoon pastime.

Dining 1

Alice's at Avaloch/Lenox, Mass.

Summer or winter, music or skiing — Alice's at Avaloch is in the midst of the attractions of the Berkshires. On one late-autumn day, we could see Catamount ski area across Stockbridge Bowl beyond Tanglewood's Music Shed as we enjoyed a Sunday brunch in the glass-enclosed Gazebo Room, in the middle of an early-season snowstorm.

Tanglewood, of course, is the main draw for Alice's new restaurant, an Alice's gone classy from the days of Arlo Guthrie and the original Alice's Restaurant in West Stockbridge, and the later Alice's Takeout beside the Housatonic River, which became the second Alice's Restaurant.

To the disappointment of some of her legion of fans who loved the rustic Alice's with the homey atmosphere, Alice, fed up with her running battle with the Stockbridge town fathers over liquor restrictions and lack of music, took her business to Lenox and finally settled into more traditional quarters in Avaloch, the old inn almost opposite Tanglewood's main gate on a picturesque hillside west of town.

No restaurant-resort could be closer to the summer home of the Boston Symphony, which assures it a captive audience during the season. But it is also a draw in the winter for cross-country and downhill skiers, serving the western Berkshires area from Butternut Basin to Jiminy Peak.

And you just might see Alice, the legend in her own time, whose creative food and menus are justly famed as is the restaurant sung about by Arlo. She lives upstairs and was on the scene at 1:30 a.m. Sunday and again at 7:30 a.m., our denim-clad waitress informed us, but was taking a break during the mid-afternoon lull when we were there.

Only the Gazebo Room was open Sunday afternoon and only the luncheon menu, featuring omelets, was available, but out of that we ordered up enough for quite a feast and a fair sampling of Alice's repertoire. Even then, many groups were enjoying a late lunch (or early supper) and the cozy bar with its fireplace blazing and moose heads studding the wall had attracted a large group of work-booted and down-vested regulars, enjoying some rather loud music from a country band.

In the Gazebo, with its high ceiling outlined with ribs of 198 (our sons counted them) 15-watt bulbs carousel style, the music is taped and classical. The decor is plain but functional — white draperies and tablecloths, bare wooden floor, lots of plants, and the only colorful accents are the bright yellow paper placemats. Nothing much detracts from the spectacular view, which is as it should be.

Our party of four sampled three wonderful appetizers, including stuffed grape leaves (with rice and mint). A large and savory cold eggplant salad was studded with onion and tomato, and flavored with olive oil. A hearty and thick meat and cabbage borscht, dotted with sour cream, was better than I've had at the Russian Tea Room in New York, although not as hot as it might have been.

Plain omelets are $1.65 with 16 additions priced from 35 cents to $1.10 for create-your-own masterpieces, including mushrooms, ratatouille, Hollandaise sauce, sausage and shrimp. Three eggs are used for each omelet, and they are immense.

We sampled three — Benedict, with ham, asparagus and Hollandaise for $3.25; super vegetarian, with tomatoes, onions, mushrooms, peppers and herbs, $3.80, and shrimp special, with shrimps, artichoke hearts and Hollandaise, $3.50.

All were chock full of fillings, with everything as fresh as could be. They were served with sensational light biscuits and sweet butter. We also had a basket of sesame-studded bread sticks, and homemade bread, the white crusty and chewy and the brown studded with caraway seeds. One member of the party tried the giant fresh ground hamburger for $2.25 that came with toast and pronounced it fine.

We also sampled a Bloody Mary ($1.75) that unfortunately seemed to be made with V-8 juice, and had a bottle of Soave for $4.75, served in place of the Chateau de Hartes Entre Deux Mers we ordered and would have preferred, although the Soave was quite acceptable.

Three fantastic desserts ($1.50 to $1.75) topped off our feast — chocolate whiskey cake, black in color and as rich as fudge; chocolate almond icebox cake with Triple Sec, a delightfully sweet and light confection, and a warm and crunchy French apple crumb cake. Apple trees grow just outside the gazebo windows and Alice has been known to pick the apples herself for the desserts.

Alice's good strong coffee (50 cents) topped this fine afternoon meal. Among many special coffees are Ethiopian Djimma and French roast for $1.50, while a selection of teas (mint, camomile, rose hip, orange and spice) is 75 cents.

Alice's main dining room, open at night and during the busier seasons for lunch, is stunning, done in pure white (chairs, cloths, draperies) with a black and white carpet underfoot. Each table has a glassed candle and three fresh red roses; a truly sophisticated atmosphere results.

The evening menu is international and changes often. A huge selection of entrees ranges in price from $6.95 to $11.95, and includes Italian, French, Russian and Chinese specialties (Szechuan stir-fried Chinese vegetables are served four ways, for example). Everything is cooked to order, and there are usually a couple of vegetarian dishes.

The old estate, once called "The Orchard" by Nathaniel Hawthorne, now has a 20-room motel. Rates change four times a year (much more expensive in the summer) and packages such as wine-tasting weekends and ski weekends are available.

Alice's at Avaloch, Lenox, Mass. 01240. Tel. (414) 637-0897. Route 183 opposite Main Gate at Tanglewood, two miles west of Lenox center. Reservations necessary for dinner, and for lunch during season (Memorial Day through October foliage). Major credit cards. Dinner, 6 to 10 p.m. Monday to Friday, 5:30 to 10 p.m. Saturday and Sunday. Breakfast and lunch served Saturday and Sunday, 8 a.m. to 5 p.m. In season, open 8 a.m. to midnight, seven days a week.

Also in the Area

J. Perspico Factor, 25 Church St., Lenox, Mass. (413) 637-2996. Continental and creative cooking are available here, with such items as mushroom caps stuffed with crabmeat, paella and the house specialty, the Tanglewood, a brochette of veal, lamb, shrimp, scallops, mushroom and onion, served with cucumber and mint sauce on saffron rice. It's open during the season until 1 a.m. seven days a week for brunch, dinner, after-concert suppers and snacks. Beer and wine.

Blantyre Castle, Route 20 and East Street, Lenox, Mass. (413) 637-0475. Dine in the only Scottish castle in Berkshire County, a baronial edifice well worth seeing, built as a "summer cottage" in 1902 for a millionaire in the turpentine business as an authentic replica of the Hall of Blantyre in Scotland. A hand-carved mantel and staircase of black oak, high-beamed ceilings, crystal chandeliers and spacious public rooms add to the luxurious feeling. Ask to view the fabulous murals of dowagers, maids and butlers in the downstairs disco which is open weekends and for special parties. Dinner entrees from $5.95 to $9.95 include lots of beef and seafood dishes (New England scallop and lobster pie is $8.50) and you can have Scotch egg sauce on your poached salmon steak ($6.95). Scottish sherried trifle, 95 cents, is a good bet for dessert. Lunch, noon to 2:30 p.m. Monday to Saturday, dinner 5 to 10 p.m. Monday to Saturday, noon to 9 p.m. Sunday.

Gourmet East, Route 2 (Main Street), Williamstown, Mass. (413) 458-9396. Szechuan, Mandarin and Shanghai cuisine are featured, including pork with scallions, shrimp in fish sauce, hot and sour soup. Dinners are $3 up and it's open seven days.

Wheatleigh, Wheatleigh Park, Lenox, Mass. (413) 637-0610. An 1894 Italian palazzo offers international cuisine, serving lunch, dinner and cocktails on the terrace. Closed Tuesday.

La Cocina, 140 Wahconah St., Pittsfield, Mass. (413) 499-4027. Home-style Mexican cooking is offered in an informal setting, with chili relleno, fish with orange sauce, boneless breast of chicken with Mexican rice. Nightly entertainment. Complete dinners from $4. BYOB. Closed Monday.

Daytrip 2

Hiking by the Housatonic
Bartholomew's Cobble/Ashley Falls, Mass.

So what is a cobble? That's the first question you'll ask and it's not likely you'll find the answer in your standard Webster's. In this case it's a local word (western Massachusetts) referring to a rocky outcrop, here the two scenic knolls of mingled marble and quartzite which rise to 100 feet above the Housatonic River which snakes its way south toward Long Island Sound.

Bartholomew, in answer to the second question, was George Bartholomew, who owned the property and farmed it back in the late 1800s, and it's kept his name ever since. The Trustees of Reservations, a private, non-profit Massachusetts corporation which acts as custodian for some 64 natural and historic areas in the Bay State, acquired the area in 1946. And I'm glad they didn't change the name to something pompous.

Bartholomew's Cobble is 200 acres of rock garden where no fewer than 500 species of wildflowers, 100 species of trees, shrubs and vines, and a respectable 40 species of ferns alone have been catalogued. That's a remarkable concentration of flora for the size of the area and in 1971 the Department of the Interior's National Park Service agreed, designating the place a National Natural Landmark (a significant illustration of America's natural history).

To enjoy Bartholomew's Cobble it isn't necessary to count wildflowers or jot down birds' names, although that's certainly a pleasurable undertaking for some. The fact is nature lovers of all persuasions can be happy here, hiking the six trails, exploring the small but interesting museum, picnicking in the meadows, viewing the landscape. Don't despair if you pass by in winter; snowshoeing and cross-country skiing are encouraged, although the museum shuts down from October to April.

The man who told me about Bartholomew's Cobble was a birdwatcher with a house on one of the Thimble Islands (see Connecticut section). He was so enthusiastic that I called up one of my friends, a dear young woman who loves wildflowers, and the two of us left our toddlers with sitters and headed for the hills.

Like most of the visitors to the cobble, we parked our car at the lot off Weatogue Road and hiked the short way up a hill to the museum, named for the late S. Waldo Bailey, the first naturalist stationed at the cobble. It makes a good starting point (except on Mondays and Tuesdays when it is closed) because you can get your own hiking map there for a few cents.

At the museum, on the advice of the current warden-naturalist, we picked up an interpretive booklet for Ledges Trail and set off, climbing first to the top of one of those knolls to enjoy a breathtaking view of the Berkshire hills and the Housatonic River Valley.

Because we were there in mid-August, my friend was determined to find some lobelia, in bloom at that time of year. We also wanted to walk along the river, which is the path taken by that trail. Ledges Trail is quite dramatic, leading first down through the dark stillness of a pine forest, then along the river on a

Location: Off Route 7A in Ashley Falls, Mass., in the state's southwestern corner. The parking lot for Bartholomew's Cobble is located on Weatogue Road; the Colonel Ashley House is nearby on Cooper Hill Road. Watch for signs.

Open: Bartholomew's Cobble Museum, Wednesday through Sunday, April 15 to October 15, 9 a.m. to 5 p.m. Cobble remains open year-round for hiking, cross-country skiing, snowshoeing, depending on the season. Col. Ashley House opens weekends from Memorial Day to late June and Labor Day to Columbus Day, 1 to 5 p.m. During the summer it is open Wednesday through Sunday, 1 to 5 p.m.

Admission: Cobble or house: $1 adults; 25 cents children.

Special Events: Annually Cobble Day is held on a Saturday in late June at both sites with a variety of activities planned, including hay rides, guided nature walks. Phone ahead for exact date.

Picnicking: At the cobble.

Telephone: (413) 229-8600.

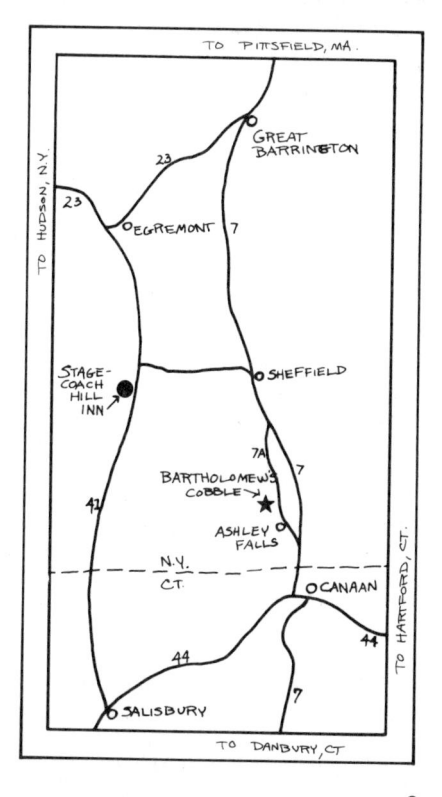

narrow ledge just above the water, then up again over the rocks of the cobble and eventually out into the meadow near the parking area.

On the way we were pleased by the many unusual ferns, some with no more than the most precarious hold in the crevice of a rock ledge. One naturalist has declared that the cobble contains "possibly the largest natural concentration of ferns in the U.S.A."

But the "fern" about which botanists are inclined to go a little dotty is the rare "Scott's spleenwort," which has been found no fewer than three times on the cobble's limestone ledges. The first was in 1906 when a Connecticut woman spotted one. In 1948 another was found by naturalist Bailey. Then in 1963 a third rare spleenwort was discovered by Mr. Bailey, who entrusted the secret of its location to another naturalist before he died. A hybrid between ebony spleenwort and walking fern, it requires exactly the right conditions for the mingling of their spores. According to records kept by the Trustees of Reservations, the rare spleenwort was still around in 1975, but I don't know where it is. Maybe you can find it.

For our part, we found our lobelia eventually — a blue one instead of the more usual red variety — and saw, too, hundreds of pretty yellow "touch-me-nots." Columbine is rampant and we imagined how lovely it must be in the spring.

The booklet for the trail recommends April for flower freaks, in particular those who are happy when they see hepatica. The advice is to wait for a warm, sunny day in the middle of the month, and visit Stop No. 11 (you need the interpretive booklet for this) where we read that "the slope overlooking the river will be aglow with a carpet of round-lobed hepatica." The concentration is noteworthy for the variety of colors, white, light blue, deep blue and lavender all represented.

In summer, from mid-June through August, the rocky ledges of the trail are decorated with the pale blue of harebell; in June and July, visitors also find the four-leafed milkweed in blossom. In the fall no fewer than 17 species of goldenrod are to be found — hayfever sufferers, beware. If you have your Peterson's wildflower guide along, you'll probably recognize scores of others.

All over the cobble you can rest on rustic benches, thoughtfully provided by the trustees. Picnicking is encouraged and highly recommended but you won't find any tables, so spread your cloth in the meadow or on a hilltop and drink in a goodly portion of nature with your repast.

The Ledges Trail takes only 45 minutes to an hour to walk so you may very well want to strike off in another direction after lunch. One that intrigued us, but that we didn't pursue, was Craggy Knoll Trail, with its Chinquapin Oak Overlook.

The reason we didn't do more hiking was because we had another plan: In the afternoon we visited the Colonel Ashley House, just down the road from the cobble, and the oldest house in this part of western Massachusetts (1732). It is also maintained by the Trustees of Reservations.

The house was the home of Col. John Ashley, a lawyer, surveyor and town official. Because of his position, our guide pointed out that the structure is somewhat elaborate for its day. In the house's lovely meeting room on the second floor (note the panelling and built-in cupboard), the Sheffield Declaration of Independence was signed three years before the national one. (Sheffield is the next town to the north).

Ashley Falls provides a lovely day trip, with a hike through the Cobble in the morning, a picnic lunch and a tour of the Col. Ashley House. After it all you can settle in for a leisurely dinner nearby if you're inclined.

And if you haven't had your fill of cobbles, there's another you can try: Tyringham Cobble, in the center of Tyringham, some 15 miles northeast of this one.

Also in the Area

Naumkeag, Prospect Hill, Stockbridge, Mass. (413) 298-3239. The 26-room, Norman-style, gabled mansion served as the summer home of Joseph Hodges Choate, the famous attorney who for almost two decades held back the 16th amendment and individual income tax. Choate also served as Ambassador to the Court of St. James. The house, completed in 1886, was designed by the New York architectural firm of McKim, Mead and White, who had also done the Boston Library, Madison Square Garden and the Pennsylvania Station. Stanford White was the designer and builder. The house, deeded to the Trustees of Reservations in 1958 by Choate's daughter Mabel, is remarkable for its gardens and landscape as well as its interior decoration and antiques. Open from 10 a.m. to 5 p.m. Tuesday through Sunday from last Tuesday in June to Labor Day. From Labor Day to Columbus Day, open weekends only, 10 to 5 on Saturdays and 11 to 4 Sundays. Admission: Adults $2, house and gardens; $1.50 house alone; $1 gardens alone. Children 6-12, 50 cents.

Dining 2

Stagecoach Hill Inn/Sheffield, Mass.

When driving through the Berkshires on a cool evening, what could be a more welcoming sight than a cozy English pub? Well, not exactly a pub, but the closest thing to it in these parts. The Stagecoach Hill Inn south of Great Barrington is a happy blend of Scotland, England and America.

Scotland sounds in the pleasant burr of bespectacled Scotty Burns, formerly of Castle-Douglas, the co-owner who greets guests and leads them into the jolly dining room.

England is in the decor — a wonderful dark, paneled bar with a blazing fire in season, uneven floors, real British beer mugs of dimpled glass hanging over the counter, and all the usual pub paraphernalia. You can even get British beer by the pint on draught.

American is the other owner, chef Wilbur Wheeler, whose elegant menu combines the best of British, French and American cooking.

You have to walk through the bar (with a pause in winter to warm your hands by the fire) to get to the dining room, with walls and tablecloths all in rosy red, bare oak floors and lanterns on the wall casting flickering shadows over all. Chintz curtains, portraits of all the "Royals" and old English hunting prints complete the old-fashioned feeling. I dined with Edward, Prince of Wales, and Princess Alexandra staring right at me — high-living Edward would undoubtedly have approved of the food!

A marvelous jellied Madrilene Muscovite, adorned with sour cream and caviar atop a slice of lemon, comes with the dinner, as do tomato or cranberry juice, chilled grapefruit or cantaloupe in season. Soup du jour on the night we dined was a very creditable mulligatawny, thick with vegetables and curry-spiced.

Other appetizers, ranging in price from $1.25 to $2.95, include avocado filled with prawns and Russian dressing, gooseliver and truffle pate, and sliced Genoa salami with oil and vinegar.

The tossed green salad served with the spicy house dressing is fine, as are the warm rolls.

Prices for entrees range from an expensive $6.50 for chopped prime sirloin steak to $11.75 for alderman's carpetbag, a sirloin steak stuffed with six oysters. We enjoyed the escargots Bourguignonne ($8.25) served in a good garlic butter (not in the shells), some lovely veal a l'estragon with very good quality veal, $8.95, and a tasty flaky-crusted steak and kidney pie, $8.25.

Other entrees offered are frogs legs, chicken Eugenie, chicken livers Rumaki, steak au poivre, blackbird pie (game hen), scallops and rainbow trout.

The well-conceived menu is marred by slightly off-putting prose under some of the entrees — such as, under the veal a l'estragon, "lush buttered young veal, simmered to tantalizing fulfillment, with a risque splash of sauterne and a

reckless dash of tarragon." Even Tom Jones might say, "too much!"
A good selection of wines is listed in a suave wine list with all the labels. We enjoyed a smooth Hungarian red, Egri Bikaver, for about $6.

For dessert, delicious apple pie, ice cream and sherbets are served with the price of the meal, and a few others are extra. I just had to try the English sherry trifle and it was fairly good, but not as tasty as British friends of mine make.

On Saturday nights, the entrees change slightly. Roast beef (with Yorkshire pudding, of course) and duckling are added, and several items including the veal are deleted.

The dining room part of the Stagecoach was built in 1829 and the pub dates from the 18th century. It is understandably popular on weekends and reservations are a must then.

Accommodations are also available in a large cottage and chalets in the trees behind the inn. Otis Ridge, Butternut Basin and Catamount ski areas are only a few minutes away, so the inn is attractive to skiers in the winter as well as to Berkshire travelers in the summer.

Stagecoach Hill Inn, Route 41, Sheffield, Mass. Tel. (413) 229-8585. About five miles west of Sheffield center, south on Route 41. Masterchange and Visa accepted. Reservations recommended, especially on weekends. Dinner 6 to 10 p.m. daily, Sunday 5 to 8:30 p.m. Closed Wednesday and in March.

Also in the Area

Sun-Inside Inn, Route 23, Monterey, Mass. (413) 528-3643. A dear little inn where the owners, Mr. and Mrs. Lancome, are French and do all the cooking. Mr. Lancome, a sculptor, displays his work in the living room adjoining the dining room. Dinners including steak chasseur, poulet Grand Vefour, coq au vin and a chateaubriand with a Bearnaise sauce made from scratch (the Lancomes grow their own tarragon, too) start at $3.75, and omelet souffle and gateau Trianon (a frozen brandy cake) are renowned desserts. Beer and wine. Dinner only, 5:30 to 9 p.m., closed Tuesday. Reservations essential September to June.

Under Mountain Inn, Undermountain Road, Route 41, Salisbury, Conn. (203) 435-0242. Just over the Massachusetts line is this handsome Colonial inn and restaurant, serving dinner Wednesday through Sunday, and brunch Friday to Sunday (clam pie is one of the brunch offerings). The 18th century taproom is a marvelously cozy place in which to have a drink. Dinner entrees are $7.95 to $11.95 and we recommend the sweetbreads highly.

Yale Barn, Route 44, East Canaan, Conn. (203) 824-5541. Country dining with an elegant air offers delicious clams linguini, scampi, broiled mushrooms stuffed with crumbs, bacon and sherry and topped with cheese, and popovers at least six inches high and light as a feather. Luncheon is served in the garden room. Open seven days for lunch and dinner, but closed from November to May.

White Hart Inn, Routes 41 and 44, Main Street, Salisbury, Conn. (203) 435-2511. This 1867 inn has a good gift shop. We like the New England taproom for dining. The bread is great here and broiled lamb chops are done just right. Surprisingly, there's classical Chinese cuisine as well as the regular menu, and in the winter, Olive DuBois assembles her famous miniature gingerbread village in the front parlor, and people come from miles around to see it. Lunch, noon to 2 p.m. Monday to Saturday; dinner, 6 to 8:30 p.m. Monday to Saturday, 12:30 to 3 and 5:30 to 8 p.m. (buffet) Sunday.

13

Daytrip 3

Historic Deerfield photo

Shh! The Village is Slumbering
Historic Deerfield/Deerfield, Mass.

Deerfield is quiet. That's the first and lasting impression, and it probably shouldn't be such a surprise, but it always is.

No matter how many times I've been to and through Old Deefield, after the pace of Interstate 91 to the west and the commerce of old Route 5 to the east, I am invariably caught up short by the village itself. For here without a gas station or a supermarket, without so much as a store, really, the New England of our mind's eye and our hearts lives on.

"The Street" (as its main road is simply called) is like no other in the country or the region. Stretching just a mile from north to south, it is flanked by outstanding examples of 18th and 19th century buildings and homes, 12 of which are exquisitely restored and open to the public year 'round.

That's why most people come to Deerfield these days, to visit the homes, drool over the furniture, the ceramics, the silver, the textiles, the construction itself. Some stay for a day or two at the Deerfield Inn so they can see everything (you can't in one day), amble up and down the streets and roads, read or rub gravestones in the burial ground, and dine in the inn's elegant dining room.

Some families come for a different reason, it's true. They arrive in September to bring their sons to the well-known Deerfield Academy, considered one of the finest boys' preparatory schools in the country and made famous in this century by its longtime headmaster, the late Frank L. Boyden.

That, after all, was why the Henry N. Flynts came, and it has made all the difference.

The Flynts, of Greenwich, Connecticut, brought their son to Deerfield in 1936, and stayed on to build Historic Deerfield Inc., which currently administers the 12 public properties (and some private ones) that make up the unique museum.

They didn't start out to do it, exactly. Like a lot of other dreamers, particularly in this part of the country, Mr. Flynt (an attorney in New York at the time) always thought he would like to own a country inn. Headmaster Boyden of Deerfield Academy thought he should own one, too — the Deerfield Inn, to be exact. The inn at that time was open only during the summer months and the headmaster said it was needed year-round to serve the needs of the academy and its visitors.

Well, the Flynts bought the reasoning — and the inn. They hired a manager to run it, true, but it started their involvement in the village. Their first foray into the purchase of antiques was to buy a few things to put in the lobby.

But they liked Deerfield so much they bought themselves a house: An antique saltbox on The Street which they restored in the mid-1940's.

In succeeding years the village became their overriding passion. They bought properties, restored them, and filled them with antiques of all sorts: Furniture, ceramics, textiles, silver, pewter. They had the advice of experts and the means to purchase extraordinarily valuable items. In about 25 years they personally selected and acquired more than 8,000 different objects for Historic Deerfield.

It was an appropriate place. Bypassed by the progress somehow connoted by highways, supermarkets and gasoline stations (none of which the village has), Deerfield was already something of an anachronism when the Flynts discovered it. And it was already conscious of its unusually rich historic heritage, including its settlement in 1669; its devastation by Indian attack during what is known as the Deerfield Massacre of 1704; its resettlement because of its fertile agricultural location in the Connecticut River Valley; its outstanding homes, built by successful, wealthy farmers; its history of Tory and Whig fighting during the Revolution, and finally, its serious attempts to preserve the past which had been started in the 19th century by Deerfielder George Sheldon and his Pocumtuck Valley Memorial Association.

All that, the Flynts had to build on, and build they did. Or rather, rebuild, resituate (the Hall Tavern and Dwight-Barnard house were moved from other locations) and restore. It soon became apparent they had a pretty big hobby on their hands and they'd better do something about it. While the Allen House was their own personal residence in Deerfield, they could, after all, only live in one house. So in 1952, in an upstairs room in their own lovely home, Historic Deerfield was born and set up to protect and continue their efforts.

Houses, a print shop, silver shop, and the tavern have gradually been opened to the public since then, many containing furnishings which belonged to families that had lived in the homes and which were persistently tracked down by the restorers. That effort continues. Most recently, in November 1977, the house in which the Flynts themselves lived, the Allen House, was opened to the public to celebrate the 25th anniversary of the founding.

(Mr. Flynt died in 1970; his wife has been an invalid for several years in Connecticut.)

As Director Donald R. Friary now sees it, the historic area is more or less complete. At least he believes quite strongly that "we have as much as we need and as much as we should handle." As it is, the buildings maintained by the foundation take a full three days to see, and contain 10,000 objects in all.

(Actually Historic Deerfield owns six other houses, three of which have architectural and historic importance. But if they were to open another, says Friary, they'd probably close one of the present ones. Enough is enough).

There is enough at Deerfield to satisfy the most avid collector. While the furniture of Deerfield is well known nationwide and has had a book written about it, other collections which are exceptionally strong are textiles (Mrs. Flynt's personal interest) and ceramics.

"Leading authorities on ceramics come here and are floored," says Friary with conviction.

Something else about Deerfield is special. Its entire collection is always on display. While this makes for a bit of crowding in some rooms of some houses, it means you won't travel all the way from home to view a rare "sunflower chest" in the Ashley house and not find it. At least under ordinary circumstances, "99 per cent" of the collection is always on view.

You can "do" Deerfield in a variety of ways, but you can't in any case see it all in one day. The foundation recommends three houses (and various combination tickets for three are sold), but the director says you can possibly do five in a day "if you really push it." Don't plan to try unless you're visiting off-season (which means not in October, when fully one-fifth of Historic Deerfield's yearly visitors come to enjoy the foliage along with the furniture or on summer weekends which are also likely to be busy.)

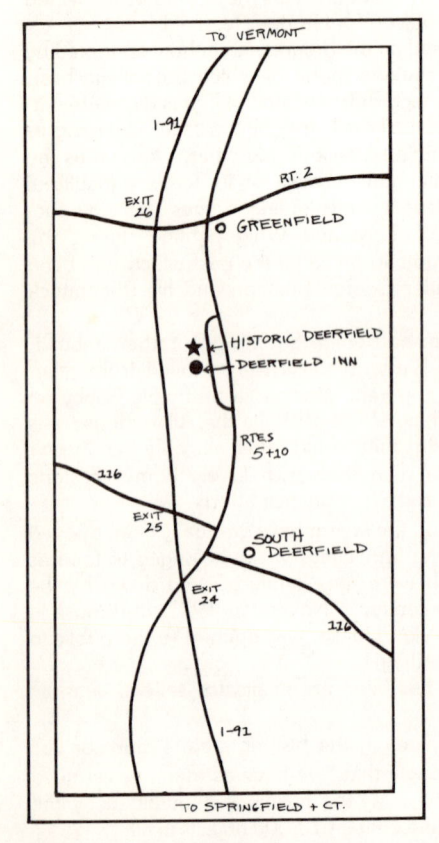

Location: Deerfield, Mass., off Routes 5 and 10, south of Greenfield. I-91 Exit 24 (northbound) or Exit 25 (southbound).

Open: Year-round, 9:30 a.m. to 4:30 p.m. Monday through Saturday, 1 to 4:30 p.m. Sunday. Closed Thanksgiving, Christmas Eve, Christmas Day and New Year's Day.

Admission: Varies, depending on houses you wish to visit. Combination tickets to tour three houses are $3.50; "All of Deerfield" ticket to all 12 houses, valid for one week, $12. Individual house prices range from $1 to $2.50 each. Children pay the same except in the Frary House, 50 cents.

Special Events: Fourth of July. An old-fashioned celebration of Independence Day, including a costume parade down The Street, an oration in the Brick Church, and toasts outside the Frary House tavern.

Tours By Appointment are a new Deerfield offering for groups of 2 to 6 with special interests. The tour is designed specifically for the group, costs $8 per person for a half-day tour with guide; $15 for the full day. Reservations required; may be made by telephone.

Telephone: (413) 773-5402.

Deerfield is lovely in almost any season, including winter, when the Christmas wreaths stay up on the doors for some time after the holiday, and when you're likely to wind up with a personal tour at a leisurely pace.

First stop is always the Hall Tavern, which serves as a visitors' center where you can purchase tickets. If you decide on a combination ticket, the "Deerfield Sampler" is a good one for first-timers. Or you can buy tickets to individual houses, and if an on-site guide is not in the particular house, one will be provided. For obvious reasons no one roams through Deerfield's houses unattended.

Deerfield recommends the Wells-Thorn house if only one can be seen, and I do too. It not only happens to be the oldest house in the historic Deerfield restoration, but is in two parts, one earlier (1717), one later (1751), giving a perfect on-site opportunity to compare.

The older part, built just 13 years after the Deerfield Massacre, has features designed to protect its inhabitants from Indians, such as high windows, and an in-the-house well so residents did not even have to step outside for water. Both front parlors contain lovely period furniture, and upstairs one room is furnished as the law office of Hezekiah Strong, who lived and worked there in the early 1800s.

If you've children in tow, by all means visit the Frary House, which is the only building of the 12 which was not restored by the Flynts, but by Miss C. Alice Baker, a cousin of the indomitable George Sheldon, and a character in her own right. The Frary House has no fewer than 14 rooms and 11 fireplaces, including a ballroom on the south side, the half of the house which was used as a tavern. My children haven't forgotten climbing up to the fiddler's balcony and looking down on that room. But possibly the best was last: A "touch it" room, unique among historic homes, where children are encouraged to explore in their favorite way every item in the room, including 100-year-old candles made from fat. (They feel just as you'd expect — greasy).

If you're a collector, a fine furniture enthusiast, or if you'd just like to get a "feel" for the way the Flynts lived during their years in Deerfield, go to the Allen House, which is individually priced at $2.50 but well worth it. Here is a treasure trove of furniture, much of it 18th century Connecticut Valley pieces in which Deerfield excels, and you will be open-mouthed when you've finished. The Rev. Jonathan Ashley House is another house for leaving you "mouth agape." Its front parlor with matching shell cupboards is, according to some authorities, one of the most beautiful rooms in America. The Rev. Mr. Ashley was an aggressive preacher and militant Tory and the stories about him are almost as much fun as the house.

You can find sustenance during all this walking and seeing at the Deerfield Inn or in good weather you can picnic at tables behind the Hall Tavern. Free daily presentations of a slide show are a good orientation to the entire town and help put the pieces together; inquire at the Hall Tavern.

Deerfield is one of my favorite places because it's done so well, remains so uncommercial (no advertising, for one thing), and because it genuinely succeeds at what so many have attempted: Preserving the past. I've never forgotten the words of one elderly lady, spoken to her companion late one summer afternoon in Deerfield. "It's just a privilege to be here," she said. And so it is.

Also in the Area

Memorial Hall, the museum of the Pocumtuck Valley Memorial Association, Memorial Street, Deerfield. (413) 773-8929. George Sheldon, a Deerfield native (1818-1916) who was one of the first advocates of historic preservation in the country, formed the PVMA and in 1880 opened the first permanent period room in America, a kitchen which may still be seen in Memorial Hall. The hall has lots of other memorabilia, is open mid-April to mid-November from 9:30 a.m. to 5 p.m. daily and on Sundays from 1:30 to 5 p.m. Adults $1.50; children 6-12, 50 cents; students $1.

Northfield Mountain Recreation Area, Route 63, Northfield, (413) 659-3713. Northeast Utilities maintains a large recreation area here, featuring boat rides on the Connecticut River in the summer and cross-country skiing and snowshoeing (with rental equipment) in the winter; also guided nature walks and special programs. The 90-minute boat ride in the summer includes a history of the river on its six mile trip south. Adults $2.50; children $1.25. Usually starts in June, but call ahead because a new boat was to be purchased. Cross-country skiing is on 25 miles of groomed trails. Price to use trails alone (with your own equipment) is $2 adults; $1 children. Varied rentals. Picnicking available (hibachis provided) in the summer.

Dining 3

Deerfield Inn/Deerfield, Mass.

It's hard to imagine anyone raising his voice, shrieking with laughter, or dropping his cutlery at the Deerfield Inn — the atmosphere is simply too refined for anything more than a discreet murmer.

Seemingly light years away from busy I-91 barely a mile away, the serenely elegant dining room of the inn, built in 1884 and serving the public continuously since then, is an oasis of graciousness in a bustling world.

With its faded (but not shabby) oriental rugs, crystal chandeliers, silver candelabra on the polished mahogany and walnut tables, reproduction Chippendale and Duncan Phyfe chairs, delicate wallpaper and many antiques from the private collection of former owners, Mr. and Mrs. Henry Flynt, the spacious dining room seems like that of a private club.

Adding to the club atmosphere is the clientele, which in the fall, winter and spring seems to consist of preparatory school boys and their well-heeled parents.

A few skiers in the winter find their way to the inn, and though you might think you'd need black ties and long dresses to dine here, you really don't have to be formally attired at all, according to the manager.

The menu, too, is quite dignified, with a choice of eight entrees and a couple of specials of the day. They range in price from $5.95 to $8.95 and include salad, vegetable, potato and beverage.

With drinks (the Bloody Mary was particularly spicy and good) came cottage cheese with chives, a mixed cheese spread (the chef's secret recipe) and packets of crackers. Later came a basket of divine hot blueberry muffins and tiny hot popovers, just right for a New England inn. All breads and pastries are baked on the premises.

Among the appetizers, escargots Elizabeth ($2.95) sounds particularly appealing; snails are stuffed in mushroom caps with garlic butter. Also offered are scampi for $2.95, prosciutto with melon, $2.50, and fresh fruit cup for 95 cents.

Cold cucumber soup (95 cents) is a refreshing cup of diced crisp cucumber in a thick and dilled sour cream base, served icy cold and enhanced by a dash from the huge pepper grinder. Soup of the day (70 cents), beef with vegetables, was thick with vegetables in a hearty rich stock.

Wines are reasonable, with Chablis $4.80, Soave $5, a white Argentinian wine for $5.25, Medoc $6, Muscadet $6.25, Johannesberg Riesling $8.75, and Cote de Beaune Villages, one of the most expensive at $13.80. We tried the house wine — a bottle of 1970 Bordeaux, Chateau La Rose Reneve, for $4.50 — which was fine. It was a distinctive touch for a house wine not to be served in a carafe.

The house salad is crisp mixed greens with cucumber, olives, onion rings and tomatoes, served on pretty glass plates with a choice of dressings. The blue cheese was thick with cheese, and the Deerfield Inn dressing, a creamy type seasoned with curry, was particularly good.

Venison steak ($7.95) and lobster saute were the specials of the night — the venison a marvelously tender and not a bit gamey dish, with an excellent sauce. Broiled Boston scrod, $5.95, done simply with a dusting of crumbs and broiled in butter, was impeccable, and the roast duckling ($8.50) with a cranberry-currant sauce was delicious.

My veal birds, $8.50, rolled with prosciutto ham, topped with Fontina cheese and seasoned with thyme, made an excellent and substantial dish. All entrees were served with baked or au gratin potatoes, and green beans with almonds.

Other entrees are trout amandine, shrimp with mushrooms, chicken cordon bleu, double-broiled lamb chops and sirloin steaks. New entrees were due to be added when a new menu was printed.

At noon the menu is more informal, with sandwiches from $1.95 to $2.50 and spinach and mushroom salad and chef's salad, $1.95 and $2.75 respectively. Eggs Benedict is $3.25 and omelets $2.95.

If you want a really light lunch, you can have soup and sandwiches in the cozy wood-panelled taproom just off the dining room, where many of the guides for Historic Deerfield eat in winter when the snack bar, open from the end of April until cold weather comes, is closed. At the snack bar and on the outdoor terrace, you can get hot dogs, hamburgers, french fries and such.

The inn also has 12 attractive guest rooms, each with private bath and renting for $28 to $30 a night. A lobby and parlor also add to the old-inn ambience.

Dining at the Deerfield Inn is a distinctive experience, with the tables set formally with English china in an old-fashioned Pink Colonial pattern, pewter cutlery, crystal goblets and wine glasses as well as crystal salt and pepper shakers, candles in huge silver candlesticks and flowers in season or, in the winter, small pots of poinsettias.

And to add a further genteel note, when the bill arrives, the shock is softened with foil-wrapped chocolate mints on top!

Deerfield Inn, Deerfield, Mass. Tel. (413) 774-3147. North end of Village Street, one block west of Route 5. Reservations recommended on weekends. Mastercharge and Visa. Luncheon, noon to 2 p.m. Monday to Saturday, to 3 p.m. Sunday. Dinner, 6 to 9 p.m. Monday to Saturday, 5 to 8 p.m. Sunday. Tea served 4 to 5 p.m. in the Beehive Parlor.

Also in the Area

Beardsley's, 140 Main St., Northampton, Mass. (413) 586-2699. Dedicated to Aubrey Beardsley, the father of Art Nouveau, is this marvelous small cafe, where the chef is a retired New York City policeman and the cuisine at night is classic French, among the best in New England. Fresh fish of the day is broiled with herb butter, white wine and lemon juice. There are many daily specials, and you can call and order ahead practically anything you'd like — lobster, rack of lamb, quail, pheasant, squab, sweetbreads and kidneys are suggestions. Quiche du jour and the pate du chef are $1.95, among the appetizers, and soups are made daily from kitchen stocks. Entrees from $7.50 to $10.95 include shrimp served on a bed of ratatouille, duckling with a brandied fruit sauce, chicken poached with a hot curry sauce and filet au poivre. At lunch, there's a fine selection of omelets ($2.25 to $2.75), salads (spinach salad is $1.95), sandwiches ($1.75 to $2.75) and homemade desserts. There's a friendly atmosphere here, and the management says that Beardsley's is as informal or formal as you care to make it. Lunch, 11:30 a.m. to 2:30 p.m. Monday to Saturday; dinner, 5:30 to 10 p.m. Tuesday to Saturday. Sunday brunch is 10:30 a.m. to 2 p.m. and dinner 6 to 9 p.m. Closed Monday night.

Goten of Japan, Route 116, Sunderland, Mass. (413) 665-3628. In this nicely landscaped restaurant, all the cooking is done on your grill-table, Teppan style. Watch the chef cut, chop, cook and flip the steak, chicken, shrimp and scallops. Complete dinners from $6.50 to $9 include soup, salad, rice and green tea. All tables seat eight, and Goten has another branch in Hyannis, Mass. Open seven days.

Jack August's House of Seafoods, 5 Bridge St. (Route 9), Northampton, Mass. (413) 584-1197. This is the original, with nothing but seafood, and there's a take-out counter. Recommended by Holiday Magazine. Closed Monday, and closes at 7:30 p.m. weeknights, 8:30 Friday and Saturday.

Hahjee's Place, Route 9, Hadley, Mass. (413) 584-9797. A gourmet Persian restaurant featuring vegetarian dishes, lamb and crepes. Brunch is served Friday to Sunday and dinner every night, entrees from $2.50.

Daytrip 4

Laughing Brook photo

A Place for Peter Rabbit
Laughing Brook/Hampden, Mass.

Jimmy Skunk, Billy Possum, Prickly Porky Porcupine, Blacky Crow, Reddy Fox and Peter Rabbit — they're all there. And there couldn't be a more perfect spot than the small outdoor zoo on the grounds of the late Thornton W. Burgess's home in Hampden, Mass. — the very place where the lovable author of nature stories brought the little animals of the woods to life in his books.

Besides visiting the small zoo, with its cages tucked into the woods near Laughing Brook, after which the place is named, you can hike over some four miles of marked trails, visit the family of geese at Smiling Pool, stop by the nature center or the live animal center with changing exhibits and displays and a snake or two, and view the studio where Burgess wrote. If you're there in the winter, you're welcome to snowshoe or cross-country ski. For the blind or visually handicapped, there is the Crooked Little Path, a "touch and see trail" with guiderope, signs in braille and animals along the way (owls, an eagle, white-tailed deer). It's a good lesson for sighted children to go through blindfolded.

Burgess was a Bay Stater by birth (born in Sandwich, Mass.) but it was at the little Cape Cod house on Hampden's Main Street that he wrote most of the 75 books that have become famous with generations of children. His column was syndicated for years nationwide in newspapers, including the old Herald-Tribune, and adults might remember him from that contact.

Burgess bought the 18th century house in 1928 as a summer home (he was

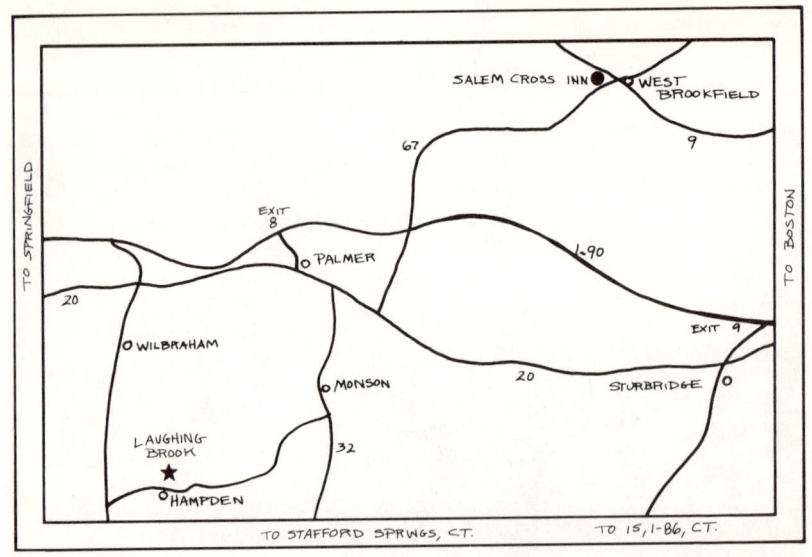

Location: 789 Main St., Hampden, Mass. Reached from Route 83 (west of Hampden) or Route 32 (east of Hampden.) Via Massachusetts Turnpike, take Exit 8, go south on Route 32, watch for signs for Hampden, which is about 6½ miles west of Monson, Mass.

Open: Year-round, 10 a.m. to 5 p.m. Tuesday through Sunday. Closed Mondays except holidays. Closed Thanksgiving, Christmas, New Year's Day.

Admission: $1.50 adults; 50 cents children. Free to Massachusetts Audubon Society members. 50 cents extra to tour Thornton Burgess's house.

Special Events: Harvest Day, Saturday in the Fall; winter festival in February.

Telephone: (413) 566-3571.

living in nearby Springfield at the time) but soon moved out to Hampden year-round, finding the ambience of the woods and streams conducive to his writing.

Here in the quiet of the Massachusetts countryside, Burgess wrote the marvelous "Mother West Wind stories" which have become children's classics. When my husband and I first visited Laughing Brook, our children were not yet old enough to read, but we bought a book anyhow "for the future." Well, the future has come and now my daughter is a genuine Burgess enthusiast, hoping to get all of his books and thoroughly delighted by a recent trip to see again the home of her hero and his animals. (She bought another book with her allowance money).

Burgess's own life wasn't the easiest or most serene, but he managed to maintain the happy outlook and love of nature that characterize the thousands of stories he penned, and that made him a favorite of neighbors in Hampden. Although his father died when he was only a year old, he seems to have spent a happy childhood learning the secrets of nature on Cape Cod which would stand him in good stead in later life.

He didn't plan to write. But he was widowed early in his marriage and left with a young son whom he used to delight with a nature story every night at bedtime. When the youngster was sent to visit grandparents in the Midwest for a vacation, the little boy became homesick for his father and the stories, so Burgess began to write a different story each day, which he then mailed to his son. That was the start of a lifetime dedication — and a new occupation.

Burgess died in 1965 at age 91 and there was some scrambling by his friends in town to prevent his house from being sold privately. The Lions Club paid $500 for an option on the property, and was able to interest the Massachusetts Audubon Society in purchasing and maintaining the site. Since then, donations of acreage have enlarged the area to its present substantial size — 260 acres.

And still local friends donate time and effort in memory of the beloved Burgess. If you visit the modest home where he lived, you will see a quilt done by local Girl Scouts and a rug hooked by a woman in Hamilton, in the design of the house, with many of the Burgess characters shown climbing about the picket fence. Story hours by "Mother West Wind" are conducted by a neighbor, Mrs. Polly Philpott, who's always on call when the people at Laughing Brook need her. It's that kind of place.

The staff at Laughing Brook also offers a number of "special days" throughout the year, including a Harvest Day in the Fall, with games, raffles, hayrides and the like; and a winter festival, usually in February, with dogsled races, ice skating and other cold weather events (call or write for complete schedule). In all, the mood at Laughing Brook is very open, friendly, and geared toward maintaining quality programs, primarily for families and children.

After visiting the zoo and the exhibit areas, you will probably want to take off on one or more of the winding trails, named after places in Burgess's books: Green Forest Trail, Striped Chipmunk Trail, Moccasin Trail and so on.

If you want to tour the house where the author lived, you must make a reservation by calling ahead. A guided tour is 50 cents extra per person, and includes the main floor only, furnished as it was when the author was there. It adds a personal note to a visit.

A popular stop is also Mother West Wind's Gift Shop, which has its own snug little building, and where the Thornton Burgess books may be purchased, as well as bird calls, feeders, butterfly nets and other nature-oriented articles.

A quote of Burgess's sums up the experience: "Nature was the first teacher . . . and is still the universal teacher. In the study of nature lies the key to the most successful mental, moral and spiritual development of the child."

Also in the Area

Norcross Wildlife Sanctuary, Wales, Mass. (413) 267-9654. More than 3,000 acres of wooded hills, lakes and streams contain a particular abundance of wildflowers, many of them unusual varieties. Founded in 1939 by the late Arthur D. Norcross of the greeting card family, it was generously endowed by him. Conservation of wildlife and the active practice of conservation for the public is the purpose of the sanctuary. From May until mid-October two-hour guided tours in mini-buses at 10 a.m. and 1 p.m. are offered to the public free (appointments must be made in advance by writing: R.D. 2, Monson, Mass. 01057 or by telephoning). Two small museums are on site; hiking trails in museum area; picnic tables available but no food sold on premises. A wide variety of courses offered throughout the year are free; no fee to visit museum or use trails. Open year-round, Monday through Saturday, 8 a.m. to 5 p.m. Closed Sundays and holidays.

Directions: Route 32 to the Monson-Wales Road; east on Monson-Wales Road to Peck Road; south on Peck Road to visitors' parking area.

Dining 4

The Salem Cross^x Inn

Olde Brookfeild, Maffachufetts

Salem Cross Inn/West Brookfield, Mass.

"He goes not out of his way who journies to a fine inn."

This quote is on the cover of the Salem Cross Inn matchbooks, and is particularly apropos. A bit off the beaten path on the Ware Road in West Brookfield, Mass., this is a real gem among old New England inns.

A good family dining spot on the traveler's way to or from Boston, it proved more reasonable and just as appealing as the famed Publick House in Sturbridge

20 minutes to the southeast, and well deserving of its three-star rating in the Mobil Travel Guide. Its cozy taproom and lounge with entertainment also appeal for a Saturday night out.

The inn's history, ambience and food combine to make it a special treat for diners.

In an area historic in Indian wars, the main house was built around 1720. Interestingly, it has been restored and expanded by a family of Syrian brothers with the name of Salem, all of whom live in the area. One brother, Richard, runs the inn and usually greets guests.

A witch mark, used to protect inhabitants against the evils of witchcraft and found on the front door latch of the main house, gave the inn its name. The door still has its small 18th century glass panes. The original King's Grant of the inn was made to a grandson of Peregrine White, the Pilgrim baby born on the Mayflower in Plymouth Harbor.

The cross, a handsome design, is used as a logo on the large parchment-type menu and also on dessert and wine lists.

The main dining room is rather typical of a good New England inn. An ell off this room, part of the original house, has beautiful walls of wide plank boards, some horizontal and some vertical, and a huge fireplace, which makes it popular in the winter. Two perfectly charming private dining rooms with round tables set with pewter service plates are in the original house.

The ceiling of the main room is low and rough-plastered, with dark wooden beams. On a summer night, fresh zinnias in miniature Mateus-shaped bottles and a candle in a wrought-iron holder brighten every table. The lighting is dim and the large windows reveal, until dark, a panorama of beautiful green lawns, trees and white fences.

Except for a middle Eastern specialty, Homus B'Taheenie, the appetizers are fairly standard, ranging from 50 cents for tomato juice or fresh fruit juice with sherbet, to $2.95 for crab or shrimp cocktail, or escargots on French bread. The homus is a zesty mixture of chick peas, garlic, lemon juice and sesame seeds, topped with chopped onion and served with Syrian pita bread.

Our only complaint about the service was that our cocktails, ordered when we sat down, took more than half an hour and several reminders to arrive, and we first were served all kinds of food, including our appetizers. Apparently the bartender, coping with a wedding reception in another room, got confused.

Crackers and butter were served right away, then a basket of hot rolls and sticky buns, and a relish tray with cottage cheese and three kinds of spicy relishes.

For entrees, broiled scrod ($5.95) was fresh and moist, perfectly done, and served with lemon butter. The excellent baked stuffed scallops ($6.50) were served in a ramekin with plenty of butter and crumbs.

With these we had an herbed pilaf of Mediterranean rice, and a choice of steamed zucchini, peas, sliced tomatoes or boiled onions. Salad was a large bowl of crisp greens with the house dressing, a tart creamy Italian. A waitress went from table to table offering steaming hot ears of corn to anyone with room left to try.

Entrees range from $5.25 to $9.25 (filet mignon) and there are different specials every day. House specialties are pork tenderloin, calves liver and bacon, baked Alaskan crab and baked stuffed filet of sole Ambassador.

A small wine list on every table offers a few popular and reasonable wines. By asking, you may see a large and elaborate list with more than 100 choices, including some extremely expensive vintage wines. We tried a featured special, an estate bottled Chablis Vaillon for $5.50, delightfully dry and light.

Children have a choice of three dinners at $3.50 including soup or juice and dessert or, for those under 10, child's portion of any other dinner for $1 less than regular price. One of ours had seafood Newburg, a special of the day.

Special pie of the day was a mouth-watering Bavarian cream, and the nut roll with claret sauce, old-fashioned pecan bread pudding with fruited sauce, and baked Indian pudding with whipped or ice cream sound interesting.

With good big cups of coffee, we tried a small glass of the liqueur Strega, appropriately an Italian name for witch. Feeling that we had been well fed and for a short time protected from witchcraft, we soon were on our way.

Salem Cross Inn, Route 9, West Brookfield, Mass. Tel. (617) 867-2345. Two miles west of West Brookfield on Ware Road. Major credit cards. Reservations recommended nights and weekends. Luncheon, noon to 2:30 p.m. Tuesday to Friday; dinner, 5 to 9 p.m. Tuesday to Friday, to 10 p.m. Saturday, noon to 8 p.m. Sunday and holidays. Closed Monday except holidays.

Also in the Area

Picot's Place, Main Street, Hampden, Mass. (617) 566-3034. This sophisticated Parisien-style restaurant is a great surprise to come upon in the small town of Hampden; unfortunately, the food has slipped in recent years. In a remodelled country store, the decor is whimsical ("un ami de General Lafayette" is the only identification of a portrait of George Washington) and a fine collection of art is spotlit on the charcoal black walls. Entrees run from $7.50 for skewered scallops to $23 for rack of lamb or chateaubriand for two, and there's a special every night (seafood crepes when we were there), including onion soup, salad, dessert and coffee. We were amused by the attire of the staff — bartender in shirt sleeves, waiter in tuxedo and ruffled shirt, bus boy in tails! We were not amused by the tough steak au poivre for $9.75, which verged on the inedible, the sauce tasting strongly of the brandy that had not been properly flamed off. A New Orleans Sunday brunch with several kinds of omelets ($3 to $3.75) and crepes ($4 and $4.50) is served from 11:30 a.m. to 3 p.m. One hopes Picot's Place regains its former outstanding reputation. Lunch, 11 a.m. to 4 p.m. Monday to Saturday; dinner, 4 to 9 p.m. Tuesday and Wednesday, to 10 p.m. Thursday, Friday and Saturday.

The Log Cabin, Easthampton Road (Route 141), Holyoke, Mass. (413) 536-7700. Enormously popular and with an immense choice on the menu (25 entrees at night), the Log Cabin across from the Mount Tom State Reservation boasts a magnificent view of the Connecticut River Valley which you can enjoy in summer while sipping cocktails on an outdoor terrace. Table d'hote dinners are $6.50 to $15 and you get more food than you can eat. Five dining rooms seat 300 people. The food is American and it's open seven days for lunch and dinner. Lunch entrees start at $3.25.

Jury's Tavern, Route 32, South Willington, Conn. (203) 429-6497. Steaks, seafood and more are served in a magnificent 1912 barn with 40-foot ceilings. Specialty of the house is mariner's catch, shrimps stuffed with scallops. Prices go from $4.95 to $9.50 and there's live entertainment in the Molly Malone Pub. Dinner only, Tuesday to Saturday, Sunday dinner 12:30 to 9 p.m.

Wheatsheaf, 2000 Boston Road, Wilbraham, Mass. (413) 543-7939. Steak, prime ribs and scallops are featured here, plus a salad bar (you can make a salad meal for $3.95). At lunch, you can sample a hot buffet that offers two kinds of soup for $2.75. Lunch is served Monday to Saturday, dinner Tuesday to Sunday.

Daytrip 5

For Knights: The Shining Armor
John Woodman Higgins Armory/Worcester, Mass.

If you've always been enchanted by the idea of "knights in shining armor," you can see what the armor was like anyhow at the John Woodman Higgins Armory in Worcester. When you get through looking, you may decide that once he was dressed up in all that forged metal, it's a wonder a knight could do anything more than just move.

I have fantasies of a Laurel and Hardy movie being done in the great hall of this museum where more than 100 medieval suits of armor are displayed. Can't you see the comedians running from suit to suit, lifting the visors, peering in — and having someone peer back?

But his collection of armor was no laughing matter to John Woodman Higgins, the Worcester native who, on a schoolboy trip to Europe, somewhat precociously purchased his first suit of armor and brought it home with him. That was just the start of a lifelong fascination with the art of the armorer, appropriate enough when Higgins grew older and became president of the Worcester Pressed Steel Co. He became so involved with his hobby that right next door to his company, Higgins had the four-story museum building of steel and glass erected in 1931.

That's nearly 50 years ago, and the Higgins Armory has been in business since then, still luring schoolboys (there were a couple there the Saturday morning our family visited) who peer at the intricate coats of mail, the suits themselves and the weaponry, and imagine what it must have been like.

It must have been awkward, heavy and clumsy to be dressed in a suit that weighed 60 to 100 pounds and to be expected to fight or joust in it. That's one impression we and our children carried home after an enthralling morning spent at the Higgins. Others were the subtle differences between one suit and another, the various styles and degree of ornamentation, and some particularly unusual features such as face pieces that look like animals or a suit of Italian parade armor that had the representation of a face on each shoulder.

My children were delighted by the suit of armor made for a dog (fashioned from a German breastplate by a member of the staff at the Metropolitan Museum of Art) and authentic child-sized armor, usually used for festivals or parades. They had fun measuring themselves against it.

From the outside, where it stands amid factory buildings that even a winter coating of snow could not sufficiently camouflage, the Higgins Armory lacks a good measure of romance. And the somewhat hokey felt heraldic banners in the stairwell for the two-flight climb didn't add to the illusion.

But once we reached the third floor and the Gothic Hall, which is modeled on the hall of the Hohenwerfen Castle outside Salzburg, Austria, and which stretches a full two floors with stained glass windows and all, the proper mood was easily evoked.

The way to see the museum, the only one devoted exclusively to armor in the country, is to start on the fourth-floor "balcony" which overlooks the main hall. It includes exhibits on ancient armor and implements, such as projectile points of stone from as far back as the Stone Age, or Greek helmets dating from 600 B.C.

Probably the best display on this floor is the Roman horse armor, made of iron scales and woven fabric, loaned to the museum by the Gallery of Fine Arts at Yale. The "stained glass exhibit" was disappointing in that it was entirely reproductions of famous windows in cathedrals of Europe, often done in a smaller size, and in a fairly dark alcove where they could not be seen to best advantage.

It is downstairs in the Gothic Hall that the bulk of the collection is displayed. This is a genuine treasure house of armor, displayed on mannequins up and down the length of the hall, and without ropes, glass cases or the like to impede one's scrutiny. In fact, you can get very close to the armor here, which is one of the best aspects of the display, and with a little care the visitor can examine it at all angles, slowly, to his own satisfaction.

It is not all alike. I had had some misgivings, I have to admit, wondering whether we and our children would feel that once we had seen one suit of armor, we'd seen them all. That was definitely not the case.

Traveling in a counterclockwise direction about the large hall, which is a rough chronological progression, we came quickly to the "touch table" at the side of the hall, where children (and adults) may finger mail, a helmet and breastplate, and above which is mounted a diagram of a full suit of armor with each part identified in four languages. This is a helpful introduction to the new vocabulary (pauldrons, vendails, rondels, falds and the like) and takes the psychological pressure off by providing an opportunity to do what we all want to: Touch the stuff.

All of the armor, except for one suit, is authentic, although a few of the suits are composites. Full suits of medieval armor are relatively rare, but there are some beautiful ones to be seen here. I remember the armor of Franz von Teuffenbach (German 1554), a beautifully etched suit, which probably took a full three years to make. The close helmet of the suit, weighing about nine pounds, was made of four pieces, each painstakingly hammered out of a piece of iron, etched and then assembled.

The dog's armor, while recreated in recent times, would have been worn by the animals when on a wild boar hunt to protect the dog from the tusks of the wild animal.

Maximilian armor, typically fluted in rows of three and so called because it was in vogue during the reign of Maximilian, was on display in two or three versions. A suit of French embossed parade armor from the 16th century was very elaborate, with the relief of famous battles displayed on the metal.

About halfway down the hall you can stop before a recreation of an armorer's forge, showing the instruments which would have been used in the creation of the suits of armor, many of which are considered fine works of art, and which the craftsmen often etched with their initials.

At the opposite end of the hall from that where we started are two mounted figures clad in armor for jousting, typically heavier than regular battle armor and having the addition of an iron mantle on the left shoulder to receive the opponent's lance. Don't miss the Japanese armor, tucked into a corner to the left and behind this display, which seems so much lighter and more flexible than the European armor.

In addition to all the armor you will want to examine shields, breast plates, lances, crossbows and one particularly gruesome looking weapon, the flail. Several oil paintings depict scenes of armorers preparing suits in their forges, and some more recent suits of armor include Flemish armor from the 17th century or French Napoleonic arms and armor.

The gift shop at the Higgins is a find for parents. Prices are still low: Imagine post cards for 5 cents, a plastic statue of a knight (it looks like metal) for 50 cents and other inexpensive mementos for the children. There is also heraldic jewelry, note paper, books on chivalry and the like.

Scholars may use a 2,000-volume library on armor by appointment.

Location: 100 Barber Ave., Worcester, Mass. Exit 19 from I-290. Take Burncoat Street to Randolph Road. Armory is on corner of Randolph and Barber.

Open: 9 a.m. to 4 p.m. Tuesday through Friday, 10 a.m. to 3 p.m. Saturday, 1 to 5 p.m. Sunday. Closed Mondays and national holidays.

Admission: Adults $1; children 25 cents.

Special Events: Occasional musical evenings; call for schedule.

Telephone: (617) 853-6015.

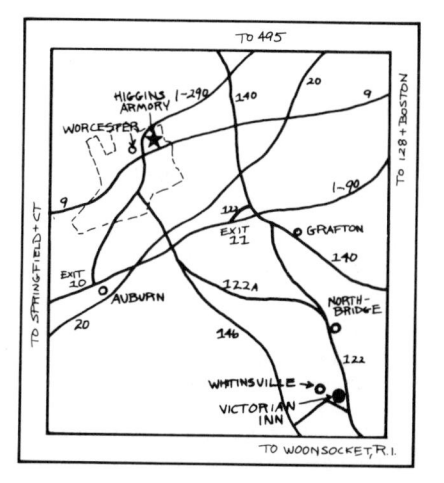

29

Also in the Area

Worcester Science Center, Harrington Way, Worcester, Mass. (617) 791-9211. This is a "see and do" museum which the kids love. Outside are polar bears in a pool with glass viewing window, two nature trails, and a three-kilometer railroad ride which tours the 60-acre site of the museum (50 cents extra for the train trip). Inside are exhibits, including a new mineral exhibit, an optical illusion exhibit and an "omnisphere," which is planetarium, oceanarium, etc., rolled into one, with daily shows. Open year-round, 10 a.m. to 5 p.m. Monday through Saturday; noon to 5 p.m. Sunday. Adults $2; children up to 16, $1; senior citizens $1. Phone for map and directions (it's a bit hard to find).

Worcester Art Museum, 55 Salisbury Street, Worcester. (617) 799-4406. With a fine, well-rounded collection, the museum was founded in 1896 and opened its first building two years later. Many out-of-towners find it worthwhile to travel to Worcester to see this museum. Besides an outstanding collection of 17th century Dutch and Flemish painting, classical sculpture, Egyptian, Persian, Indian and Far Eastern art are offered. Open 10 a.m. to 5 p.m. Tuesday through Saturday, 2 to 5 p.m. Sundays. Gallery tour Sunday at 3 p.m. Closed Mondays, New Year's Day, Christmas, July 4, Thanksgiving. Adults $1; children and senior citizens 50 cents. Museum Shop.

Picnicking: Green Hill Park, Worcester. Playground facilities and barnyard zoo.

Dining 5

The Victorian/Whitinsville, Mass.

In a house that Mark Twain would have adored, imagine dining in the elaborate Victorian manner, surrounded by literature. Thousands of books line the walls of the elegant library dining room of the Victorian, with subjects from soup to nuts — "The Complete Walker," "Exploring the Upper Atmosphere," "The Saint in New York."

In the tiny town of Whitinsville, 15 miles southeast of Worcester, Orin and Martha Flint, who met when they were in college in upstate New York and whose ambition it was to own a country inn, bought four years ago for a bargain the beautiful house that industrialist James Whitin built in 1871. Standing empty, it was about to be torn down for a new supermarket.

The Flints, who scoured the countryside for pieces of Victoriana, have done a superb job of renovating the Whitin mansion, creating an atmosphere of what they call the Golden Age of 100 years ago.

From the moment you are welcomed by the delicately painted flowers and birds on the inn's sign, drive up the curving driveway to the spotlighted and curlicued white wooden inn, open the beautifully etched glass doors and stand in the spacious entrance hall, you are in another world.

Ahead, the broad staircase curves around to some comfortable guest bedrooms on the second and third floors. The small dining room in the blue and gold parlor with its blue moire paper and intricately draped gold brocade window coverings is on the left.

What a handsome room the main library dining room is on the right! With its faded oriental rugs, lacy white curtains, dark wood panelling, fireplace, crystal sconces and red leather chairs, it is the epitome of Victorian comfort and luxury.

Carnations adorn the spacious, blue-clothed tables, and wine and water are served in lovely crystal goblets. White wine arrives in elaborate silver buckets, and even the inn's homemade dill bread comes on a silver tray.

After serving medium-sized drinks ($1.95), the waitress, demurely clad in a pretty flowered gown, recites the appetizer choices of the day, which are included in the price of the meal. We were served the quiche of the day instead of the crepe we ordered, but it turned out to be a marvelous shrimp quiche with a flaky crust and a hint of tomato in the composition. The Oysters Florentine was superb — three huge oysters, served in their shells on rock salt, were nestled on beds of spinach and doused with a Mornay sauce.

We were a bit disappointed that no veal dishes were listed on the menu (only seven entrees and no specials of the night, as we had heard). But we did have a superlative filet of beef served with Bearnaise sauce ($11.95) and leg of lamb ($10), a trencherman's portion, served with silken mashed potatoes and gravy. It was good, but not the pink color I would have liked. With these entrees came tiny French peas and mushrooms.

Other entrees range in price from the day's omelet for $7.25 to prime ribs for $11.50. Shrimp scampi is $10.25 and sole amandine $9.

We enjoyed a hearty bottle of 1973 Guigal Cotes du Rhone, $7.50. The wine list is carefully selected with mainly French wines and a few Californian, starting at $4.75. Muscadet can be had for $6.25 and for the big spender, Chateau Lafite 1966 for $70. A carafe of house wine is $4.50.

Salad, happily served after the entree in the continental manner, consisted mostly of iceberg lettuce, but had an extremely interesting vinaigrette dressing with the addition of slivered almonds.

It was impossible to think of dessert after all this, so we simply enjoyed the fine coffee and a glass of spicy hot mulled wine in a tiny cordial glass on a doilied plate, served to all diners. It sounds incongruous, but was a novel way to end the meal.

Also a bit incongruous was the choice of background records — most were classical and gentle, but a disco "hustle" slipped in and really seemed out of place.

At lunch, dishes range from $3.50 to $5.95 and include such items as omelets with chicken livers, spinach and sour cream, or crabmeat and cream cheese, as well as chicken, lobster or seafood salad, crepes and chilled salmon steak with herbed mayonnaise. A Sunday brunch is served and features eggs Benedict as well as quiche, onion soup or full dinners.

The Victorian Inn is set on several acres of beautiful grounds where guests can ramble to a nearby pond or ski cross-country through pine groves.

The guest rooms all have luxurious bathrooms, and some have king-size beds. We wish we could tell you that Queen Victoria slept here, but she didn't. But Joanne Woodward and Paul Newman did while on an inn-hunting trip through New England. Guess they, too, wanted to experience some of that atmosphere of the Golden Age.

The Victorian, 583 Linwood Ave., Whitinsville, Mass. Tel. (617) 234-2500. Take Exit 11 from Mass. Pike and Route 122 south to Linwood Avenue (just across railroad bridge), west toward Whitinsville. Reservations recommended at night. Major credit cards. Luncheon, 11:30 a.m. to 2:30 p.m. Tuesday to Friday; dinner, from 5:30 p.m. Tuesday to Saturday, noon to 8 p.m. Sunday. Closed Monday.

Also in the Area

El Morocco, 100 Wall St., Worcester, Mass. (617) 756-7117. Arthur Fiedler dines on shish kabob ($5.95) when he eats here, but you could have kibbee, stuffed eggplant, squash, grape leaves or cabbage for $3.75. If you don't like Lebanese food, there are prime ribs and steaks. A nice selection of baklava and Arabic pastries is offered, and on Wednesday nights, belly dancing. Open 11:30 a.m. to midnight daily except Sunday, when it closes at 9 p.m.

Putnam and Thurston, 27 Mechanic St., Worcester, Mass. (617) 753-5427. An old (from 1858) downtown standby, they have great baked stuffed shrimp and also specialize in beef. Dinners range from $5.50 to over $10.95; child's plate up to $3.50. Hours are 10 a.m. to 11 p.m. daily; Sunday noon to 9 p.m. except for July and August, when the restaurant is closed Sundays.

The Publick House, Route 131, Sturbridge, Mass. (617) 347-3313. This big venerable inn, charming and hospitable, serves breakfast, lunch, dinner and supper from 7:30 a.m. to 11 p.m. every day. It's popular with visitors to Old Sturbridge Village, so reservations are advised at night. The Tap Room, with huge open hearth, has the most atmosphere of the several dining rooms. Worth trying is the lobster pie, a house specialty, with a cracker topping. Dinners, semi a la carte, range up to $10.95, and children's plates are available.

Daytrip 6

A Walk Among Wild Flowers
Garden in the Woods/Framingham, Mass.

If you're on the trail of the trailing arbutus — or any other wild flowers for that matter — congested, suburban Boston may not seem the place to look. As a matter of fact, it's the best place in the entire Northeast.

For Framingham's Garden in the Woods, the headquarters of the New England Wild Flower Society, is a 43-acre site boasting, quite simply, "the largest collection in the Northeast of native plants growing in natural surroundings." It is also stunningly sited, lovingly maintained, and the best-marked of any visited by this writer.

And it's sure to have some trailing arbutus — or mayflower — the state flower of Massachusetts.

The approach to Garden in the Woods makes your visit all the more dramatic. After driving through an uninspired tract of small ranch houses, you come upon the entrance gates for the shady, quiet area.

If you visit between late April and mid-June (which the society recommends as the best time because of the number of native plants in flower), a hostess in the parking lot will help you park your car, bike or scooter, or any other vehicle you might have along, including baby strollers which are prohibited from the self-guiding trails. If you're as serious about wild flowers as the society is, you might leave behind children as well, since they're only permitted in certain areas. Smokers are asked to abstain, and picnics are not allowed.

The restrictions may seem a bit harsh. But once you see the area, you'll understand why they're necessary. Wild flowers, quite simply, don't follow the rules as you might like. To survive, much less thrive, most varieties require the very natural, undisturbed kind of location which they have in Framingham. As a result of the precautions and the careful maintenance, thrive they do.

When we visited in May, an avowed wild flower enthusiast and I were enchanted from the start by the masses of white trillium in full bloom in the area just beyond the parking lot. They were surrounded by wild azaleas, both white and pink varieties of bleeding heart, and rhododendron about to pop into bloom. It was a good introduction to the area as a whole.

Once you've parked your car, you're welcome to "freshen up" in the attractive Nature Center, where you will also find charts of wild flowers along with cards in full color to tell you "What's Blooming." For novices, that's a help. Here too is an extensive library and books for sale on wild flowers and conservation.

The visitor to Garden in the Woods may select any of a number of self-guiding trails, ranging from a half-mile to a mile and a quarter long. You'll get a map to the area when you pay your entrance fee, but serious gardeners also may want to invest in the 64-page book, "Will C. Curtis Garden in the Woods," for $3. An illustrated guide to plant material growing in the garden, it is also useful as a general wild flower guide.

It was Curtis, a landscape architect, who acquired the land for the garden back in 1930 and who, with his partner Howard O. Stiles, developed an outstanding plant collection on it. In 1964 the men offered the site to the New England Wild Flower Society, if an endowment fund could be raised. It was, and in May 1965 the area was deeded to the society and opened to the public.

Your walk through Garden in the Woods should be leisurely, allowing for discoveries along the way, and you should plan ahead for uneven terrain by wearing sturdy walking shoes.

The main trail begins off the center of the parking lot where the information shelter is. As we went we saw more white trillium, dwarf coreopsis and a tiny wild

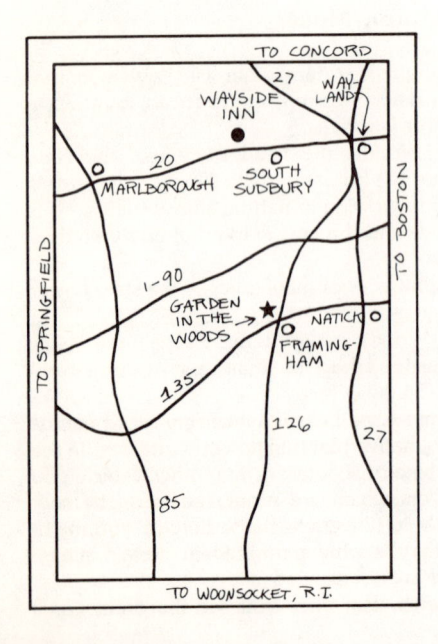

Location: Hemenway Road, Framingham, Mass. Exit 12 from Massachusetts Turnpike (eastbound). Follow Route 9 east to Edgell Road; left on Edgell for two miles to Water Street; right on Water Street a short way to Hemenway Road. Signs posted.

Open: April 1 to Nov. 1, Monday through Saturday, 8:30 a.m. to 4:30 p.m. Closed Sundays. Open holidays except Sundays.

Admission: Adults $1; children 50 cents. Members of New England Wild Flower Society, free.

Special Events: Annual "Plant-Book-Sale," second Saturday of June, 11 a.m. to 3 p.m.; wide variety of donated native plants for sale reasonably. Plants also available for sale throughout growing season.

Telephone: (617) 877-6574 or (617) 237-4924.

iris (Iris cristata); next a splendid rock garden, which contains many cultivated plants from the Eastern United States, as well as some wild ones. An elderly lady ahead of us, obviously well-versed in the area, kindly stopped every few feet to point out varieties we were pondering.

Which brings up this suggestion: Take a camera, or at the very least, a notebook, so that you can record flower varieties which you might want to have in your own yard at some future date. Many of the varieties are marked. If not and you have a question, society volunteers are usually eager to help.

We followed the Lady Slipper Path along a brook, traversing it at one point via a fallen pine bridge which the adventuresome can take. Others may prefer to stay on terra firma, which is okay, too.

It is impossible to mention all the flowers and trees that are crowded into this marvelous place. Suffice it to say the area is chock-full of the loveliest ferns, flowers and pine trees you can imagine. Additionally, there is a Western Rock Garden, something of a surprise, which contains cacti and other varieties of plants from the southwestern United States.

Allow at least an hour and a half for your walk. At the end you will surely want to investigate the wild flowers on sale the day you visit — in fact this feature alone draws many gardeners to the area. I purchased two Iris cristata plants that day, which continue to enchant me at home with their tiny purple blooms, and two wild yellow primroses which, I have to be honest, didn't make it.

But the sale area acts as an informal exhibit, where you can really see the flowers at close range and increase your ability to spot them when you're out in the woods on your own another day.

Garden club groups may visit and have a guided tour for a fixed price. Call ahead.

Also in the Area

Stony Brook Wildlife Sanctuary, off Route 115, Norfolk, Mass. (617) 528-3140. Maintained by Massachusetts Audubon Society, this 101-acre sanctuary is operated beside the 200-acre Bristol-Blake State Reservation, which includes pond, woodland, boardwalk over marsh and trails. It's open year-round from sunrise to sunset. Pamphlet to self-guiding nature trail may be purchased for 25 cents. No charge to hike trails.

Dining 6

Longfellow's Wayside Inn/Sudbury, Mass.

Ghosts of the past still seem to hover over the Wayside Inn, extolled by Henry Wadsworth Longfellow in *Tales of a Wayside Inn* ("As ancient is the hostelry — As any in the land may be . . . ").

A sense of history exudes from the sprawling complex that attracts a myriad of people for dining and tours of a 5,000-acre preserve including gift shop and chapel in sylvan solitude, just off the Boston Post Road in South Sudbury, west of suburban Boston.

The oldest operating inn in the United States, the restored building shows no sign of the disastrous fire of 1955. But it does bear the touch and largesse of Henry Ford, who took the inn under his wing in 1923 and deeded it in 1944 to the Wayside Inn Corp., whose trustees run the inn today much as the 18th century visitor would have found it.

From the Old Barroom, oldest section of the two-room tavern built on the site of the Black Horse Tavern in 1702, a delightfully warm room with glowing fireplace and wide planked floors, to the Longfellow Parlor, furnished with pieces mentioned in "Tales," the entire establishment shines with authenticity and an aura of American history.

You should not necessarily expect, when dining at a National Historic Shrine, to have a memorable gourmet meal, but you can expect at the Wayside Inn to have good fresh food, fairly reasonably priced, and fascinating surroundings.

New England and regional specialties are included, of course, and one of the house specialties is fresh scrod, baked with a cheese sauce. The floury sauce tends to detract from the impeccably fresh fish, but it can always be scraped off! Baked jumbo shrimp with Wayside stuffing are delicious; the filet of sole with crabmeat stuffing and lobster sauce, adequate.

Prices at night range from $5.50 for chopped sirloin to $12.75 for a 1 1/2-pound Maine lobster. Most are in the $6.75 to $8.75 range and include appetizer, vegetables, salad, dessert and coffee. A few appetizers and desserts are extra, $2 for oysters on the half shell or shrimp cocktail, 50 cents for Creme de Menthe or strawberry parfait, or strawberry shortcake.

We started our meal with French onion soup — pleasant if not memorable. A crock of cheddar cheese spread and crackers enhanced the generous cocktails beforehand and we also nibbled on fresh vegetables and a good mixture of marinated vegetables, including mushrooms, carrots and peppers. The muffins and rolls are made of wheat flour and corn meal ground in the inn's own gristmill and are superior.

The wine list is not extensive, but we were pleased with our bottle of Moselle for $7.

For dessert, the fresh-baked blueberry and deep dish apple pies are outstanding, and the Norwegian ice cream cake is also a fine choice.

Other entrees include prime ribs with Yorkshire pudding, roast Massachusetts duckling with orange sauce, and broiled fresh swordfish.

At lunch time, everything is a la carte and the entrees range from $3.25 for a cup of soup with a roast beef sandwich, to $4 for fresh bay scallops. The only item more expensive is a filet mignon for $8.75.

The large Colonial Dining Room where most patrons dine exudes an air of simplicity and cleanliness. The shining wood floors, gold cloths and napkins, pretty flowered china, flowered draperies and sconces on the walls convey an impression of bygone days. Some prefer to eat in the cozier Taproom.

On a Saturday night, when about 800 meals are served (never try to go on a weekend without a reservation), things get rather bustling and noisy, and the waitresses are somewhat harried.

We think the Wayside Inn is a welcoming place in winter, when the fires are lit, but on a glorious May day, with the towering oaks just coming into leaf, the wide green lawns, sturdy wooden furniture under the trees, stone walls and flowering shrubs, the first glimpse of the Wayside's rosy-red colored facade is an unforgettable one. And that's what you'll remember probably long after you forget what you ate!

Longfellow's Wayside Inn, Route 20, South Sudbury, Mass. Tel. (617) 443-8846. Take Wayside Inn Road north off Route 20, west of South Sudbury. Reservations recommended on weekends. Major credit cards. Luncheon, 11:30 a.m. to 3:30 p.m.; dinner, 5:30 to 9 p.m. Sunday dinner and holidays, noon to 8 p.m. Closed Dec. 25.

Also in the Area

The Pillar House, Route 16 at 128, Newton Lower Falls, Mass. (617) 969-6500. This beautiful restaurant, in a gracious mansion built in 1828, is jammed every weekday for lunch and dinner but, astonishingly, is so successful it can close on Saturday and Sunday. It's a complex of several dining rooms, old-fashioned parlors to wait in, and a huge bar upstairs with a tartan rug and lots of plants. Lunch prices run from $3.25 to $7.75 for entrees; sandwiches and salads are in the $2.75 to $5.50 range. At night, with emphasis on beef and seafood, entrees are from $7 for breast of capon to $14 for lobster. You can make a reservation, or wait your turn. Hours are 11:30 a.m. to 9 p.m. Monday to Thursday; to 10 p.m. Friday.

The Every Day Gourmet, Mill Pond and Speen Street, Natick Mass. (617) 653-8010. A gourmet shop, a cooking school and a small restaurant are under the roof of the Every Day Gourmet, which serves lunch from noon to 3 p.m. Friday and Saturday and brunch from 10 a.m. to 2 p.m. Sunday. You can sit at a counter and watch your meal being prepared by the chef. A different menu is featured every week, with a soup for $1.50, a choice of two entrees ($2.75 to $5) and a dessert (something smashing like a chocolate almond torte) for $1.50. French menus dominate, but sometimes they switch to Chinese, Spanish, Italian or Greek. Soups are inventive: Cold orange or apricot in summer, New Orleans cream of scallion in winter. Only 18 can be served at a meal, so call ahead to make a reservation, find what is on the menu and bring your own wine.

Burnham's 1742 Manor, 366 Pleasant St., Ashland, Mass. (617) 881-1742. In a converted Revolutionary house, Burnham's is noteworthy for unusually good value. Menu favorites here are baked stuffed haddock, southern fried chicken and pecan pie. Lunch prices range from $1.75 to $2.50; dinner from $3 to $6.95. There's outdoor dining on a large patio in summer, and the house wine, Tavola, is only $2.25 a carafe.

Daytrip 7

Fruitlands Museums photo

Utopia Was Here
Fruitlands Museums/Harvard, Mass.

People who visit Fruitlands are interested in one or more of the four museums on the open hillside site, each of which celebrates an interest of the founder, the late Clara Endicott Sears. The best-known of the four was also the first, the house that gives the site its name, and where an unusual experiment in communal living was conducted before the Civil War.

When you think about communal living today, certain images come to mind: A run-down farmhouse peopled by long-haired men and women who survive on bean sprouts and wheat germ, and prefer peace to prosperity. They wear plain, loose-fitting clothes, live off their own land and do their own thing. Meanwhile, their neighbors, living lives of ordered conformity, regard them with suspicion, if not horror.

Actually, that's pretty much the way it was in 1843 when Bronson Alcott, educator (and father of Louisa May), and Charles Lane, an English reformer and mystic, led a group of New England Transcendentalists (including Alcott's family) into the rural countryside at Harvard to start their experiment in the communal life. They called themselves a Con-Sociate family, moved into the old red farmhouse on Prospect Hill, and tried to bring about a New Eden. They called it Fruitlands, or maybe they didn't, but that's what Louisa May Alcott called it years later when she wrote a humorous piece about the venture called "Transcendental Wild Oats" (you can buy a copy at the museum store). The name would have been appropriate, and ironic.

The group, shunning animal products because they believed in freedom for animals as well as people, ate only fruit (mainly apples) and vegetables. The diet was meager since they also refused to eat vegetables that showed their "lower nature" by growing downward, for example beets, carrots or potatoes, and water was the only beverage.

Nor was diet the only hardship. The Transcendentalists carried the ban on animals to extremes — refusing to use them for labor, to use manure to grow crops, even to wear woolen clothes. Then, because slaves were used to pick cotton, they banned cotton clothing as well. They garbed themselves in linen tunics (designed by Alcott) and canvas shoes, which was okay in June when the experiment began, but less so when the chill winds of autumn and winter began to blow. By January 1844 the venture had ended.

Fruitlands wasn't quite as well known as that other Transcendental attempt at communal life, Brook Farm, which lasted five years. But it continues to interest, intrigue, even inspire those who visit the house today where Louisa May Alcott, at 10, giggled with her sisters in their attic bedroom, where her mother faithfully if not fervently made meals for an assorted and changing cast of characters of which she was usually the only woman, and from which her father periodically went off to proselytize about the new religion. (Possibly too periodically; supplies and enthusiasm dwindled on the home front in his and Charles Lane's frequent absences.)

The wild-eyed utopians (who believed in knowledge received intuitively and the power to "transcend" one's senses) were usually no more than 12 in number. But others visited, like Alcott's friend and former neighbor from nearby Concord, Ralph Waldo Emerson. Wrote Emerson prophetically after a visit to Fruitlands: "I will not prejudge them successful. They look well in July. We shall see them in December."

Because of the Transcendentalists' brief occupation of the house (barely seven months) and its establishment as a museum so long afterward (1914), there is little furniture from the Alcott period. But it is furnished as it might have been when the Transcendentalists were there, including the attic bedroom for the Alcott girls.

An exhibit at the house introduces the visitor to the Transcendental movement in general, in which says Director William H. Harrison, "interest has been increasing right along." Theology and philosophy students are among the visitors. Some come just to see the historic place, some to do scholarly research in the fine library, some because of an interest in the Shakers.

Which brings us to our second museum. Going from the Transcendentalists to the Shakers might seem an abrupt jump, but at Fruitlands there IS a connection and an appropriate one. For one thing, at the same time the Con-Sociate Family was doing its thing, the United Society of Believers, as the Shakers were officially known, had a village of their own just across town. Charles Lane even joined up for awhile after the Fruitlands experiment fizzled (he unjoined later).

But the real reason the Shakers have a place at Fruitlands is because of Clara Sears. Miss Sears, a member of a distinguished and well-to-do New England family, arrived in Harvard in 1910 to build a summer place and stayed to build a museum. She first became interested in the Transcendentalists' farmhouse down the road from her own house, bought and restored it and opened it to the public.

Next she turned her attention to the Shakers, even compiling a book about them, *Gleanings from Old Shaker Journals,* published in 1916 and credited with some of this century's interest in the sect. One thing led to another; specifically, Miss Sears bought one of the Shaker buildings from the then-defunct Harvard group, had it moved across town to the Fruitlands property, filled it with Shaker furniture and crafts, and opened it in 1920. The collection of Shaker objects at Fruitlands is considered quite fine.

At that point Fruitlands was (and still is) of particular interest to students of religious movements. But Miss Sears's interests could not be so confined. She delved next into the history of the North American Indian and (you guessed it) an Indian museum appeared on the property in 1930. It is filled with dioramas, artifacts, baskets and other crafts of Indians north of Mexico.

Finally, another of Miss Sears's personal enthusiasms, art, came to have its place. A collector of primitive portraits done by early American artists, and of paintings of the Hudson River School, she opened the Picture Gallery in 1940. Its collection is outstanding, and still being added to.

You should visit the Fruitlands Museums for all or any of these four major reasons, but also for the ambience of the whole, for it is a special place. The ap-

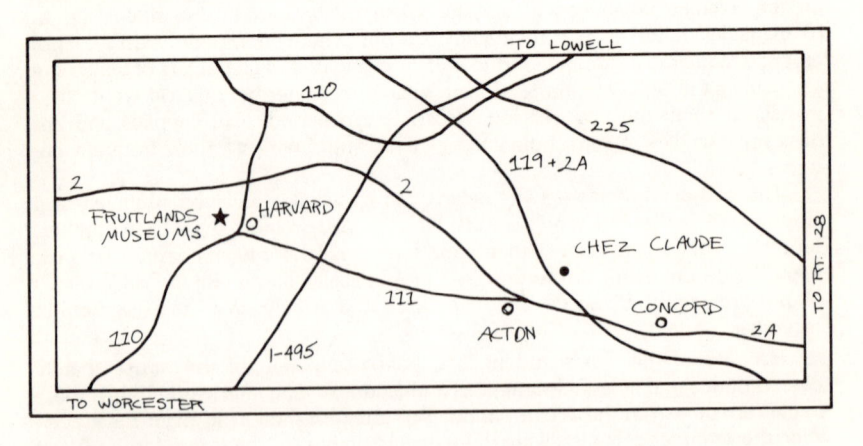

Location: Prospect Hill Road, Harvard, Mass. Two miles south of center of Harvard, via Routes 110-111. (The town is not near the university, which makes for confusion. It is actually closer to Worcester).

Open: May 30-Sept. 30, Tuesday through Sunday, 1 to 5 p.m. Closed Mondays except when a holiday.

Admission: Adults $2; children 50 cents.

Telephone: (617) 456-3924.

proach up Prospect Hill Road is memorable for the view that comes almost as a shock: A magnificent panorama of the Nashua River Valley with Mount Monadnock and Mount Wachusett in the distance. Many visitors like to linger on the terrace of Prospect House on the grounds, where there is a snack bar, to rest and gaze out across the valley of a summer's afternoon.

Allow at least two hours in good walking shoes to climb up and down the hillside where the buildings are clustered (they are not far apart, but the incline is appreciable). You probably won't be crowded because Fruitlands doesn't advertise, except by word of mouth. "We used to," says director Harrison laconically, "but we got all the Sunday drivers from Boston."

It is fortunate in these generally lean times when a museum doesn't have to beat the bushes for patrons or depend entirely on donations and admission fees for survival. Miss Sears's generous endowment protects Fruitlands from all that and serves to keep it the serious, tasteful spot that it is.

Picknicking is not permitted, but since it is only open afternoons, the snack bar staves off hunger. A small shop sells postcards and books and absolutely no gimcracks.

Also in the Area

Orchard House, Lexington Road, Concord, Mass. (617) 369-4118. About 15 miles east of Harvard is the home of the Alcott Family from 1858-1877 in Concord, with much Louisa May Alcott memorabilia. She wrote "Little Women" here in 1868. Open early April to mid-November, daily from 10 a.m. to 4:30 p.m. and Sundays 1 to 4:30 p.m. Adults $1.25; children 50 cents; senior citizens $1.

Ralph Waldo Emerson Memorial House, 28 Cambridge Turnpike, Concord, Mass. (617) 369-2236. The home of Ralph Waldo Emerson and family contains all family pieces and is very much the way it was when Emerson lived there. Open mid-April to end of October, daily, 10 a.m. to 5 p.m. (last tour starts at 4:30). Adults $1.25; children 75 cents.

Dining 7

Chez Claude/Acton, Mass.

No one seems to know whether the charming red house that houses Chez Claude is 150 or 200 years old, but everyone around Acton knows about the fine Provincial cuisine and good value offered there.

Even Bostonians make the trip to dine in one of the four dining rooms (three tiny ones in the original house, and one a bit larger recently added on) and to sample the dishes of chef-owner Claude Miquel. He's from Paris, and his wife Trudy, who serves as hostess, is French-Canadian. They moved to their present location in April 1977 after operating another Chez Claude for several years in Acton.

One good reason for Chez Claude's popularity is the price of entrees. They range from $5.40 for filet of sole Meuniere to $9.50 for Chateaubriand or

Tournedos, and include potatoes, vegetable of the day, salad and coffee — quite a bargain.

Another reason is the informal and friendly atmosphere — we spotted many gentlemen in somewhat casual attire on a Saturday night. White paper placemats protect the white tablecloths, and candles flicker in old wine bottles covered with wax drippings.

In our small dining room (four tables), floors were bare wood, but softly draped flowered Austrian-style curtains and a creamy caramel color on the walls softened the room. Rough beams from the original structure are exposed and on what looks to be an original brick wall, copper pans glow.

Chez Claude has only a beer and wine license, but offers a comprehensive list of aperitifs, including a good selection of domestic and imported sherries, champagne, port, madeira and vermouths. We enjoyed a Kir (white wine and creme de cassis) for $1 and Lillet blonde on the rocks, $1.30.

As you would imagine, the wine list is extensive, and the bottles are stored in a special room just inside the main entrance. We noted a Chateau Margaux 1973 for $18, one of the most expensive, Graves for $6.50, Cote de Rhone $5.50 and

Chez Claude Restaurant

Medoc $6. We selected a 1973 Pinot Noir for $6.50, with a rather sharp but pleasing taste. The house wine is, surprisingly, Carlo Rossi.

Pate du chef for $1.80 (an artful combination of pork and chicken livers) was a thick slab laid atop a bed of Bibb lettuce. Strongly seasoned with thyme and baked with a bayleaf on top, it was marvelous with the house crusty French bread and sweet butter.

The French onion soup with grated cheese (small $1.30 and large $1.80) was mellow, with lots of a very mild cheese like gruyere melting on top.

Other appetizers include quiche Lorraine for $1.80, lobster bisque for $1.50, and shrimp cocktail or escargots de Bourgogne, $3.00.

Next was served a simple and classic salad — Bibb lettuce, tossed masterfully with a delicious vinaigrette dressing.

Two special veal dishes were offered that night — one was veal Normande, done with apple slices, cream and the Calvados (apple brandy) of Normandy. The other, which we tried, was an excellent veal marengo, in a casserole with white wine, mushrooms, cream and tomato, faintly peppery and very flavorful.

We also tried a Chez Claude specialty, roast duck with orange sauce for $8. This was outstanding; the duck roasted for a longer time as requested so the skin would be extra-crisp, with a zesty orange sauce and orange segments.

All entrees are served with potatoes Anna, which are also called potato cakes with butter, and a vegetable of the season. Ours were carrots, slightly undercooked so they were crunchy, with parsley and onions.

One of the best sounding entrees is another house specialty, rack of lamb with mustard and garlic coating, $18 for two. Chateaubriand Bouquetiere is $19, and other entrees include trout amandine ($6.50), frogs legs in garlic butter ($7), coq au vin and beef Bourguignon ($6) and crepe maison with shrimp, scallops, lobster and crabmeat ($8.50).

Desserts are fairly standard (chocolate mousse, creme caramel, etc.), but we tried the special of the night, an extraordinary almond pie with apricots (1.50), with a crumb crust, a strong almond flavoring, and the texture of a pecan pie. Coffee is a good strong French blend.

For luncheon, served only from Wednesday to Friday, entrees are $3.20 to $4.80 and include many items on the dinner menu, as well as omelets, crepes and chicken salad. Potato, vegetable and salad are included.

Altogether, Chez Claude lives up to the reputation extolled by the natives. And the prices for such fare are a pleasant surprise.

Chez Claude, 5 Strawberry Hill Rd., Acton, Mass. Tel. (617) 263-3325. Just off Route 2-A on the north side, two miles west of the Concord traffic rotary. Reservations recommended at night. Major credit cards. Luncheon, noon to 2 p.m. Wednesday to Friday; dinner 6 to 9:30 p.m. Monday to Saturday.

Also in the Area

Bull Run and Sawtelle House, Route 2A, North Shirley, Mass. (617) 425-4706. Just a few miles from Harvard, this establishment, dating from 1740, with its tap room, eight dining rooms and four fireplaces, serves from 11 a.m. to 11 p.m. daily, even Christmas. Prime rib is the specialty; all vegetables are fresh and all bread and pastries homemade. Dinner entree prices range from $5.95 to $9.50; at lunch from $2.50 to $3.25. Wednesday nights there's a "pocket theater" with plays like "Come Blow Your Horn," and cake and wine is served at intermission. On Friday and Saturday nights, in the Sawtelle House, named after the first tavern owner in Shirley, supper theater features musical variety shows. You enter Bull Run's grounds over a wooden bridge copied from one designed for Eli Whitney in 1620.

The Mileaway, Federal Hill Road, Milford, N.H. (603) 673-3904. Not far across the state line in a lovely old barn, once the recreation room of the Hood family (of Hood Dairy fame), this restaurant specializing in veal dishes (the owner is Swiss) has a warm and relaxed feeling, and a nice view of the Monadnock Mountain range. Full-course dinners are $6.25 to $9.95, and include beef fondue, sauteed sweetbreads, Wiener schnitzel and Holstein schnitzel. You can even get a whole Maine lobster dinner for $9.95, and scrod and bluefish are sometimes the daily fish specials. Customers love the dessert trays of Swiss pastries. It's closed Monday and Tuesday, open Sunday from noon to 7:30, and all other nights from 5 to 9 or 10 p.m.

Cafe L'Orange, 87 Thoreau St., Concord, Mass. (617) 369-8700.) Rather casual and contemporary is this nice little cafe, specializing in country French dishes. It's on the second floor of the Concord Depot, and is open for lunch, 11:30 a.m. to 2:30 p.m. Monday to Saturday; dinner from 6 to 9 p.m. Monday to Thursday, to 10 p.m. Friday and Saturday, and for Sunday brunch.

Daytrip 8
By the Sea, By the Sea

Cape Ann/Rockport and Gloucester, Mass.

Seeing Cape Ann in a day is like trying to do Europe in a week, but it's better than nothing. You cannot see or do everything, so you should judiciously avoid any temptations of the kind. Instead, spread yourself on a golden strand for at least half a day, allow another few hours to poke in some shops or dawdle over a late afternoon drink by the water's edge, and wind up the whole with a marvelous seafood dinner and a bottle of wine.

You must go in the summer, but not on the weekend, arrive early and stay late, and, if it's raining, wait for another time.

There are things to see, of course. Two rather major tourist attractions are in Gloucester: Beauport and Hammond Castle. And Rockport has some interesting places, too: The Sandy Bay Historical Society, the Paper House, the Rockport Art Association. But they are rainy day things.

A bright day is for sunning and swimming and sandcastling; for walking, watching and whistling. The beaches and their breezes are for flying kites and playing frisbee and the towns and their shops are for slow ambling, from one to the next, just for the fun of it.

This, the "other" cape of Massachusetts, is, of course, no new star in the summer resort sky. For more than 100 years, visitors have been heading to Rockport in search of fresh air and seafood, finding rooms in private homes, strolling the lanes, stopping to watch a lobsterman haul his catch or an artist paint his canvas.

They've come to Gloucester, as the expatriate American poet T.S. Eliot did as a child, to spend summers in the fancy homes on Eastern Point, or to go down to the harbor to watch the fishing boats come in.

Fishing in Gloucester is serious business, with more than 100 million tons brought in annually from the rough waters of the North Atlantic and the treacherous seas of St. George's Bank. (If you want to know just how dangerous a business it is, pick up the map "Shipwrecks of Cape Ann" by Paul Sherman). Rudyard Kipling wrote about Gloucester fishermen in *Captains Courageous* and Winslow Homer painted them, and they both spent time here (in the village of Annisquam) getting the feel of it.

Unlike Cape Cod, with which Cape Ann would under no circumstances compare itself anyhow, this smaller, more northerly chunk of land jutting into the Atlantic has managed to stave off the progress connoted by the golden arches of a McDonald's or the high-rise of a Hilton.

Motels there are, but for the most part they're small, homey affairs (except for a couple in the Bass Rocks section of Gloucester). And restaurants there are, but generally under the individual ownership of private entrepreneurs, rather than the chains that stretch their sameness across the country.

Rockport is, in addtion, "dry." It's been that way since 1865 when a group of irate townspeople, mostly women, formed the famous "Hatchet Brigade" and entered the taverns and groggeries where they split open the casks and let the liquid run out into the streets.

If you want a cocktail, you must go to Gloucester to get it. A few restaurants, such as the homey Old Farm Inn in Pigeon Cove are happy to have you bring along a bottle of wine to sip with your supper; some others frown on the practice. It's best to check ahead when you're making reservations, and you should.

Art is also big business on Cape Ann and you're likely to find someone setting up an easel near you on the beach, or by the rocks, or just about any place you are. Art galleries line Main Street and Bearskin Neck in Rockport, and are beginning to do the same on another neck, Rocky Neck, in East Gloucester. That is a place that is picking up steam as a spot for gift shops and boutiques as well. My favorite restaurant on all of Cape Ann, the Rudder, is there, and I think happily of the evenings we have sat on the back porch that overlooks Gloucester Harbor, watching the boat lights dance on the waters.

The Rudder is a good place to end the day, but the beach is the place to start, and there are several good ones, the best in terms of sand and size probably being Good Harbor Beach in Gloucester, reached via Thatcher Road (Route 127-A) as you swing north toward Rockport.

Move back one space and get to Cape Ann. This is a cinch; just follow Route 128 north of Boston to the end and you're there. Pick up 127-A just after you leave 128.

Good Harbor beach has amenities for the daytripper (like rest rooms, snack bar and changing facilities) that you won't find on most of the smaller, more private Rockport beaches. And parking is permitted, for a price. It is a marvelous long stretch of golden sand, where the generally clear waters of the cape may be gentle or rough, and are usually invigorating.

There's an old concrete pavilion with its wood planked "boardwalk" over the sands where they dispense coffee and pastries for beach breakfasters (among whom I am firmly included) and hot dogs and hamburgers for lunch. Good Harbor Beach is long enough for a good "constitutional" — a walk or jog by the water's edge — before you settle into the softer sands to read the Boston Globe, snooze or watch the bikinis. Most of Cape Ann's bikinis wind up on this beach.

If, however, you are searching for a smaller beach, you can drive on up 127-A, take a right at South Street and Penzance Road (they converge there) and another sharp right onto South Street, following it to the end and Cape Hedge Beach.

Cape Hedge is best at low tide when the sand is the consistency for sandcastles, and not so good at very high tide when all that's left is a rim of stones and pebbles where the faithful perch precariously trying to keep their towels dry. But Cape Hedge Beach has a spirit all its own, and does not have so much as a snack bar to infringe on its lack of commerciality. If you have your own picnic in tow and you're willing to park rather far up the street (sticker parking only near the beach and Rockport police are merciless), you will probably love this beach.

Around the corner is an even smaller, more pebbly beach, known as: Pebbly Beach. Take the south end of Penzance Road from South Street (near Cape Hedge beach) to find it.

In Rockport center there are two more beaches, Front Beach and (what else?) Back Beach. Front Beach has restrooms and a float from which you can dive and it's so picturesque, with a crescent of Rockport's shops all cheek-by-jowl behind it, that painters often work there, but the two-hour parking meters are hard to get unless you arrive very, very early. You can park at a distance and walk.

After the beach, or possibly before, you might do a complete circuit of Cape Ann in your car, which usually takes under an hour and puts it all into perspective. Starting in Rockport, take 127 up to Pigeon Cove, through the hamlet of Lanesville (another beach), into the village of Annisquam, and back out and on to Gloucester, thence back via 127-A to Rockport. (Annisquam hides itself off 127 so turn right at the Community Church and drive down into it to see the pretty homes and harbor).

You'll see that unlike that other cape, this one is accessible simply because it's that much smaller. You **can** manage to see it in a day. After the beach, in the mid to late afternoon, you can either do "Beauport," the unusual 40-room "cottage" on Eastern Point Boulevard, Gloucester, which is only open weekday afternoons, or you can head for the shops of Rockport, with their infinite varieties of clothing, gifts and artwork (mostly seascapes).

Bearskin Neck is a popular place to prowl, but Rockport's Main Street is wonderful, too, and some fine women's clothing shops are on Broadway. You can

Getting There: Route 128 north to the end. The route around Cape Ann is 127, which passes through the centers of both Gloucester and Rockport.

Picnicking: Plenty of places, but a few of the better-known ones are: Stage Fort Park, overlooking water in Gloucester, picnic tables, playground equipment, public restrooms; Millbrook Meadow, King Street, Rockport, a verdant and cool spot with trees and pond, hidden behind the houses on the street; end of the breakwater at Bearskin Neck, Rockport, where you can perch on rocks or a couple of benches and eat your sandwiches; Halibut Point Reservation, off Gott Avenue, Pigeon Cove, Rockport, 10-minute walk along a dirt path leads to a stretch of flat coastal rocks suitable for picnicking and enjoying the sun and sea.

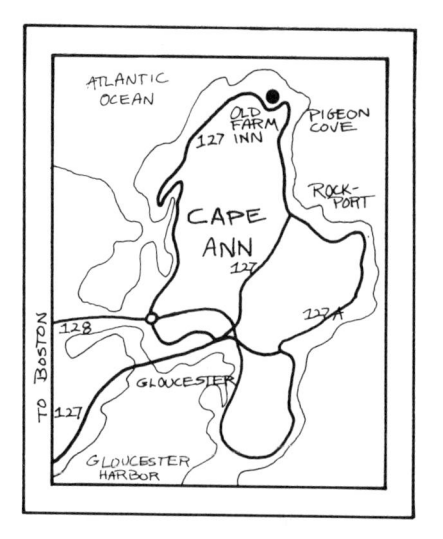

munch some homemade fudge from Tuck's on Main Street, or lick an ice cream cone as you wander.

And when the shadows lengthen you can go to your restaurant, where you will linger into the night, extending the pleasures of a day on Cape Ann.

Also in the Area

Hammond Castle, Hesperus Avenue, Gloucester, Mass. (617) 283-2080. The medieval-style castle built by the late John Hays Hammond Jr. houses a fine collection of art objects, particularly sculpture, and the largest privately owned organ in the world. The organ occupies the place of honor in the Great Hall of the castle, and organ concerts are conducted on a regular schedule. A guided tour of the castle includes a courtyard filled with tropical plants and its own rain system, a treasure chest said to contain the bones of one of Christopher Columbus's crew, and rare tapestries. From the castle you can see the ocean, and the reef of Norman's Woe, made famous in Longfellow's poem, "The Wreck of the Hesperus." Open daily April through November, 10 a.m. to 4 p.m., December, February and March, reduced schedule. Closed January. Adults $2; children $1.

Beauport, Eastern Point Boulevard, Gloucester, Mass. (617) 283-0800. The unique creation of interior decorator Henry Davis Sleeper, this mansion has more than 40 rooms, each decorated in a different style or period. There's an amazing collection of objects. Open June 1 to September 30; tours Monday through Friday at 1:30, 2:30 and 3:30 p.m. Adults $2.50; children under 12, free. Run by the Society for the Preservation of New England Antiquities.

Paper House, Pigeon Hill Street, Rockport, Mass. This rarity was built over 20 years ago with newspapers specially treated and rolled. Desks, chairs and lamps are all made of paper. Open daily from 10 a.m. to 5 p.m. Admission, 25 cents.

Sandy Bay Historical Society, 40 King St., Rockport, Mass. Paintings, ship's models, tools of fishing and granite industries are on display. Open daily from 2 to 5 p.m. Free admission.

Dining 8

Old Farm Inn/Rockport, Mass.

Imbued with a quaint, almost "down-East" flavor is the Old Farm Inn, picturesquely situated at Pigeon Cove, near Rockport. The little red inn with the white trim and ponies grazing in the back yard has been owned for 14 years by the Balzarini family.

The whole clan gets into the act. John Balzarini is the main chef, his wife Mabel is the gracious hostess, his sisters Rose Dayton and Regina Runsala are salad girl and baker respectively, daughter Faith Keating is a waitress, grandson Kirk Keating a busboy, granddaughter Karen Keating a busgirl, and granddaughter Kristin Keating helps with the washing, while Charles Balzarini, John's brother, tidies up in the mornings.

Together they run a fine operation in the inn, thought to date back to 1799.

The first thing you see as you step inside is a 70-year-old large black cast-iron stove (the Old Farm Indian pudding slowly bakes in another one in the kitchen). A coal fire casts a welcoming glow on a nippy night, and the cozy dining room welcomes you with its yellow woven mats, hurricanes lamps, antiques and old pieces of china in corner cabinets.

Rockport is bone dry, by the way, so if you'd like a drink or wine here, bring your own. Setups are cheerfully provided as are crackers and a zippy cheese spread. Crisp relishes (changing weekly) and fabulous oatmeal bread, served in a loaf, help to stave off hunger pangs.

The clam chowder is decidedly not from a can — thick, piping hot, and with lots of clams as well as the usual potatoes.

Seafood is the obvious choice here near the rocky shore. We loved the Old Farm Inn's special crabmeat-mushroom pie, with plump whole mushrooms and ample crabmeat topped with buttery bread crumbs, and the crabmeat Rockefeller, huge chunks of fresh crabmeat served in a Mornay sauce. We also enjoyed another delectable specialty, the roast duck, crisp and golden, served with rice and wine or orange sauce.

The house salad dressing (served on mixed fresh greens) is loaded with blue cheese and is delicious. Fresh vegetables, changing with the season, are served with all entrees.

Lobsters caught by local fishermen come baked and stuffed, in lobster pie or salad bowl or Newburg. Prices in 1977 were $10 to $12, quite a bargain.

Children's platters are in the $3 to $4 range, and our junior gourmet said the boneless fried chicken and acres of French fries were the best he ever tasted.

Entrees range in price from $5.50 for that old New England favorite, Finnan Haddie, to $8.50 for broiled sirloin steak.

Except for the above mentioned Indian pudding, served steaming hot with ice cream melting over it and utterly yummy, desserts are fairly standard.

At lunch, when entrees range from $3.75 for chicken pie to $5.95 for petite sirloin steak, there's something called Uncle Charlie's rum bread pudding that I plan to try on my next visit!

Service when we were there was spectacularly fast, so much so that we felt rushed. However, it's polite, so if you want to linger a bit, I don't suppose they'd throw you out.

Sunday brunch is also served, featuring pancakes and all manner of omelets.

During the summer, outdoor dining is available on a front terrace. Old Farm Inn also has overnight accommodations with six rooms in a small guest house adjacent to the main inn. There's even a suite with two fireplaces!

We asked Mr. Balzarini what he does in the winter months when the inn is closed. "I sure as heck don't go down south," he said. "You can have Florida!" What he does is create a few new dishes for next year's menu, get the inn ready for its spring opening, and enjoy the winter on the rockbound coast.

Old Farm Inn, Granite Street, Pigeon Cove, Rockport, Mass. Tel. (617) 546-3237. Two miles north of Rockport on Route 127. No credit cards accepted. Luncheon, 11:30 a.m. to 2 p.m. Tuesday to Saturday; dinner, 5 to 9 p.m. Tuesday to Saturday. Sunday brunch, 9:30 a.m. to 2:30 p.m., dinner 4 to 9 p.m. Closed Monday and mid-November to end of March.

Also in the Area

Woodman's. What's a trip to the shore without fried clams? Woodman's, a glorified clam shack off Route 128 six miles west of Gloucester, without a single frill, serves some of the best we've ever tasted. They're dipped in evaporated milk and cornmeal before being deep fried, and do they melt in your mouth!

What's a trip to New England without a clambake? Woodman's is also famous for these, and serves them in the summer for a rather bargain price of $7.50, including steamed clams and broth, corn, hot dog, boiled lobster, watermelon and soft drink. Hours for the clambakes are 5 to 8 p.m. Wednesday and Saturday, and 4 to 8 p.m. Sunday.

Draft beer is 75 cents here, and there's a full bar, but don't expect any amenities. The salt on the plank tables comes in the original Morton's carton.

Fried clams are $1.75 for a small carton and $5.50 for a large — the small carton is enough for a feast. Combination plates (with great French fries and onion rings) are in the $2.75 to $4.25 range for chicken, shrimp, scallops and lobster.

Hours are 11 a.m. to 10 p.m. every day in the summer, to 9 p.m. from Labor Day through the winter.

Woodman's is on Route 133, Riverfront, Essex, Mass. Take Exit 15 from Route 128 North. Tel. (617) 768-6451.

At **Eddie Donovan's** fish store on the Bearskin Neck corner of Tuna Wharf in Rockport, smack in the middle of the craft shops, you can buy lobster, boiled, cracked and dished up for $2.39 for 1 1/8 lb. Take and enjoy on the wharf or find some rocks!

Rocky Neck in Gloucester is an artists' enclave with several interesting restaurants on the water, interspersed among the art galleries. At the **Rudder** you can eat in the dining room or on an open porch in charming surroundings on such delicacies as baked stuffed shrimp, lamb with garlic sauce, shad roe and sponge cake with hot blueberry sauce. The restaurants and most galleries are closed in the winter.

Daytrip 9

Art in a Many Splendored Place
Gardner Museum/Boston, Mass.

Things haven't changed much in 75 years at the Gardner Museum in Boston, which is the way its founder would have it. The tiny but dynamic Isabella Stewart Gardner provided in her will not only for the museum's support, but for its preservation intact, just as she left it at the time of her death in 1924. Not a painting may be moved.

And while the museum was generously endowed by Mrs. Gardner to provide for its future, the future did not include additions or subtractions. Nothing is bought, nothing sold. It is, as they say in the trade, a "closed collection." All of which sounds a bit stuffy, while the Gardner is not at all. The collection of art is so enormous, and so spectacular, that it would take many visits before it could even begin to pall on the average visitor. And there are some things that change at the unusual museum: Magnificent floral displays in the central courtyard, for one thing; and the concerts, three of which are presented weekly (except July and August) free of charge.

Music, flowers and art were three passions of the transplanted New Yorker, who married a Boston man and proceeded to shock proper Bostonians who found her a bit, well, independent. She did what she pleased, and pleased whom she would, and the motto of her museum reflects that attitude: *C'est mon plaisir* — "it is my pleasure."

It likely will be yours, too, although one staff member says that visitors "either love it or they hate it," a reflection of the strong impact that Isabella Stewart Gardner continues to have on those who view her collection.

Modeled after a 15th century Venetian palazzo, its central courtyard rising the full four stories of the building to an overhead skylight, and its interior crammed with mosaics, arches, railings, murals, frescoes and the like from European buildings, the very physical makeup of the Gardner is not easily forgotten. The building is wedded to the collection and vice-versa to a degree rarely achieved.

In spite of Mrs. Gardner's reputation for flamboyant high spirits, it was a sad event that provided the impetus, in a roundabout way, for the museum. The death of her only child, an adored son of two in 1865, plunged Mrs. Gardner into a depression and illness from which she had still not emerged two years later. Her husband, John Lowell Gardner, took her to Europe in an attempt to divert her.

Europe fascinated Isabella Gardner, in particular Venice, where she and her husband spent long periods on subsequent trips. She became interested in art and began to acquire objects she liked.

Italian Renaissance was the period that first inspired her; as time went on, and with the advice of knowledgeable friends, she delved into other styles and periods including her own 19th century America. The painter John Singer Sargent was a friend; he is, as you might imagine, well represented at the museum which became Mrs. Gardner's home, and which she, but no one today, called Fenway Court.

The Gardners decided to build a museum which would evoke memories of their beloved Venice, and they hired Boston architect John Sears to do the design. But Mr. Gardner died before the land had even been bought; his death shocked Mrs. Gardner into a frenzied acceleration of the pace she had been keeping.

She bought land in an area known as the Fens, then on Boston's outskirts, and took off for Europe to look for the columns, fireplaces, arches, fountains and other architectural elements which she would incorporate into her building. Italian builders were imported for the work, partly because, since they didn't speak English, they couldn't leak the secret of what Mrs. Gardner wanted to be a surprise.

Surprise her friends she did — at a gala New Year's Night celebration in 1903 when the museum was officially opened, lighted for the event with strings of lanterns and flickering tapers. Visiting the Gardner today, it is easy to imagine such a scene, and such a woman.

My visits to the museum have been on gray or rainy days, but they are among

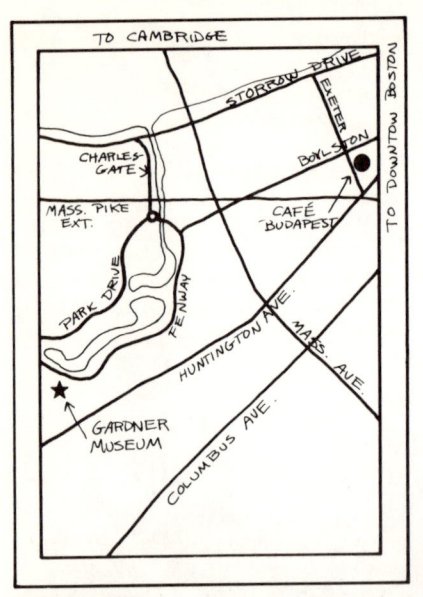

Location: 280 The Fenway, Boston, Mass. Public transportation: From Park Street Station take the Arborway or Huntington car. Get off at Louis Prang Street.

Open: Year-round Tuesday through Sunday, 1 to 5:30 p.m. Closed Mondays, national holidays and the Sunday before Labor Day. From September to June, the museum is open late on Tuesdays until 9:30 p.m.

Admission: Free except on Sundays, $1.

Special Events: Music concerts offered free three times weekly; Sunday and Thursday at 4 p.m.; Tuesday evening at 8 p.m. in the Tapestry Room, second floor. Program information available at beginning of month for entire month.

Telephone: (617) 566-1401. For information on concerts, (617) 734-1359.

the best. It is simply a delightful experience to step inside and see ahead the marvelous open courtyard, banked with masses of blooms (all grown in greenhouses on the same property), brightening up an otherwise gloomy day.

It is not easy to get around the Gardner; that is, it is not easy to put an order to what you're seeing as you go from room to hall to chamber to chapel, but that's not the visitor's fault. Mrs. Gardner displayed things as she liked; in some cases a very famous painting is hung in a dark corner while some little object, which happened to catch her eye, is given a place of importance. Unfortunately, the staff can't change it. So if you're serious about knowing what you're seeing, and not missing the high points, it's wise to invest in the official guide which takes you from object to object, room to room, in the manner the museum is laid out ($2 at the museum shop).

The collection of paintings, sculpture, furniture, textiles, ceramic, glass, manuscripts and rare books takes up three very large floors (the fourth, Mrs. Gardner's apartment, now houses director Rollin van N. Hadley and his wife). The impression is of tremendous ornateness: Dark woods and gold gilt (on frames, on dishes, on frescoes), deep red brocades and intricate carvings. There is the feeling of a cathedral, a castle, a manor hall all rolled into one.

There really is a small chapel in the building, a perfect jewel on the third floor, where annually on April 14 an Anglican High Mass is said to commemorate Mrs. Gardner's birth date. (Friends of the Museum attend and breakfast afterward.)

The concerts in Tapestry Hall, with its polished mosaic floor and fine acoustics, are often outstanding, calling on guest soloists who have appeared with the neighboring Boston Symphony, chamber groups, or music students from Boston's wealth of colleges, among others. You can just walk in and sit down (first come, first seated) on Sunday or Thursday afternoons or Tuesday evenings, when they're scheduled.

The floral displays are very popular, and change with the seasons. Four fulltime gardeners grow the poinsettias for Christmas, jasmine and azaleas for spring, lilies and cineraria for Easter, and chrysanthemums in the autumn. They don't just decorate, but truly **fill** the courtyard with their blooms and their fragrance. They also grow the orchids for which the museum is famed. Look in the bay window of the Chinese Loggia on the main floor for some of these.

Your trip through the museum will take you past paintings by many masters: Vermeer, Titian, Rubens, Rembrandt (his only known seascape for one), past medieval arches and Renaissance fireplaces, past ornate tables and carved wooden thrones and pews and chairs. The more you'll see, the more you'll marvel.

There are marvelous eclectic touches: A collection of manuscripts and letters of famous poets, musical instruments, Japanese screens, even toilet articles in a guest room on the main floor. You'll get a look at the woman herself, in paintings by John Singer Sargent, one of which, in the Gothic Room, portrays Mrs. Gardner at 48 and was a favorite of hers.

Allow at least two hours, more if you can, to immerse yourself in the museum built to please Isabella Stewart Gardner.

Also in the Area

Museum of Fine Arts, 465 Huntington Avenue, Boston, Mass. (617) 267-9300. Just around the corner and up the street from the Gardner Museum, this claims to be the second most comprehensive museum in the Western Hemisphere with collections from antique to contemporary objects. Open Tuesday, 10 a.m. to 9 p.m.; Wednesday through Sunday, 10 a.m. to 5 p.m.; closed Mondays, New Year's Day, July 4, Labor Day, Thanksgiving, Dec. 24 and Dec. 25. Admission: Adults $1.75, children under 16 free. Free from 5 to 9 p.m. Tuesdays and $1.25 all day Sunday. For recorded listing of events phone (617) 267-9377.

Institute of Contemporary Art, 955 Boylston Street, Boston, Mass. (617) 266-5151 or 266-5152. Housed creatively in a renovated police station in Boston's Back Bay, this gallery features changing exhibitions by contemporary artists. Open Tuesday through Saturday, 10 a.m. to 5 p.m., Wednesday until 9 p.m.; Sunday, noon to 5. Admission: $1 adults; 50 cents children, students, senior citizens.

Dining 9

Cafe Budapest/Boston, Mass.

Considered by many to be Boston's best restaurant, the elegant and terribly Old World romantic Cafe Budapest is situated in a rather unlikely place, the basement of the Copley Square Hotel, not one of Boston's best hotels.

It's the kind of lavish place where you'd expect to see Zsa Zsa Gabor dallying with an admirer in one of the intimate alcoves off the lounge, sipping champagne and eating something with lots of whipped cream on top. Actually, she has dined here, on chicken paprika, we're told!

Although Cafe Budapest is in the expensive category at night (a la carte entrees run from $8.50 to $15.50, and drinks are a hefty $2.35), you can get a table d'hote lunch including soup of the day, salad, entree, pastry and coffee for

$6.90. You're not likely to have as inexpensive a lunch as my husband and I enjoyed once, however.

In town for a convention during the January 1978 Blizzard, we staggered through the drifts to the Cafe Budapest about 1 p.m. At the foot of the stairs, the captain informed us that Edith Ban, the autocratic Hungarian who owns the restaurant and always dresses in white (fetching culottes and blouse that wintry day), had decreed that the first patrons to brave the storm were to have lunch as her guests. And we were they!

We slowly dried out from all that snow, sipping from a bottle of the delicate Hungarian wine, Badacsonyi Keknyelu, listening to gypsy music on tape and enjoying the splendor of our own "private" dining room and staff. We felt like Hungarian royalty, although Mrs. Ban, a practical businesswoman, admonished us, "don't tell the rest of your convention that lunch is on the house!"

The soup of the day, a peasant soup combining pinto beans, Hungarian sausage and ham in a thick liquid, was hearty enough for a blizzard and, topped with the thinnest of fried noodles, was truly outstanding. Crusty, sesame-studded hot rolls were served with sweet butter.

The baked paprikas chicken pancakes were actually crepes, exquisitely thin and wrapped around tender pieces of chicken in a wonderfully rich sauce, dusted with the true Hungarian paprika, rosy and piquant. A small salad of cucumber — marinated, sliced razor-thin, very crisp and also anointed with paprika — accompanied this fine dish.

Gypsy baron rice pilaf proved to be a melange of beef and lamb cubes in a flavorful rice pilaf laced with peas, and served with lightly marinated and shredded red cabbage. It was a most satisfying meal.

Our Hungarian strudel, with the flakiest melt-in-your-mouth pastry, was thick with apples and accompanied by fragrant Viennese coffee, served in glass cups (the beans are ground fresh every hour). Hungarians claim their pastry is better than Vienna's and judging from the strudel, they may be right.

At other meals here we've had the stuffed mushroom pancakes, the mushrooms being stuffed with delicate minced turkey breast and served with a cranberry and cinnamon relish. We've also tried the authentic beef goulash, which an Austrian friend, who is manager of a fine hotel, says is absolutely the best in the world.

At night the menu takes on a bit of French accent, so you have such curiously named dishes as "stuffed cabbage a la Hongroise," and goulash changes to goulache!

Most of the entrees are middle European, although chateaubriand, tournedos, steak au poivre and fresh flounder filet appear. Sweetbreads a la Hongroise sous Cloche is the most expensive entree at $15, but the potpourri full-course dinner for two and mixed grill a la Hongroise for two are $29.95 and $32.50 respectively.

If you are really in the mood for splurging, imported Beluga caviar is $14 an ounce, and goose liver with truffles, $9. Hungarian geese are force-fed on corn soaked in milk to fatten their livers, which are highly prized.

Desserts are $1.90 to $5.50 (crepes flambees). A Gundel pancake for $3.50 with almond-orange cream filling, raspberry souffle topping and chocolate sauce sounds enticing.

All kinds of teas ($1) and coffees ($1 to $2) are available to round off the meal, as are Tokay dessert wines for $1.75 a glass. The bottles of unusual Hungarian dinner wines on the all-Hungarian wine list run from $6.50 to $9.

If you have any romance in your soul, you'll love the decor at Cafe Budapest.

From the main dining room, all in red and white and dark woods, with old Hungarian flasks, walking sticks, wine jugs and decorated plates on the walls, to the small blue dining room used at night, with handsome stencilling done by a Provincetown artist and glazed ceramic della robbia all around the arched entranceway, to the dining room off the lounge all in pink except for some green chairs (pink is so flattering to a lady's complexion), it's almost too pretty and old world for words.

A Russian pianist and Hungarian violinist at night in the lounge provide more romantic atmosphere, and here, ensconced in French Louis XV-style gilt and brocade chairs, you can have crepes flambeed at tableside.

Mrs. Ban has come a long way from Brookline, where she learned the old Hungarian recipes at her mother's original restaurant, to the Holiday-award winning Cafe Budapest.

Cafe Budapest, 90 Exeter St., Boston, Mass. Tel. (617) 734-3388. In basement of Copley Square Hotel, just off Boylston Street near Prudential Center. All major credit cards. Reservations required at night. Luncheon, noon to 3 p.m.; dinner, 5 to 10:30 p.m. Monday to Thursday, to midnight Friday and Saturday, 1 to 10:30 p.m. Sunday.

Also in the Area

The Hermitage, 955 Boylston St., Boston, Mass. (617) 267-3652. Imperial Russian cuisine is offered at this elegant (and expensive) restaurant with its very modern decor, tucked away on two levels in the basement of the Contemporary Art Institute. Items like Russian eggs, herring, smoked sturgeon, caviar, bliny with smoked salmon or smoked sturgeon, roast veal Prince Orloff and steak tartare are on the menu. A chef's special luncheon costs $5.95 to $7.95, and you can get flavored Russian vodka or Slavic beer. Hours are noon to 2:30 p.m. daily except Monday, dinner from 6 to 10 p.m. Monday to Thursday, to 11 Friday and Saturday, and Sunday brunch, noon to 3 p.m.

The Modern Gourmet, or **Chez La Mere Madeleine,** Piccadilly Square (Union Street), Newton Center, Mass. (617) 969-1320. Gourmets from across the country trek to the unlikely and hard-to-find basement location of Madeleine Kamman's famous cooking school and restaurant. Reservations are a must, and you'll probably have to make them weeks in advance. Dinner is served from 6 to 9 p.m. Tuesday through Saturday, and is a la carte (different cuisines, sometimes cuisine nouvelle) on week nights, prix fixe classic (and very expensive) on weekends.

Anthony's Pier 4, 4 Northern Ave., Boston, Mass. (617) 423-6363. Many famous people have dined here (Richard Burton and Elizabeth Taylor, to name two). You can see them all in pictures on the walls of the largest of Anthony Athanas's chain beside Boston Harbor, where 600 diners can be seated at a time. Extravagance is his byword, with lots of seafood, lots of dining rooms, lots of plants and ferns, lots of nautical mementos — in fact, lots of everything, including quantity of food and value. It's all a bit overwhelming but fun, and the views of the Boston skyline, the planes landing and taking off at nearby Logan airport and the passing ships add even more color to this vibrant establishment. Anthony's is open daily, 11:30 a.m. to 11 p.m., with Sunday dinner, 12:30 to 10 p.m.

Daytrip 10

A Trove of Chinese Treasure
Museum of the American China Trade/Milton, Mass.

Museums which specialize have a particular appeal. That's why, when I noted on a UNICEF note card that the Chinese porcelain vase design was from the Museum of the American China Trade in Milton, Mass., I was anxious to visit.

Milton is a suburb south of Boston, whose main business district may be a bit rundown at the heels, but whose massive homes and estates bespeak an elegance that is still present. It was there when the wealthy shipping captain Robert Bennett Forbes bought property and had an unusual house built for his widowed mother and sisters on Adams Street in 1833.

The house has its own story. The architect was Isaiah Rogers (1800-65), from whom the captain bought the plans for $52.50. Rogers had a unique reputation in Boston at the time as the father of luxury hotels; it was he who designed the first hotel of that kind in the country, the Tremont House. The house plans which the captain bought were for a Federal design with Greek Revival features, which now include some Victorian overtones added in the late 1800s. The unusual cupola at the top provided a skylight for a billiard room, as well as a marvelous view out over the water to Boston Harbor.

If it all sounds rather strange, it is, but at least you won't find it difficult to spot the gray mansion with black trim when you drive along Adams Street in Milton. And while you won't get to climb up to the cupola, the view from the grounds on a clear day takes in a hefty slice of Boston and its teeming harbor.

The house remained in the Forbes family for its entire history as a private residence, and in a way, it's still in the family. It is museum curator H.A. Crosby Forbes, the grandson of the seafaring captain, into whose hands the house passed in the early 1960s, and who decided to turn it into a museum in 1965.

The China trade was the obvious focus, for items brought back on Captain Forbes's ships were still in the family and could form the core of the collection. They did then, the curator notes, but an active acquisitions program over the years has reduced that original group of Chinese objects to about five per cent of the total collection.

It is some collection. Inside the house you find yourself in the world of the Orient, in the only museum in the country devoted exclusively to items of the rich and varied China trade which flourished between 1784 and 1832. It has the largest collection of Chinese export furniture and silver to be seen in America, and possibly the largest collection of Chinese porcelain (well over 1,000 items) on display at one time.

The captain who brought back many of these Oriental riches was born in 1804 and by the time he was 19 captained his own ship between Boston and China. When he was 28 he retired from the trade, but in those 10 or so years he was an outstanding merchant seaman.

He wasn't alone. Our guide pointed out that following the Revolutionary War, the British retaliated by closing their ports. That was a devastating blow to our shipping merchants, because the young nation had ships and men, but no place to go to barter for goods. In 1784 the *Empress of China* left for Canton from New York City and that was the start of the thriving trade.

56

All this doesn't really come into focus until you reach what the museum refers to as the "China trade room" on the main floor, third room on the guided tour. Mounted on the walls of the room are various views of Canton, the major port with which foreigners dealt, showing the "hongs" by the water's edge where the shippers would establish headquarters while gathering items for the ship. Often they would be in China for as long as six months, waiting for orders to be filled and making "deals" for the items they wanted.

In the China trade room, the visitor sees examples of what we traded with the Chinese (spices, furs from the Northwest Territory, sandalwood from Hawaii, and opium which we got from Turkey and which eventually got the British into the Opium Wars). From the Chinese in return we got silver flatware (notice how exact are the copies of British designs); intricately carved ivory fans, porcelain, elegant fabrics (note the laces in this room) and furniture in both Eastern and Western styles. Tea, too, and some of the large crates in which it was shipped are on display.

The "Chinese parlor" in the front of the house — the first room we visited — sets the mood. I was enchanted by the wallpaper in the room, an exquisite, bright design of flowers and butterflies, which copies an old Chinese paper and was made, so our guide explained, of silk applied to paper and then handpainted by Chinese artists. It is stunning.

Over the fireplace in this room is a painting of Houqua, the Chinese merchant with whom the Forbes family dealt in their trade, a Mandarin whose own fortune was in the millions of dollars when he died. It was he who took the young Robert Bennett Forbes under his wing when the young captain first arrived in China.

The old dining room of the house, into which we went next, has a wonderful Chinese export black and gilt lacquer tea table with enamel decoration, which is given the place of honor in the room. The museum was delighted when it was able to acquire the table; you will be delighted to see it. The enamel insets in the ornate base are truly gorgeous, and the table is surrounded by Chinese bamboo furniture, quite rare in that very little bamboo has survived from the 1800s. Don't sit down.

On exhibit in the dining room, where we were inclined to linger, was an exceptional collection of teapots on loan by Mrs. Harry T. Peters Jr. of New York City. The 38 pieces, ranging from the 17th to 19th century in age, were marvelous, and would that we could have sat at the tea table and been served from one of those delicious pots!

All of these items so far have had a real Oriental look to them as you would expect. But what about the Chippendale lady's desk in the corner? So begin some of the surprises in the collection: Exact copies of English (and American) designs, made by the Chinese for export here.

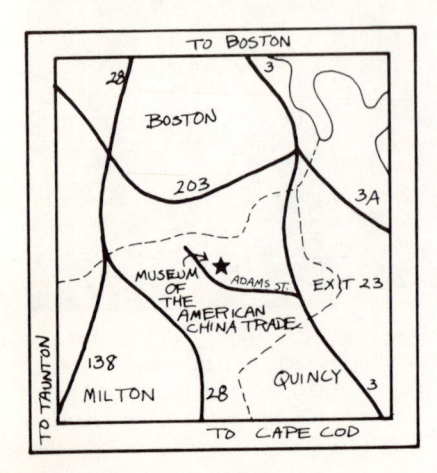

Location: 215 Adams St., Milton, Mass. Take Exit 22 from the Southeast Expressway (Route 3). Follow Adams Street west to museum.

Open: Year-round, Tuesday through Saturday from 2 to 5 p.m. Closed holidays.

Admission: Adults $3; children $1.50, Special group rates.

Telephone: (617) 696-1815.

The popularity of Chinese tableware during the first decades of our new nation is apparent here, too, in a collection of plates owned by famous early Americans. Note the oval dish from a service owned by George Washington, a part of Thomas Jefferson's set or the Chinese Imari plate, one of a set owned by Paul Revere. Some of these plates, you will find, contain the eagle motif, symbol of a proud new nation, used by the Chinese to please their customers.

Upstairs my co-author and I were intrigued by the furniture, particularly the marvelous Ning Po bed (named for a port on the coast famous for furniture making) of Chinese hardwood inlaid with bone. Like all of the export furniture, it can be taken apart in relatively small pieces for ease in moving and shipping.

Other favorites in the musuem: The collection of miniature vases, used as samples from which the American merchant could take orders as to she e and color; a collection of snuff bottles; a sewing table fitted with ivory, and the "Sunday box" created by non-Christian Chinese for the rigidly Puritanical American children who could only play quiet games on the Sabbath.

The porcelain room downstairs is last, and for many it will be best. Note the enormous fishbowl on the floor. The designs on the plates are marvelous — bright and intricate, the hallmark of Chinese artwork. My favorite: A plate from the Tao Kuang period with a chrysanthemum and grasshopper decoration.

We were sorry not to find more interesting Chinese items in a museum shop; a few things were sold by the door (note cards, coasters, some books), but it was a disappointing selection.

The museum owns the Holbrook House next door, which is open to groups of 10 or more only, on advance reservation. We didn't see that house, but understand it contains a few period rooms furnished with Chinese export furniture and a ceramic gallery with 700 to 800 items. The museum's Asian textile collection is also there.

The China Trade museum has an active membership of Sinophiles from across the country, issues a newsletter regularly and plans wonderful trips to the Orient. For information, write the museum.

Also in the Area

Trailside Museum and **Blue Hills Reservation,** 1304 Canton Ave. (Route 138), Milton, Mass. (617) 333-0690. This 7,000-acre reservation intersected by roads, hiking trails and bridle paths has a large museum at the entrance from Route 138. The area is somewhat hilly, to the extent that it includes the highest coastal point of land from Maine to Mexico, and if you want, you can hike 20 minutes up the hill to the weather observatory, which has the longest continuous weather record in North America, dating from 1834. During the 1938 hurricane, the second highest reported wind speeds in North America, 186 miles an hour, were recorded there. The area is gorgeous, with miles of well marked trails, two of which, the red dot or green dot trails, are short, right outside the museum. Outside there are also an otter and turtle pond and cages for small animals. The museum is open Tuesday through Sunday, year-round, 10 a.m. to 5 p.m. under the auspices of Massachusetts Audubon Society. Adults 50 cents; children 25 cents.

Picnicking available at picnic tables provided in area. Winter visitors can ski here at small ski area, which even boasts a chairlift.

Kendall Whaling Museum, off Route 27, Sharon, Mass. (617) 784-5642. A fine collection of artifacts and photographs about whaling. Open Monday-Friday, 10 a.m. to 4 p.m. Adults 50 cents; children 25 cents.

Dining 10

Joyce Chen/Cambridge, Mass.

It's a hike across town from Milton to Cambridge, but no lover of things Oriental should miss the place where the Julia Child of Chinese cooking holds forth.

Joyce Chen, that diminutive lady whose cooking programs on public television got a lot of us madly chopping and stir-frying, opened her restaurant near Fresh Pond about four years ago.

This is an area where there is no shortage of restaurants, Oriental and every other ethnic persuasion you can think of (Harvard Square is aglut with them). But Joyce Chen's is packed every night.

We think the draw is a combination of her popularity, and the fact that you get good value for a reasonable price.

The Chinese buffets are especially well received, and quite a bargain — $6.50 on Tuesday and Wednesday nights from 6 to 8 p.m., and $4.75 for the vegetarian buffet on Monday from 6 to 8:30 p.m. Needless to say, these attract a lot of impecunious students, taking advantage of "all you can eat."

The handsome menu is also informative (Joyce Chen can't get out of the habit of instructing us, I guess), describing many of the cooking methods used in the Szechuan, Hunan and Peking cuisines she features. Of course, she has many of the Cantonese dishes so familiar in this country as well.

We ate at Joyce Chen's on a Wednesday night and had a fine time trying the dishes in the buffet, served piping hot in a steam table and replenished every few minutes.

Starting with tiny fried wontons, crisp and delicious, and tender Peking chicken wings, we proceeded to beef with broccoli, a Cantonese stir-fried dish, with beautifully green small spears of broccoli and wonderfully tender beef. Then came a sensational Szechuan spiced chicken, cut into tiny cubes, in a delicate sauce laden with peanuts, and a dish of meatballs in a fiery black bean sauce.

Also in the buffet were dishes of tiny shrimps with fresh young Chinese peapods; a sweet and sour chicken, the chicken in deep fried puffs and the vegetable laden sweet and sour sauce served separately; Kan Shao green beans, stir fried the Szechuan way over very high heat, firm and fresh, and, of course, rice, plain and fried, with bean sprouts and other vegetables.

Accompanying this feast was a recommended bottle of a rose, dry with a touch of coarseness, Bouquet de Provence, for $4.50. It had a very interesting though rough flavor, and was just right for the Chinese buffet.

Another wine to go with the food is a Lirac Lisarique Vintage for $4.85, and Paul Masson and Mateus wines are also offered. Sake is $5.75 a bottle and you can have red, white, rose or plum wine for $1 a glass, while domestic beers are under a dollar and Heineken and Kirin, the delicious Japanese beer, are $1.20.

Several interesting soups are served at Joyce Chen's, including a fish soup with fresh coriander and ginger root; Joyce Chen special soup, assorted meats and vegetables topped with crackling rice, and a pork and Szechuan pickles soup. Serving four, they range in price from $4.50 for the fish to $1.95 for wonton soup.

My favorite soup in all the world is hot and sour Peking soup, which I make myself when the urge for it gets too strong, and Joyce Chen's is a delight to body and soul, a superb and spicy blend of bean curd, pork, exotic vegetables like tree ears and tiger lily buds, shreds of beaten egg, and fresh scallions cut into minute pieces on top. It's a bargain 75 cents for one; $1.95 for four.

Peking duck is $8.50 a half and $16.50 a whole, served with Mandarin pancakes, and should be ordered a day ahead. Other exotic specialties are Bon Bon Chicken, cold chicken shreds and cucumbers in a very spicy hot sauce (served cold — it sounds great for summer), and hot spiced bean curd with minced pork. Few of the many main-course dishes cost more than $4.50, and a lot are considerably less.

Daily luncheon specials for $2.50 include soup of the day, appetizer, three entrees, fried rice, fortune cookies and tea — a fragrant pot full.

There's even a dieter's menu and dishes will be prepared to the spiciness of

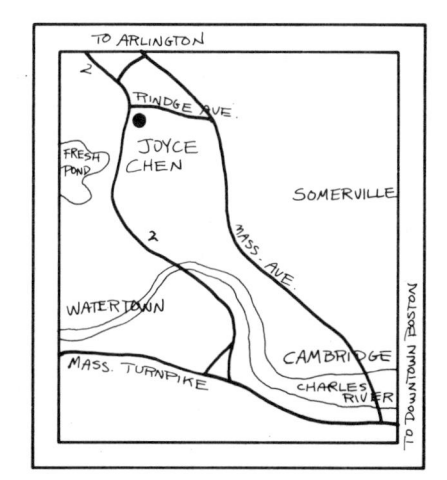

Joyce Chen, 390 Rindge Ave., Cambridge. Mass. Tel. (617) 492-7373. East off Alewife Brook Parkway just north of Fresh Pond Shopping Center, 1½ miles northwest of Harvard Square. Mastercharge and Visa. Reservations accepted. Hours: Noon to 10:30 p.m. Sunday to Thursday, to 11:30 p.m. Friday and Saturday.

your choice, also without cornstarch, salt, fat or MSG, if ordered that way.

Joyce Chen's does not suffer from the super-carved wood-exotic decor of some Chinese restaurants, nor the Chinese laundry effect in others. It's a sort of Danish-modern, low-key approach, with the main dining room on two levels, bare wood floors, hanging plants and skylights. The only touch of Oriental is a glass case near the entrance filled with Chinese objets d'art. It's bustling, and you can expect to wait at least a few minutes for a table.

If you can't wait until your next trip to a Chinese restaurant for a bowl of hot and sour soup, you can purchase all the ingredients at Joyce Chen Unlimited, Madame Chen's new shop at 172 Massachusetts Ave. in Arlington, where she carries fresh and packaged Japanese, Chinese and Korean foods, imported cookware and gifts.

Also in the Area

Milton Hill Restaurant, 36 Eliot St., Milton Village, Mass. (617) 896-3034. Conveniently close to the Museum of the American China Trade is the Milton Hill, on the ground floor of an apartment complex. The decor is Yankee-type with captains' chairs and one wall of brick. Lots of soups and sandwiches are served at lunch time, and at night, dinners are in the $5 to $6 range, with a salad bar. Hours are 11 a.m. to 9 p.m. Tuesday to Saturday, 8:30 a.m. to 9 p.m. Sunday.

Faneuil Hall Marketplace, Boston. Everything you've always wanted to eat but didn't know where to find is available at the Quincy Market and South Market, the complex of eateries, wholesale and retail, and smart shops giving new life to the historic Boston waterfront area. You can mingle with the crowds inside Quincy Market and build your own meal from the various stalls (Anna's Fried Dough, Baby Watson Cheesecake, Ming Tree, Nutcracker, Belgian Fudge, Black Forest Deli, the Juicerie and more) or dine elegantly at one of the several full-fledged restaurants. Cherrystone clams and oysters on the half shell with Michelob on tap are available at the Walrus and the Carpenter's raw bar, a fisherman's platter at the Fisherman's Net, an avocado sandwich at Nature's Banquet, a spinach salad at Rebecca's — all reasonably priced, too. Watch sensational chocolate chip cookies coming out of the oven at the Boston Chipyard, build a yogurt sundae at the Yogurt Shop, or sample a ham croissant from Charcutrix. Get a draft beer or glass of wine from Ames Plow Tavern and you can sit at one of the umbrellaed tables outside the South Canopy. At Seaside, a very "with-it" and contemporary restaurant in the South Market, the seafood casserole Florentine for $8.50 is excellent, as is the house spinach salad. Crickets, another fairly large restaurant, has an enticing outdoor cafe. You are also close to the fantastic Italian food available in Boston's North End, and the venerable Durgin Park is just around the corner.

Daytrip 11

Cape Cod's Dolls
Yesteryears Museum/Sandwich, Mass.

An antique grandfather clock that keeps perfect time is generally respected; in this case it is nothing short of remarkable. For the clock, the Venetian glass lamp that can be lit with a match, and all the other charming antiques in the house are actually less than Lilliputian in size.

The entire setting is in miniature, dates from 19th century Germany, and is complete in every tiny detail, including the dollhouse in which the furniture is displayed, and which was itself modeled on the actual house of the couple for whom it was a 50th anniversary gift. (Their grandchildren, I think, reaped the benefits).

"Millie Roth's dollhouse" (after the woman whose family thought of the gift) can be found at one of the largest and most fascinating doll and miniatures museums in the country, if not the world.

So when the inevitable rainy day pops up during your vacation on Cape Cod, head over to the unspoiled town of Sandwich for a morning or an afternoon or (if you're a collector) a whole day at the Yesteryears Museum, right in the center of town. (The library is across the street for any boys in your party who wouldn't be caught, dead or otherwise, in a doll museum).

Serious collectors of dolls, dollhouses and miniatures are inclined to go a little crazy here, and understandably so. Retired Army Col. Ronald Thomas, whose wife, Eloise, began the collecting in earnest in the 1940s, remembers one such woman who flew to the Cape in her own plane, spent every day of an entire week at the museum, and then took the Thomases out for dinner every night "to discuss dolls and doll collecting."

You needn't allot that much time. In fact, says the colonel modestly, the collection can be seen in as little as an hour to an hour and a half. Perhaps so. But after an intense two-hour tour one rainy winter afternoon (when Colonel Thomas obligingly opened up and turned on the heat for me), I'd recommend allowing the better part of a half day, so you'll not just glance at, but really see, this outstanding array.

It's worth it. Not only are there dolls of every size, description and age, but you'll see some of the rarest early dolls from Germany, France, Japan and our own country to be found anywhere.

There is, for example, what the colonel unabashedly says is "the oldest mechanical doll in the world," a 300-year-old Oriental doll whose head moves, while a rooster perched nearby flaps his wings. It still works. Then there is a genuine Bru doll, worth several thousands of dollars, made by the French master who was known as "the Rembrandt of the doll world."

I remember a rare 300-year-old Japanese doll dressed in "fingernail brocade" which was made with solid gold thread filaments and remains untarnished because it was. And Col. Thomas points with pride to the exceptionally rare Japanese doll, the "naughty boy" doll, a classic, discovered by the Thomases during their tour of duty in Japan around 1950 and authenticated by the curator of the doll collection at the Imperial Museum, with whom they had become friendly.

Those tours of duty during the 20 years the colonel spent in the Army (especially stays in Germany and Japan) are obvious in the strength of the Japanese and German parts of the collection. But there are American dolls, too, one being an authentic "Joel Ellis" doll from Springfield, Vermont, carved in wood in 1873, and valued for the intricacy of its parts as well as its rarity. Ellis was a dollmaker for only a few months.

Americana enthusiasts also will stop longer to view one of the first Goodyear patented rubber dolls; an antique rag doll from Pawtucket, R.I.; the Edison phonograph doll of 1889 which could "talk" when a tiny record was inserted, or the doll heads made by Ludwig Greiner of Philadelphia, about 1858. Greiner is revered as the first American doll maker, and he was, not surprisingly, a German by birth.

But some of these rarities, over which the colonel waxes increasingly enthusiastic, might be missed if you don't go slowly and carefully, reading each of the hand-printed identifying labels as you do. The Yesteryears Museum is basically self-guiding, with the dolls of one period or country following a display from another country or period in no discernible order (there isn't any, says the colonel, because it's more interesting this way).

And dolls aren't the only thing you'll be looking at, nor are they necessarily the most fascinating part of the museum for everyone. If your weakness is for miniatures and dollhouses, as is mine, you will find the collection in Sandwich not far short of Valhalla.

Dollhouses there are, nearly 50 of them, including an outstanding group of German ones where the rooms, typically, are strung along horizontally, with open roofs, to aid in "playing" with the dollhouse people. Millie Roth's is one of those. There are marvelous American houses, too, a particularly charming one being the "Captain's House," displayed outside the glass cases, and a marvelous white specimen furnished with lovely Victorian miniatures and copied on an actual house in Mattapoissett, Mass. You can still go to Mattapoissett to see the original, the colonel points out.

Not a whole house, but just a miniature kitchen, was traditionally given a little German girl on her fifth birthday to introduce her to the domestic and culinary arts. They were originally made in Nuremburg, so dubbed "Nuremburg kitchens," and the museum is famous for its collection of them.

My favorite might well be the kitchen with all the cookware and canisters in blue and white with the tiny inscriptions "kaffee" and "zucher" clearly readable.

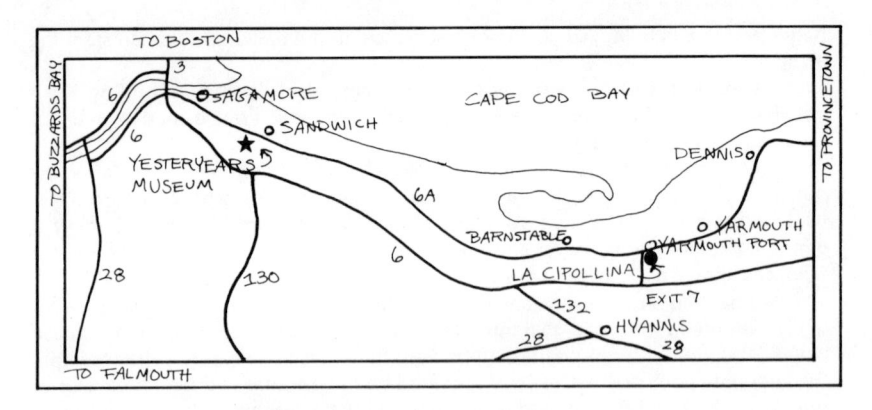

Location: Corner of Main and River streets in former church building, center of village of Sandwich. Can be reached via Routes 6A or 130.

Open: Mid-May to mid-October, Monday through Saturday, 10 a.m. to 5 p.m.; Sunday, 1 to 5 p.m.

Admission: Adults $1.50; children and senior citizens, $1. Family maximum of $5.

Special Events: Sale in the Collectors' Shop in October each year; average savings, 10 to 20 per cent.

Telephone: (617) 888-1711; if no answer, (617) 563-6673.

That kitchen has a working vegetable shredder as well as a stove that heats up via an alcohol burner, but then the charm of the Nuremburg kitchens was that everything from meat grinder to rolling pin traditionally worked.

The oldest Nuremburg kitchen, a very rare one, dates from 1740, and is resplendent with its copper and brass utensils and pewter plates.

More enchantment comes when you see the tiny grocery stores, toy shops and candy stores, some of them acquired intact, others composed by Mrs. Thomas. Do stop on the first floor to see the grocery store with all ingredients made from real candy, including marzipan sausages strung above the meat counter.

And don't miss the very rare set of miniatures carved by a Japanese master, Nanasawaya, in the early 1800s, and claimed by Col. Thomas to be unquestionably the "finest collection of Japanese miniatures in the world." The set takes up an entire large case and is noteworthy for the dolls of carved ivory, the wooden furniture decorated with real gold leaf and, if you please, a solid gold teapot.

These are only highlights — and not all of them — of a collection crammed into two full floors of what was, until quite recently, an operating church and no ordinary one at that. The building is of interest in its own right for it is the site of the original parish established by the Pilgrims back in 1638 and used most recently by the Unitarians into the 1960s.

The Thomases leased the building in 1961 for three years, but didn't know if they'd have to turn it back to its worshippers eventually, so rather than remove the pews, they mounted their display cases atop them. You'll see them on the second floor of the museum, which is the first area visited by the tourist.

The final stop is for some of the best. It is a visit to the "Collector's Shop" where antique dolls are for sale (some as high as four figures), and where miniatures and doll clothes can be found. This is the place to come if you're furnishing a dollhouse. The Thomases also carry on an active mail-order business and research service, answering questions about dolls and miniatures from extensive files and their own knowledge. Just drop them a line.

A special aspect of this museum is the loving care with which it is maintained, and the personal interest the Thomases take in it. It's very much a family affair: Eloise Thomas is director; her husband, president of the board, and their daughter Mary, who lives across the street, the business manager. Col. Thomas laughingly adds that four granddaughters are on hand during the busy summer season when some 25,000 to 30,000 visitors stop by, making it the best attended doll museum in the country.

Also in the Area

Heritage Plantation of Sandwich, off Routes 6A and 130, (Box 566), Sandwich, Mass. (617) 888-3300. The 76-acre former estate of Charles O. Dexter has magnificent rhododendrons, at their best in May and June. Now an educational, non-profit museum, the plantation includes varied exhibits of Americana including antique automobiles (displayed in a reproduction of the Shaker round barn of Hancock, Mass.), a military museum with antique firearms and military miniatures which once belonged to Josiah K. Lilly Jr. of the pharmaceutical family, and an arts and crafts building with working carrousel. An annual antique car show and competition is held in July. Other special events and frequent concerts can be determined by writing or phoning in advance. Visit takes 2½ to 3 hours. Adults $2.50; children 75 cents. Special group rates. Open daily April 30 to mid-October, 10 a.m. to 5 p.m.

Picnicking — Just outside Heritage Plantation in a picnic grove.

The Town of Sandwich is Cape Cod's oldest, settled in 1637, and miraculously retains much unspoiled charm. Drive around and enjoy the lovely old homes, one of which, the Hoxie House, considered the oldest on the Cape, is open to the public from June 18 to Sept. 30, 10 a.m. to 5 p.m. daily and 1 to 5 p.m. Sundays.

Dining 11

La Cipollina/Yarmouthport, Mass.

There are more good restaurants on Cape Cod than you can shake a whisk at, but not many of the best are open year-round, and few dish up the lively foods and regional specialties of Italy.

Not far from Sandwich, however, is the delightful La Cipollina (The Little Onion) in Yarmouthport, a North Shore town that seems to have more than its share of interesting restaurants.

With an intriguing menu and with Marietta Bombardieri Hickey, its animated owner, keeping a firm hand in the kitchen, La Cipollina is a real treasure. It's tucked away in a small white Cape Cod house on Route 6A, and is locally very popular.

In the small, square and rather plain dining room, large abstract paintings cover the walls and classical music on tape provides a pleasant background. Sturdy oak chairs ring the tables and a rear wall of glass looks out on a nicely landscaped little garden, sheltered from the parking lot by a stockade fence. The only jarring note was the tablecloths — a rather hideous shade of bright green, embossed plastic.

Italians always seem to be celebrating life and their cuisine, with its beautiful fresh vegetables and fruits, zesty sauces and artful antipasto arrangements, reflects this love of the good life.

The owner's antipasto alla Marietta is truly a work of art — $3 for a small platter that turned out to be more than enough for two, including boiled ham, salami, prosciutto, mortadella and capicola, all rolled up in little packages, bean and tuna salad, hot peppers, hardboiled eggs, artichokes, tomato and two kinds of olives.

With crusty Italian bread and butter, this was a meal in itself. But we pressed on through the menu, and next came the "zuppe" of the day, a hearty, delicious white bean soup, laced with salt pork.

The house salad, insalata di verde misto, is a nice simple presentation of fresh mixed greens, tossed with an Italian dressing fragrant with herbs. The special garlic bread, which is drenched in butter and heavily garlicked, is well worth the 50 cents extra per person.

The luncheon special of the day was anatra in agro dolce, duck served with rice in the Sicilian manner, plus soup and salad for $4.95. It was so astonishingly good that we had to find out how it was done. The duck is roasted for several hours to get rid of all the fat. A sauce made with stock, vegetables, red wine, onion, cloves and bay leaf is strained and reduced. Then are added brandy, apricot brandy, wine vinegar, honey and arrowroot, which makes a sensational topping for the duck, served with pignola nuts and with its skin crackling. A wonderful rice pilaf accompanies this.

Vitello alla Milanese, breaded veal cutlet with butter and lemon, was made with first class veal, very delicate in its puffy golden batter, and served with a side order of linguini, red or white. The white, tossed with cream, butter and cheese and flecked with herbs, was a perfect accompaniment for the veal.

A liter of the white California house wine accompanied this feast. A most comprehensive wine list has a good selection of French, German and California whites and reds, plus a very interesting array of Italian wines, the whites costing from $6 to $8 a bottle; the reds $6 to $14 (for a 1964 Barbaresco).

A few desserts such as spumoni, tortoni and cheese cake are offered. You'd think one wouldn't have room for any more, but the special dessert of the day was dacquoise, an irresistible cake made of meringue layers with praline butter, whipped cream, almonds and chocolate. It was absolutely sumptuous, but French, and the only non-Italian item on the menu. With a cup of the good fresh roasted coffee it was a perfect ending to an outstanding meal.

Entrees at night range from $4 to $7 for the pasta dishes, in the $7 range for the many veal dishes, and up to $10.75 for steak. The menu is extensive, with such not-often-found items as osso buco and risotto Milanese.

Italian restaurants always seem to be a little more jolly than other kinds and this is no exception. You should bring with you a big appetite and an appreciation for the Italian cuisine, the source of all the great cuisines of the Western world. Mangia bene!

La Cipollina, Route 6A, Yarmouthport, Mass. Tel. (617) 362-2636. South side of Yarmouthport's main street in center of town, just east of Hyannis-Yarmouthport Road. Major credit cards. Reservations recommended for dinner. Luncheon, 11:30 a.m. to 3 p.m. daily; dinner from 5 p.m. daily. Sunday brunch, 11:30 a.m. to 3 p.m.

Also in the Area

Eli's, Route 6A, East Sandwich, Mass. (617) 888-9893. Moderate prices and a menu studded with Greek and mid-East specialties as well as more usual offerings are the attractions here. Eli's sandwich special at lunch is a mixture of pan-fried minced lamb and beef with cracked wheat, flavored with Oriental herbs, served in Syrian bread, with lettuce, tomatoes, onions and feta cheese, all for $2.50. At night entrees are $6.95 to $9.95 (for a 1 1/2-pound lobster stuffed with shrimp and scallops) and a well-chosen wine list has many $6 bargains. Eli's is closed Monday and Tuesday.

Old Yarmouth Inn, 223 Main St. (Route 6A), Yarmouthport, Mass. (617) 362-3191. This venerable inn serves complete dinners for $5.75 to $6.25, including broiled fresh Chatham scrod with lobster sauce. It's open daily except Monday, noon to 3 and 5 to 9 p.m., to 10 p.m. Friday and Saturday.

Daniel Webster Inn, Old Main St., Sandwich, Mass. (617) 888-3622. Although built just a few years ago, this inn welcomes travelers back to the 17th century with its ambience of the original 1694 structure that Daniel Webster reserved a room in. Classic dishes such as beef Wellington, veal Oscar and steak au poivre are featured, along with ample seafood and daily specials. Entree prices are $6.95 to $12.95. An overnight accommodations package plan includes full dinners, except in summer. Breakfast, lunch and dinner are served daily to 9:30 p.m., to 11 p.m. Friday and Saturday.

Anthony's Cummaquid Inn, Route 6A, Yarmouthport, Mass. (617) 362-4501. Tourists line up for hours (no reservations taken) to get a table at Anthony's, a glamorous hostelry in the old Cummaquid Inn recently acquired by Anthony Athanas. Perhaps it's for the extras — giant hot popovers, marinated mushrooms, plates of vegetables, cheese and crackers. The menu is all beef and seafood, and the bouillabaisse is a good buy at $7.50. In summer, you can wait on an outdoor patio and watch the spectacular sunsets over Cape Cod Bay. Anthony's serves dinner only from 5 p.m. on, except for Sunday, from 12:30 p.m.

Daytrip 12

Just Milling Around
Slater Mill Historic Site/Pawtucket, R.I.

A spool of thread seems like a perfectly ordinary item until you visit a place like the old Slater Mill in Pawtucket, R.I. After that, it's a sure bet you'll have more respect for thread.

For instance, suppose you had to make your own? That's how it was done in those early homes in America and the first stop on a tour of the Slater Mill Historic Site is the 18th century Sylvanus Brown house, where the story of hand weaving is told.

In all there are three main buildings, all impeccably restored, at this riverside site in Pawtucket; a fourth (to house a steam engine already owned by the Old Slater Mill Association) is in the works. For now, in addition to the Brown House, visitors tour the old stone Wilkinson Mill, which houses an authentic 19th century machine shop, and the big wooden Slater Mill itself, which was the first cotton mill in the country and where visitors follow the whole process from bale to bolt in the production of cotton thread and cloth.

Because Pawtucket is such an industrial city and the mill site so old, I had expected the neighborhood to be like one of those dreary New England mill towns of the 19th century. Not so: This part of downtown Pawtucket has been renovated, is new and clean and a pleasure to visit. The vista from the mill site across the river, or across the river to the site, is lovely. And the deep red of the Brown house, the solid gray stone of the Wilkinson and the pale yellow of the Slater Mill building make a most esthetically pleasing group.

The Slater Mill is an "educational" site in the full sense of the word and I think 11-year-olds who are studying the Industrial Revolution for the first time, or mechanical engineers interested in early machines, would love the place. But almost anyone should come away with a new sense of how it was when mass production wasn't a household phrase.

Our guide to the site was an ebullient young man in denim overalls and work shirt, whose enthusiasm for machinery and mills made the 90-minute tour perfectly enjoyable. And while he wasn't quite as much at home at the spinning wheel as he was later in the machine shop, he did a creditable job in the Brown house, explaining the process of spinning wool from the natural product, or of working with flax after the plant itself was pounded to reveal the tough inner fiber.

What many people don't realize is the high value of textiles prior to their industrialization. Sylvanus Brown, the owner of the house, who was a millwright and pattern maker in Pawtucket, left an inventory of his belongings, which at the time of his death amounted to $97 worth. Of that, fully $40 was for bed linens, tablecloths and other textiles. A tablecloth, our guide told us, might easily cost three times the price of a table, reflecting the greater amount of time required to produce it.

The struggle to produce that cloth becomes abundantly clear in the large L-shaped kitchen underneath the house, where a "flax break," spinning wheel and hand loom are on display and demonstrated. At most, two or three yards of cloth could be woven by a housewife in one day. Modern day weavers will attest that it is not speedy work.

Stepping from the Sylvanus Brown house, then, to the great stone Wilkinson Mill, is like going from one chapter to the next in one of those old fifth-grade social studies texts. And the interior of the Wilkinson, with its outstandingly recreated machine shop of the mid 1800s, is like stepping into a photograph from such a text.

You must remember the pictures of those graven-faced men, women and children working in America's early factories from sunup to sunset. The interior of the Wilkinson looks just like that. It is a good job, said to be one of the finest, if not *the* finest reconstruction of its kind in the country.

This is where mechanical engineers tend to go a bit crazy. In fact, their professional organization, the American Society of Mechanical Engineers, has recently designated the Wilkinson Mill a National Historic Mechanical Engineering Landmark.

But even non-mechanical types find the Wilkinson Mill a fascinating place (it's my favorite of the three buildings). We visited on a gray day in November, but were not treated to any indoor lighting because machinists in the mid-19th century would not have had any, even in gray November. That lent even more authenticity to the spot.

With a flip of the switch, guide John had the entire place humming (all machines powered centrally by the main source). Currently that source is the local electric company; the next project of the mill association is to restore water power to the Wilkinson via a water wheel which will be built soon. These people, you see, are purists. (An archaeological dig underneath the building has been conducted prior to clearing the site for the wheel and has revealed some habits of mid-19th century machinists, like what they had for lunch — fresh peaches for one thing).

In the mill, as we went from machine to machine, John pulled a wooden handle to activate the particular one under consideration, and discussed the dangers as well as the delights provided by the swiftly turning parts. In particular, the fly planer is potentially so dangerous that guides are not permitted to operate it, he said. The machines, all in working order, include a rare wooden lathe which makes wooden bobbins, old iron cutting lathes, an early jig saw, table

71

saw, and that Daniels fly planer which revolutionized the American building industry by standardizing lumber sizes.

Last stop on the tour is the Slater Mill itself, a pretty pale yellow building with bell tower on top, from which the call to work was issued each day.

The mill was named for Samuel Slater, who came in 1789 from England to America at the age of 21, fresh from a seven-year apprenticeship in a large textile mill. What he knew about mill operations was vital to men like Moses Brown, a Pawtucket businessman who was trying to operate a small textile mill on the banks of the Blackstone River. Slater and Brown joined forces, and the Slater Mill rose to the fore in a city that led the entire nation industrially from 1780 to 1820.

The mill is such an authentic replica of those days that CBS and the BBC, among others, have done on-site specials on the industrial revolution from the Slater. Inside, the visitor follows the process of cotton weaving from the weighing of a bale of cotton (it should weigh 500 pounds; the scale was to keep the suppliers honest) to weaving cloth via the first fully automated power loom. The precision with which such patterns as herringbone and the like were created on those early looms is impressive. In fact, says museum curator Gary Kulik, industrialists from as far away as England and Japan have traveled to Rhode Island to visit this mill.

The area around the buildings, while not large, is very pleasant, and you can walk up along the river for a short way to look at the dam, the last before the Blackstone eventually empties into Narrangansett Bay.

When you've finished you can go to the small but fine museum shop (which is where you bought your tickets to begin with). The mill has a nice arrangement with Rhode Island craftsmen who display and sell their wares here. Such items as handwoven placemats and pillows and rag rugs are not only beautiful, but appropriate. Weaving supplies are available; also large wooden bobbins that can be used as candlesticks, and note cards, books and the like.

And after the mill (or before) there is all of Providence, just down the pike, with Brown University, the Rhode Island School of Design, shops and historic homes to satisfy a variety of tastes.

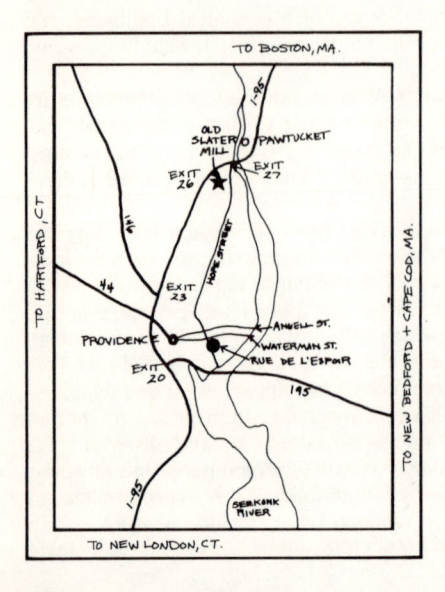

Location: Roosevelt Avenue, Pawtucket, R.I. Center of downtown area, reached via Route I-95 north from Providence, Exit 28 (School St.). Turn left, cross river and take your first right.

Open: Daily, Memorial Day through Labor Day, Tuesday to Saturday, 10 a.m. to 5 p.m.; Sunday, 1 to 5 p.m.; closed Monday. Labor Day through December and March through Memorial Day, Saturday and Sunday, only 1 to 5 p.m. Closed January and February.

Admission: Adults $2; children 75 cents.

Telephone: (401) 725-8638.

Also in the Area

Picnicking: Slater Memorial Park and Zoo. Route 1-A, Pawtucket. Train and kiddy rides in park as well as picnicking facilities. Zoo. Open 8 a.m. to 10 p.m. year-round; zoo open 10 a.m. to 4 p.m.

Museum of Art, Rhode Island School of Design, 224 Benefit St., Providence, R.I. (401) 331-3511. One of the nation's fine small museums, it has 19th century French art, classical Greek, Roman and Etruscan art, etc. The adjoining Pendleton House is the earliest example of an "American Wing" in a U.S. museum. Open Tuesday, Wednesday, Friday and Saturday from 11 a.m. to 5 p.m.; Thursday, 1 to 7 p.m.; Sunday, 2 to 5 p.m. Closed August, Thanksgiving, Christmas, July 4. Adults $1; children 25 cents. Free Saturdays.

Roger Williams Park, 950 Elmwood Avenue, off I-95, Providence, R.I. (401) 941-3215. This famous 430-acre public park has waterways, drives, rose, Japanese and Hartman outdoor gardens, park museum and planetarium, zoo, and paddleboats and motor launch in summer.

Dining 12

Rue de l'Espoir/Providence, R.I.

Providence has never been known as a mecca for gourmet dining (even the Mobil Guide does not list a single restaurant for Rhode Island's capital city).

We were almost reduced to writing about the downtown McDonald's — an institution which every downtown should have and one which comes in handy everywhere. But continued scouting turned up more possibilities, and we are happy to share a fortunate find: Rue de l'Espoir.

Informal yet sophisticated, chic and charming, there's very much of a Left Bank bistro feeling here. It's quite noisy, and the youthful staff scurry about wearing tan T-shirts with the restaurant's name on the sleeve and big white French aprons.

On the city's East Side in the historic and interesting Brown University area, Rue de l'Espoir serves casual fare: Soups, quiche, crepes, salads and sandwiches. At night there also is a changing plat du jour, which could be veal, scallops, chicken or pork.

In this cozy restaurant on several levels, checked gingham napkins in red, yellow, green and blue add a touch of color to the unusual tables topped with quarry tile. On the walls are chrome-framed Toulouse-Lautrec posters and, just inside the front door, a wall of artistically arranged copper molds, cooking utensils and the like. The floors are bare and the ceiling an antique pressed tin — perhaps that's why it seems so noisy.

You sit at the tables on mismatched wooden kitchen chairs or at green-cushioned booths, which are rather uncomfortable since you can't lean back. Even the W.C. has a French flavor; it's co-educational, with Mesdames et Messieurs on the same door!

There's only a wine and beer license, and you can get a terrific assortment of imported beers (Wurzburger, St. Pauli Girl, Molson Golden Ale, etc.) for $1.15. Aperitifs are $1.25 or $1.50, and seven white wines (starting at $4.50 — Pouilly-Fuisse is by far the most expensive at $9.75) and six reds ($5, to $6.95 for Baron Phillippe de Rothschild Mouton-Cadet) are offered. We thought our bottle of Beaulieu Vineyard Chablis quite a bargain at $4.50 — it was bone dry and served in huge globe glasses.

The soup of the day ($1.50) was vegetable, but was much less prosaic than the name. In a flavorful chicken broth were suspended morsels of velvety minced chicken, cauliflower, corn, carrots and onions, and large pieces of spinach. Served piping hot, it was really outstanding.

The house pate ($1.95) was a smooth blend of chicken livers and cognac, served with Carr water biscuits and pearl onions. It tasted great spread on diagonal and toasted slices of warm Italian bread, served peasant-style from a big woven basket and wrapped in a colorful gingham napkin. You could take all the bread you wanted and it was so good we asked for a refill.

A special crepe and quiche are served every day — fresh mushroom quiche on the day of our visit, and salmon crepes. We tried the salmon crepes, a hearty portion topped by a suave white sauce (the salmon was canned but was acceptable anyway). Also canned were the artichokes in the artichoke and mushroom salad, but the salad was nicely put together with a generous amount of fresh mushroom slices on romaine lettuce and a marvelous curry dressing. This was $3, and all the crepes, Swiss Gruyere, ratatouille, onions and mushrooms and sour cream, onions and mozzarella are $2.25 to $3. Egg and spinach pie with salad or quiche Lorraine with salad are $2.75, and you can buy the whole pies for $10.

The house salad is 95 cents alone and is tossed with an oil, vinegar, mustard and herb dressing.

For a lightish (and healthy) lunch, you can try the cheese board — $3.95 for fresh fruit, bread, crackers, house salad and a choice of two kinds of cheese, two ounces each. I would prefer more of a choice and fewer ounces, but the cheese is all prepackaged.

Two rather caloric desserts are the chocolate mousse cake, layers of cake filled with a rich mousse and an added layer of raspberry preserves, and a Charlotte Malakoff, a fabulous concoction of lady fingers, whipped cream, nuts, kirsch and strawberry preserves. Each is $1.50 and well worth it.

The special house coffee is one-quarter espresso and the beans are ground fresh every day. Sugar is served in antique tin molds. Tea served by the pot (six different kinds) is 50 cents, and a pot of espresso for two is $1.15, for four $2.

The restaurant's owners, two young women, Debbie Norman and Grace Kohn, also run Panache not far away at 125 North Main Street. A bar with live entertainment, it serves light meals, quiche, salads, sandwiches and desserts.

But we prefer Rue de l'Espoir, which has a nice neighborhood feeling about it along with its flair. Every neighborhood should have one!

Rue de l'Espoir, 99 Hope St., Providence, R.I. Tel. (401) 751-8890. One mile east of downtown, southeast of Brown University campus. Reservations not required. Major credit cards. Luncheon, 11:30 a.m. to 2:30 p.m. Tuesday to Friday; dinner, 5 to 9 p.m. Sunday to Thursday, to 11 p.m. Friday and Saturday. Closed Monday.

Also in the Area

The Left Bank, 220 S. Water St., Providence R.I. (401) 421-2828. A fine Sunday brunch is served here, with live chamber music a delightful accent. The Left Bank has thick stone walls (it's in a renovated warehouse) and a simple decor (when we were there the walls were covered with stunning works by a local photographer). You can get spicy Bloody Marys in a big carafe, lovely fresh melon, super eggs Benedict and good crepes Florentine, except that our spinach was gritty, as it was in the day's spinach quiche. There are several interesting cappuccinos with different liqueurs, hot cider and mulled wine. At night, some specialties are veal Marsala, steak au poivre, shrimp with tomato and garlic sauce, and roast duckling. Chicken and fish specialties change daily, as well. Lunch is served from 11:30 a.m. to 4 p.m. Monday to Saturday, and dinner from 5 to 10 p.m. Sunday to Thursday, to midnight Friday and Saturday. Sunday brunch is 10:30 a.m. to 3 p.m.

Arboretum, 63 Warren Ave., East Providence, R.I. (401) 438-3686. It used to be the Odd Fellows Hall and then an auto parts shop, but now it gleams with shining wooden floors and bare tables, a myriad of plants and flowers, huge glass windows and Mexican rush chairs. Lunch is served from 11:30 a.m. to 5 p.m. Tuesday to Saturday, and the owner told us she was considering opening evenings. Her constantly changing menu has a fascinating selection of soups, seafoods, salads, quiches, casseroles and crepes. Salade Nicoise, French peasant soup, Armenian wedding soup, moussaka, broccoli quiche, crepes Divan are among the offerings, and they make their own yogurt for the chilled cucumber and yogurt soup, and ambrosia, yogurt with fresh and dried fruits, nuts and honey. Prices are in the $1.95 to $4.50 range and there's a full bar.

David's Pot Belly, 100 N. Main St., Providence. (401) 351-4927. You can play backgammon at David's Pot Belly, or eat eclectic food from copper tables. There's a huge selection of imported beers, 14 kinds of tea, intriguing espresso combinations, and some 45 different omelets from $3.25 to $3.75. These are served with potato pancakes, applesauce and Syrian bread, and you can have them with sweet potato, artichokes, raisins, all kinds of berries, peanut butter and octopus — now there's a combination for the books! Baked eggs, meal-sized salads and chopped steak platters with choice of fillings also are featured and, at night, steak casseroles with a variety of fillings ($8.95) make a hearty dinner. Hours are 11 a.m. to midnight Monday to Thursday, 11 to 1 a.m. Friday and Saturday, and 4 to 10 p.m. Sunday.

Daytrip 13

Where Topiary is Tops
Green Animals/Portsmouth, R.I.

The *flora* turns out to be the *fauna* (or vice-versa) at Green Animals in Portsmouth, R.I. And even though one may not think of camels, elephants, giraffes or lions as native to this climate, they were the original four residents of the unique topiary garden on a small country estate overlooking Narragansett Bay.

Formal gardens, in the Williamsburg tradition, are not unknown in this country. But the animal garden, like that in Portsmouth, combined with geometric figures (note the spiral) are less common, and the brochure printed for visitors proclaims Green Animals "the finest topiary in the country."

Allowing for a little poetic license, it is a splendid place. The art of fashioning living plants into the shapes of animals and geometric figures has been carried to the point where no fewer than 85 pieces of topiary are on view. Add to that the seasonal displays of annuals and perennials (when we visited in October, the chrysanthemums were especially profuse); throw in a vista of sea sparkling under a brilliant sun, and long manicured lawns extending down to the water's edge, and you have an idea of what this place is like.

Green Animals became a public garden, in the fullest sense of the word, after the death in 1972 of its owner, Alice Brayton. Miss Brayton, a founder of the Preservation Society of Newport County, which manages a number of Newport's finest old homes as museums, willed the estate to the society. Prior to that, on her own impulse, she would open her gardens to visitors and friends, so that Green Animals had gained something of a reputation around Newport before it was opened to the public.

The story of its creation is interesting. Alice Brayton's father, Thomas E. Brayton, who was an executive with a cotton manufacturing company in Fall River, Mass., bought the estate (consisting of seven acres of land, a white clapboard summer residence, and a few outbuildings) in 1872. A few years later, noticing that one of the Portuguese employees at the cotton company was doing a creditable job of landscaping, he invited Joseph Carreiro to be his private gardener.

At that time, the estate was little more than pasture land. But Carreiro, a native of the Azores, and familiar with topiary gardens from Europe, began the creation of the formal garden after having been told to "do what you want" on the Brayton estate.

Brayton's estate passed into the hands of his daughter in 1940, and she made it her permanent residence. A horticulturist in her own right, Alice Brayton devoted great interest to the garden which by then was being managed by Carreiro's son-in-law, George A. Mendonca, who lives on the property and is responsible for the garden today.

The loquacious Mendonca, whose garden has been featured in national magazines on more than one occasion, remembers how he got his job — and his wife. A native of nearby Middletown, R.I., and the son of a tree surgeon, Mendonca says "it got into my blood when I was about 10 years old." Years later he got a job on the Brayton estate, and met and married the daughter of his boss.

Patience is required to create a true topiary: An average of 16 years before a

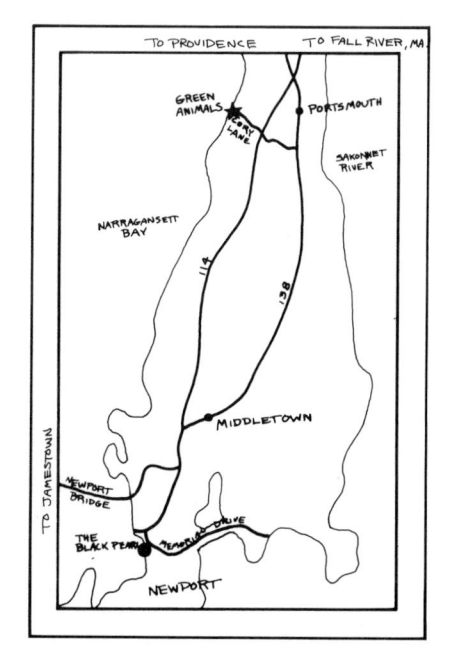

Location: Cory's Lane, Off Route 114, overlooking Narragansett Bay in Portsmouth, R.I.

Open: May 1 to September 30, daily, 10 a.m. to 5 p.m. and October weekends, 10 a.m. to 5 p.m.

Admission: Adults $1.50; children 6 to 15, 75 cents.

Telephone: (Superintendent's cottage) (401) 683-1643.

full-sized animal is created, Mendonca explains. The animals, or geometric shapes, usually of privet, sometimes boxwood, are trained while they are growing, without the help of a frame. "They're all self-supporting and free-standing," he says proudly.

The four large animals, camel, giraffe, lion and elephant, at the corners of the original garden, are evident soon after the visitor begins his walk. "Did you see how the giraffe has a short neck?" asks the garden superintendent.

Mendonca explains that during the hurricane of 1954, when Miss Brayton was 76 years old, the topiary garden was badly damaged. The giraffe, which was her favorite animal of all, lost its head in the high winds of the storm. According to the story, she said sadly to the affable Mendonca, "I'm afraid I'll never live long enough to see a new head on my giraffe."

Mendonca, in a flash of creativity, carved some of the giraffe's long neck into a head, thereby shortening the neck. Meanwhile, Miss Brayton lived another 18 years.

Today, visitors wander through the garden on their own, assisted by a printed guide which they receive when they pay their admission. Other shapes which our family remembers include a horse and rider, ostrich, rooster, donkey, bear, mountain goat and dogs. While most of the topiary garden seen today was begun by Carreiro, his son-in-law works on new forms as time permits. (His own sons may not follow in the family tradition; all three were in different lines of work at this writing).

In addition to managing the garden, Mendonca has begun creating wire forms for tabletop topiaries which he sells as a sideline in the small garden shop on the premises. Also on sale are plants, postcards and some wonderful salt marsh pottery.

Gardeners needn't think that all they'll see at Green Animals is topiary. There are the seasonal displays, and some unusual other plants, including a whole area with dwarf fruit trees. I have a lasting impression of a hardy orange with thorny branches and miniature fruits, some of which were lying on the ground in October. I picked one up and took it home in my pocketbook. And for at least a week afterward I was treated to the most wonderful aroma, every time I reached inside for anything.

No, Green Animals won't take an entire day, but it can be the highlight. Allow an hour to two. Nearby Newport should be included in your itinerary, with its famed mansions along the Cliff Walk, Touro Synagogue, the renovated waterfront area, and marvelous restaurants and shops. Even the Tennis Hall of Fame, for addicts.

Also in the Area

Prescott Farm, 2009 W. Main Road (Route 114), Middletown, R.I. (401) 847-6230. This group of restored buildings includes an operating windmill which was originally located in Warwick, R.I., and which still grinds cornmeal (on sale at the museum Country Store). Also on the property are General Prescott's guardhouse, c. 1730. Nearby is the Samuel Whitehorne House, c. 1811, open by appointment. Buildings are operated by the Newport Restoration Foundation. Open May 1 to October 31, daily 10 a.m. to 5 p.m. Adults $1.50; children 75 cents. Open weekends year-round. Not far from Green Animals.

Newport with its mansions, Touro Synagogue, restored waterfront area (fine boutiques and restaurants) is just south of Portsmouth on the same Aquidneck

Island. It is a city for more than a day, but any one of its fascinating areas or homes might be combined with your trip to Green Animals. Touro Synagogue is a favorite place of mine, 72 Touro St., Newport. Built in 1763, it is open from late June through Labor Day, Monday through Friday, 10 a.m. to 5 p.m.; Sundays, 10 a.m. to 6 p.m. A beautiful colonial house of worship.

Dining 13

The Black Pearl/Newport, R.I.

A staggering 1500 meals a day are served in the summer from the tiny but organized kitchen at the Black Pearl. With its picturesque setting by the water on Bannister's Wharf and its colorful outdoor cafe (tables shaded by Cinzano umbrellas), the Black Pearl is fantastically popular and quite an "in" place on the Newport waterfront.

Yacht owners and their crews, the rich and not-so-rich, blue-jeaned youths and tourists of all ages mingle here, drawn, no doubt, by the informal milieu and good, solid and reasonable food of the Black Pearl Tavern (the fame of the clam chowder has spread beyond the borders of Rhode Island).

In the Black Pearl's other dining room, the formal Commodore's Room, the cuisine is elegant French and expensive, and even very young gentlemen must wear jackets and ties.

The tavern is hectic, crowded, noisy, smoky and fun. Customers often are still lined up at 2:30 p.m. for late lunch. Ladies with a need for the one ladies' room wait five deep in the extremely narrow corridor (a 15-minute wait is not unusual) while harried staff race back and forth to the kitchen, yelling "coming through" and brandishing heaping plates of food. It's a wonder there aren't more bowls of chowder on the floor than on the tables!

The chowder — creamy, chock full of clams and laced with dill — is served piping hot and with a huge soda cracker, for $1.25 or $1.75. Lobster bisque and onion soup gratinee are also $1.75, and the onion soup, with lots of onions in a good strong stock, is topped with an oversized cracker heaped with cheese instead of the traditional crouton.

Omelets and crepes are served from 11 a.m. to 3 p.m. Plain omelets are $2.50, with a 25-cent surcharge for ham, cheese or mushrooms. Crepes are $3.25 to $3.50 — ratatouille, chicken and mushrooms, and lobster and native seafood.

Very popular with customers are the hamburgers ($2, with 25 cents added for cheese or bacon) served in Syrian bread or onion roll, with a pile of crisp and tiny French fries. The Pearlburger, $2.50, adds the middle Eastern salad tabbouleh (mint, cucumber and rice) to the hamburger and it's especially delicious.

Hefty roast beef, turkey, and ham and Swiss cheese are $2.50, and a ham Reuben $2.75. The chef salad is $3.25, as is spinach salad, a healthy plateful with thinly sliced marinated onions, lots of fresh mushrooms and crisp bacon bits and a nippy hot dressing including mayonnaise, mustard, oil and herbs.

A special of the day was bouillabaisse ($5.25), a huge bowl but not altogether the classic version. It included large pieces of Dover sole rolled up, clams and mussels, in a fantastic saffron-y broth, delicious when sopped up with the tavern's good French bread. Usually about five daily specials are written on a blackboard, and a couple of others on the day we were there were chicken livers in a Madeira sauce (4.75) and rainbow trout ($7.50).

A glass of the house chablis, Inglenook, and a draft beer (Heineken or Michelob) go nicely with the meal.

Also offered, all day, are a few more substantial entrees: Filet of sole Duglere, sauteed Cape scallops, soft shell crabs with almonds, veal scallops prepared two ways and prime New York strip steak. These range from $6.25 for the sole to $8.75 for the steak.

Desserts are limited to sherbet, mousse and a delectable brandy cream cake; the latter two items are $1.50. Espresso is 75 cents and made as strong as it should be on the Black Pearl's special machine. You can also get cafe au lait and cappuccino. The cappuccino Black Pearl, $1.95, is enhanced with Courvoisier and Kahlua.

In the fancy Commodore Room, very pretty with its view of the harbor through small paned windows, the fare is rich indeed, with such appetizers as toast Normande (goose liver, cream of artichoke and mushrooms on toast) for $2.75; Gruyere cheese, batter dipped and deep fried, $1.75; escargots Narbonnaise (snails on cognac, ham, walnut and tomato sauce) $2.75, Strasbourg foie gras for $7.50 and Beluga caviar $9.

Lobster (no fixed price), Dover sole, frogs legs, veal scallops and a house specialty, roast duckling with green olive sauce, are offered, ranging from $7.85 to $12. Tournedos au poivre or Bearnaise are $10.50 as is steak Diane, and for $21 you can have filet of beef, rack of lamb or grilled prime rib for two. The wine list here is extensive.

It's an elaborate menu, and we are impressed with the fact that it can be done from such a miniscule kitchen. However, we prefer the tavern side, with its low-ceilings, dark beams, old charts on the walls, and woven blue and white tablecloths. Whether in the high season, or decorated for Christmas in Newport, it's fun!

The Black Pearl, Bannister's Wharf, Newport, R.I. Tel. (401) 846-5264. On waterfront off America's Cup Avenue, just south of Treadway Inn. Reservations recommended in Commodore Room. Mastercharge and Visa. 11:30 a.m. to 1 a.m. Monday to Saturday, noon to 1 a.m. Sunday. Dinner in Commodore Room, 6 to 10:30 p.m. Hours slightly limited in winter. Closed February.

Also in the Area

La Petite Auberge, 19 Charles St., Newport, R.I. (401) 849-6669. In the 1914 Decatur House, chef Roger Putier opened his small and rather formal restaurant, featuring classic French cuisine, in 1975. Everything is elegant here, from the lace tablecloths layered over pale blue linen, to the extensive menu. Dinner entrees range from $7.50 (filet of sole Meuniere) to $10.75 for beef Wellington, lobster tails in champagne or broiled lobster with herbs, and bouillabaisse (only on Fridays) is $12.25. At lunch, salade Nicoise is $2.75, avocado and lobster salad $3.95, and omelets are in the $2.50 range. At night you should make reservations; coats and ties are a must. Hours are noon to 2:30 p.m. for lunch, 6 to 10 p.m. for dinner, Sunday dinner 5 to 9 p.m.; closed Mondays in winter.

The Clarke Cooke House, Bannister's Wharf, Newport, R.I. (401) 849-2900. Beside the Black Pearl, and with a good view of the hustle and bustle of the harbor, is this colonial-style restaurant in the restored home of a Newport merchant. The menu offers French and continental specialties, with entree prices ranging from $6.25 (native fish in season) to $10.75 (steak au poivre or filet Dijonnaise). Early diners can have a less expensive meal; sunset dinners are served from 5:30 to 7 p.m. (to 6:30 on Saturday) for $7.50 — including a glass of wine, dessert and coffee. For lunch, there are crepes, omelets, salads and soups, $1.25 to $3.75. Open every day for lunch and dinner.

The Pier, West Howard St., Newport, R.I. (401) 847-3645. Also on the water and extremely popular is the Pier, with its early American decor and seafood-laden menu. At lunchtime the clam chowder, seasoned with celery seed, is good, and the cold seafood platter for $4.95 includes half a lobster, clams, shrimps and crabmeat. At night, the fresh fish of the day is $5.25, and a house specialty, New England lobster pie, is $8.90. A happy hour, 4:30 to 6:30 p.m. Monday to Friday, features giant cocktails with hot hors d'oeuvres. Open daily for lunch and dinner; Sunday dinner, noon to 10 p.m.

Soups and Crepes Unltd., 190a Thames St., Newport, R.I. Right opposite the Treadway Inn is this pleasant little restaurant, where you can get soups, $1 or $1.25; crepes, $2.15 to $3.85; salads, $1.25 to $3.50; omelets $2 (extra ingredients 50 cents) and dessert crepes, $1.50 to $2.50. Open for lunch and dinner every day (serving all day Saturday and Sunday) except Monday night.

The Inn at Castle Hill, Ocean Drive, Newport, R.I. (401) 849-3800. Built in 1874 as the home of naturalist Alexander Agassiz, this charming country mansion is worth a visit just to see the Oriental rugs and carved Victorian furniture in the sitting room. Three handsome dining rooms, all furnished differently, serve continental food, and a sophisticated bar has a piano player. Poached salmon Hollandaise, scampi and scrod are among dinner items ($7 to $11.50) and at lunchtime, the usual crepes, sandwiches and omelets. In the summer, you can enjoy sandwiches and drinks on an outdoor patio. Come for Sunday brunch (noon to 3 p.m.) and revel in the spectacular views of Narragansett Bay and the open Atlantic.

Daytrip 14

Biking, Boating and Beaching
Block Island/Rhode Island

A boat ride, a bike ride and a beach are always a hard act to follow — throw in an island and you've got the ultimate day trip. You've also got Block Island, R.I., which suits the category to a fare-thee-well because it's accessible (just one hour from its most frequently served mainland port), casual (very) and varied.

Block Island is a sunshine place and a summer place and, for the most selective, a September place (but then the ferries are fewer and farther between). It is open and rolling and "see-worthy" for hikers and bikers; yet its main town, indeed its only town, Old Harbor, is right at the ferry slip so that the more leisurely-paced can mosey about the shops and lunch in a restaurant without need of transportation. And its exquisite natural resource, State Beach, with lifeguards, bathhouse and the amenities, is also within walking distance as are bike and moped rental shops for those who decide they'd rather not. Walk that is.

Like a Bermuda of the north, Block Island's flat to gently rolling roads, lined as they are with honeysuckle and roses, lure cyclists by the hundreds. They pay an extra $1 each way to ship their two-wheelers over the stretch of water from Point Judith in Galilee, R.I., to the town of New Shoreham (the official but little used name for Old Harbor). Bike rentals run $3 to $5 a day; mopeds, $20 to $25. It is not so large an island — seven by three miles — that much of it can't be seen in a day. The ferry from Point Judith is the best way to get there for daytrippers because sailings are frequent (six a day, each way, on the average) and the ride is just over an hour. You can leave the mainland around 9:30 a.m., return via a 5 or

6 p.m. boat (8 p.m. on Fridays) and have seven to eight hours on the island. People for whom the boat ride is the best part may opt for a longer (two and a half hours) sail from New London, Conn., or from Providence (three and a half hours) or Newport (about two hours).

The ride is sometimes smooth and sometimes not. Many people recall Block Island as the other half of weather reports which began "from Newport to Block Island" and the stretch of sea between the two does have its choppy days. The island is windy, and while I've always had a ferry go on time as planned, they don't always. There are days in the winter when it's not unusual if they don't go at all.

But it's those same winds that provide natural air conditioning in the summer, so much so that not one island hostelry depends on the artificial sort.

Because of the salubriousness of its summers, in fact, Block Island has been a favorite destination of vacationers for years. It reached a heyday of sorts around the turn of the century, when the island became a "watering spot" of some note and large steamers made regular trips from New York and Boston.

They don't any more. But the old Victorian hotels, with their gingerbread trim, are standing yet, many of them refurbished and thriving as the island ex-

Location: 14½ miles off the coast of Point Judith, Galilee, R.I.; 28 miles by water from New London, Conn., both of whose ports have daily ferries in the summer (the rest of the year you must go from Galilee).

How to Get There: By ferry from Point Judith, Newport or Providence, R.I.; New London, Conn., or Montauk, L.I., in summer. By plane from Westerly, R.I. The most frequent and fastest service is between Point Judith (Galilee) and Block Island. Earliest ferry from Galilee is generally 9:30 a.m. for the one-hour trip; last boat from Block Island is usually 6 p.m. (Fridays, 8 p.m.; Saturdays and Sundays, 5 p.m.). Also fast commuter service on hydrofoil from Point Judith at unscheduled times. Adult same-day round trip is $4.75; children under 12, $2.25. Bicycles cost an additional $1 each way. Schedules and prices can change. For information call Interstate Navigation Co. at Point Judith: (401) 783-4613.

Beaches: State Beach is the great beach, stretching up the eastern coast of the island from behind the Surf Hotel for miles. There are a public changing pavilion and snack bar.

Bike Rentals: Average $3 to $5 a day, available many places. Mopeds (at approximately $20 to $25 a day) are also available.

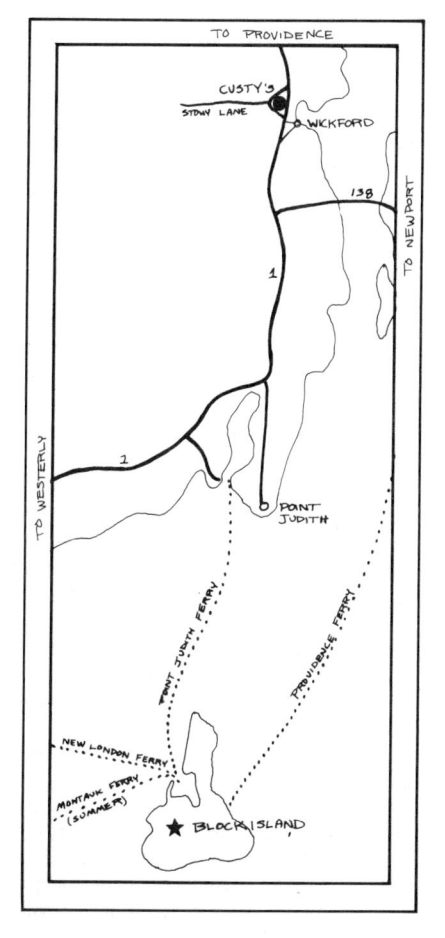

periences a rebirth of sorts. It never died. But since the mid-'60s there's been a resurgence of interest, much of it from families who rent or who buy, pushing real estate prices up so fast that even realtors find the pace breathtaking.

They come, according to one of those real estate people, because of the "freedom and no crime." They also like a "less manicured place" than, say, Martha's Vineyard or Nantucket. It's true that Block Island is not a pretentious place. Only one private club, and that a sailing club for children, does not make for great class distinctions. So if you're the type who likes to show off your poncho or your pedigree, you might better head to the classier Massachusetts islands.

Block Island is casual almost to the point of being scruffy. If jeans are in everywhere, they are *de rigueur* here. Cut-offs, faded jeans, ripped jeans — worn with sweatshirts and foul weather gear — form a kind of costume on the island just as doing your own thing is a kind of canon.

Because of that casualness and freedom, daytrippers have loved Block Island for decades. They come with their fishing poles, their swimsuits and their picnics; with their cameras, their cousins and their kids, just to "get away from it all" at a place where they truly can.

The last time we were there we met a man from Hartford who said he goes out every Saturday in the summer in search of blues and stripers and other denizens of the deep, fishing from the breakwater by Ballard's Hotel in Old Harbor. Others fish from their own boats or from deep sea fishing party boats, of which there are many. Fishing gear may be rented or purchased on the island and surf casting may be done anywhere.

If you don't care about fishing or about cycling, you ought to about swimming because it is so good at State Beach (which begins behind the big old Surf Hotel in Old Harbor and extends for miles along the island's East Coast). The water is clear, the sand is deep and because it is protected, the swimming is generally not rough. It is a wonderful beach for kite flying (those breezes again) and for frisbee games.

The town of Old Harbor is the place where daytrippers can shop, pick up picnic supplies or sit down to lunch (outdoors or in). The gift shops are mostly in the ceramic lobster-Kodak film category (I said the island wasn't fancy), but one of them, the Ragged Sailor, is several notches above and represents island craftsmen and artists. Luncheon can be eaten outside at picnic tables at Ballard's or at a small sandwich shop, or inside in a number of small restaurants that line the main street and that have a habit of changing names and owners. Best idea is to ask when you get there.

The Block Island Historical Society, at the corner of Old Town Road and Ocean Avenue, is worth a visit. It is open weekdays in the summer from 11 a.m. to 4 p.m. (adults, 50 cents; children, 25 cents). Exhibits include a typical Block Island "double ender" boat, a Santo Domingo mahogany desk from 1720 and an aerial map which shows the island in entirety — you can decide for yourself if it looks more like a pork chop or a pear.

And if toward the end of the afternoon you just want a place to sit down and rest before the ferry blows its whistle, you'll find it — and a water fountain — at Esta's Park, a postage-stamp piece of land overlooking the harbor and provided with benches, flowers and some poetic inscriptions along the fence: "Sunny beaches, cooling breeze, sky blue waters, sheltered lees; with all these joys, the world is blessed, so do sit here and take a rest."

There's more, but that's the gist — unsophisticated, uncomplicated and uncommonly welcoming — Block Island.

Dining 14

Custy's/North Kingstown, R.I.

You're just off the boat from Block Island and if the trip hasn't been too rough, all that salty air has made you hungry. You feel like some lobster? Have we got a place for you! Have one, two, five, fifteen lobsters, if you want, at Custy's in North Kingstown.

Custy's boasts the "world's most talked about buffet," describes itself as the "eighth wonder of the world," and has the customers to prove it.

On a summer Thursday night, despite a telephoned assurance that a party of two could be seated right away, we endured a nearly two-hour wait for a table. "And that's nothing," our waitress informed us. "You should see it here on a Saturday night!"

Once inside, the world's most talked about buffet is almost everything it's cracked up to be. For $15.95 a head you get all you want to — or can — eat, from a mind-boggling assortment of fare ranging from the mundane to the sublime.

The chief drawing card, of course, is the lobster. The thought of indulging in unlimited amounts of fresh boiled lobsters from the waters of nearby Narragansett Bay draws people from across the country.

It's an interesting if not edifying experience — if you put aside objections to a slam-bam, thank-you-ma'am approach to gluttonous dining.

Custy's white exterior resembles a bowling hall and the interior decor is unmemorable, but that's not what you are coming here for anyway.

No reservations are taken in the summer, and crowds mill around the foyer (which has a schlock souvenir stand) and outside the front entrance. There are a couple of cocktail lounges and if you're told they are full, don't necessarily believe it. After a boring half hour of waiting, we marched through the entire restaurant and up a flight of stairs marked "cocktail lounge," finding it almost empty.

Ninety minutes later, after sipping a drink VERY slowly on a rooftop patio, we were finally seated in one of the three downstairs rooms, at a table squeezed jaw-to-jaw in a row with other singles and doubles, making for friendly dining!

Our waitress intoned directions: "Proceed down to the buffet, take one plate, go past the salads, the vegetables, the shrimp cocktail, the lobsters. Fresh fruit is here, the desserts over there. Place your order for steak at the grill. Take only one plate, but go back as often as you like."

Her warning about one plate was echoed in the line ("only four shrimps at a time and one lobster per plate") as well as on the wall ("Eat all you want, but please no food leaves the premises. Do not embarrass yourself or us").

The buffet is really something . . . gorgeous fresh fruit salad on display in a half watermelon, many cold salads, pickles, vegetables, huge shrimp stuck into a pineapple, baked stuffed chicken breast and, of course, the lobsters. Most of them are one-clawed and small, but pristinely fresh. There are baked stuffed shrimp as well, and an absolutely beautiful display of fresh fruit of every sort — melons, strawberries, grapes, plums. A grill across the room offers small steaks cooked to order, roast beef, ham and garlic spare ribs.

After we staggered back to the table with our loaded plates, we asked the waitress for a wine list. "There isn't one," she informed us, "but we have Gallo wine in carafes. And if that isn't dry enough for you, we have sauterne!" Not being overly fond of Gallo or sauterne, we settled for a couple of Falstaff draft beers, which went nicely with the food.

In dress at Custy's, anything goes! There was not a tie in the place and a lot of overweight customers were in cutoffs and muscle shirts, perhaps to show off some stunning tattoos. Casual is the word and Tom Collins the drink — the party of six next to us upstairs nursed six Tom Collinses while waiting for their names to be called.

The 350 seats in the restaurant turn over at least three times on a busy summer night, when the family-owned business goes through 3,000 pounds of lobsters. Stock comes from two of their own fishing boats, plus extras. The 10-year-old business has expanded three times, so it must be profitable.

Ninety percent of the customers choose the buffet, although there is a limited regular menu as well (single lobster, $3.35; a special of three lobster tails, three claws and two jumbo shrimp for $9.75; jumbo shrimp cocktail $3.75).

Go prepared to wait, wear something loose, be sure to have a hearty appetite, and you'll receive good value for your $15.95 — it's not exactly my cup of tea, but I seem to be in the minority!

Custy's, 7769 Post Road, North Kingstown, R.I. Tel. (401) 885-2650. Route 1 north of Wickford, near Quonset Point. Reservations not accepted in summer except for parties of 12 or more; accepted rest of year. Major credit cards. Buffet hours, 5 to 11 p.m. Wednesday to Friday, 2 to 11 p.m. Saturday, 1 to 8 p.m. Sunday. Lunches and dinners served a la carte, 11 a.m. to closing. Closed Monday and Tuesday.

Also in the Area

1661 House, Spring Street, Old Harbor, Block Island, R.I. (401) 466-2421. A favorite eating spot on the island, the dining room in this old seaside inn is particularly attractive, all yellow and white and welcoming. Entrees on the menu include flounder stuffed with oysters and walnuts, a specialty; broiled scallops, frogs legs and sirloin steak. Items, ordered a la carte or with complete dinners, range from $6 to $10. Children eat from the same menu at reduced prices. A specialty is Johnny Cakes with syrup, served with home baked rolls. Luncheon is not served, and for the day tripper, probably the only time you could stay for dinner would be Friday, when the last boat back to Point Judith is at 8 p.m. Reservations required.

The Merciful Lion, Waites Corner Road, West Kingston, R.I. (401) 789-1971. Nary a bit of meat, fish or even eggs is on the menu in this vegetarian establishment, owned and run by a group of dedicated vegetarians from the nearby University of Rhode Island, but it's still a most interesting and varied fare. Miso (a Japanese broth) and the day's soups are kept hot in crockpots, and the garden salad is a work of art. Great hearty breads are served, and you can buy loaves to take home. Spinach pie, curry and pilaf, eggplant mozzarella and tempura are among the dinner entrees, $3.25 to $3.95, and appetizers include tabouli, stuffed mushroom caps, hommos and soyballs with cocktail sauce. Fresh-pressed apple juice smoothies (fruitshakes) and exotic teas and coffees are offered, and, on the munchkin menu for the kids, Aunty Em's sensible protein supper and wizard's crystal yogurt bowl are a couple of the imaginatively named goodies. Lovely pottery is sold here, and in keeping with the peaceful aura, there's a small sitting area with books for browsing and toys for children. Bare stained floors, macrame dividers, patchwork curtains and old dining room tables and chairs add to the charm. Merciful Lion is open for lunch and dinner from Wednesday to Saturday, and there's a very popular Sunday brunch (11:30 a.m. to 2:30 p.m.) for $3.95, and dinner, $4.95, from 5 to 8 p.m.

Cafe in the Barn, Route 6, Seekonk, Mass. (617) 336-6330. The front part of the barn dates from 1864 and has survived hurricanes, fires, floods, neglect and the honky-tonk of Route 6. Inside is a most attractive restaurant, a fine gourmet shop and a greenhouse supplying the plants that hang all over in huge woven baskets. The Barbadian chef has cooked for British royalty, but now he concentrates on us hungry commoners, with a menu featuring steaks with different sauces ($7.95 to $10.50), specials every night of chicken, fish and lamb, and appetizers like pate Strasbourg, ratatouille, and melon and prosciutto. Desserts are superior: Blueberries Romanoff, violets in summer snow, Mom's pantry pie and black velvet cake. At lunch, there are items like capricious crepes, fat-farm omelets and chicken salad Cleopatra (with mayonnaise, dill, nutmeg, avocado and almonds). Beers, wines and a good selection of aperitifs are available. Lunch is served from noon to 3 p.m. every day except Sunday when there's a brunch from 11 a.m. to 4 p.m., and dinner is served Thursday, Friday and Saturday from 6 to 10 p.m.

Daytrip 15

How to See the Seaport
Mystic Seaport/Mystic, Conn.

Go to the head of the class if you know what a gimballed bed is.

If you don't, go to Mystic Seaport, where you'll see more than one gimballed bed (the captain's, on the whaleship *Charles W. Morgan* is one). You'll also see and learn about most aspects of life at sea (and on shore) in 19th century America.

The seaport, celebrating its 50th anniversary in 1979, is something of a venerable institution in Connecticut's southeastern corner, for years ranking as the state's No. 1 tourist attraction and bringing in all manner of secondary development like motels, restaurants, shops and even an aquarium (with which it has no direct connection).

But Mystic Seaport, with its strong educational orientation, tries its best not to go the commercial route and to stick to its original purpose: "The preservation of America's maritime heritage."

With a few reservations, it does a good job. On the 17-acre immediate site (it owns 40 acres in all), visitors climb aboard preserved sailing vessels, watch cooking demonstrations over open hearths, view working craftsmen, learn about whaling and whalemen, watch planetarium programs which teach about navigation via the skies, and in general get a strong taste of the lure, the lore and the life of the sea during the last century.

The seaport is most appropriately located. No Disney World carved from a swamp, it evolved from what was for years an operating shipyard where the Greenman family of Mystic launched nearly 100 vessels of all sizes and configurations between 1838 and 1878. At the same time Mystic had become important as a whaling port, and the small town's merchants owned no fewer than 18 whalers at the height of the whaling trade in the 1840s.

The *Charles W. Morgan* wasn't one of them. But it is the last of its kind — the only wooden whaleship surviving from the 19th century fleet of American whalers, a property of which the seaport is immensely proud, and the one which probably attracts the most visitors in the course of the year. It has been designated a National Historic Landmark.

The *Morgan*, with its graceful masts poking up from Chubbs Wharf where it is tied on the Mystic River, is a floating exhibit, one which can be boarded, as can two or three other of Mystic's larger ships, and whose importance is explained by an "interpreter" aboard. These guides are on hand at most of the major exhibits, and some not-so-major ones, to answer questions, explain and, if they're not too pressed by crowds, get into an enthusiastic conversation with visitors about their particular area of expertise. In between, you're on your own to wander as you will.

The *Morgan* is not to be missed, any more than the presentation on "Whales, Whaling and Whalemen" which is generally a daily event in the Campbell Room, downstairs from the seaport planetarium. Together the ship and the demonstration provide a graphic and exciting account of whaling in the last century, from the thrill of sighting one of the great ocean mammals, to the thrill of coming home with the hold filled to overflowing with barrels of whale oil. By the time you're finished, you'll probably know your odonceti from your mysticeti, too.

Mystic Seaport photo

There's more than whaling demonstrations at Mystic, so much more, in fact, that visitors are hard-pressed to take it all in in one day. (For the sticklers who insist on seeing everything, the seaport sells a two-day ticket which can be used on two consecutive days).

In general, one day is enough. The key to getting your money's worth is to arrive early (when the gates open if possible), stay late and keep moving.

I've been to Mystic in summer and winter, and summer is better. It's also crowded, sometimes hellishly so. Best of all can be late Spring or early Fall, when the weather is balmy but there's still room to breathe. The seaport is open all year, it's true, but in the winter the schedule is curtailed, a number of the buildings aren't open, and it takes more than a pot-bellied stove to warm up a whaler.

When everything is in full swing, Mystic really hums. The shipcarver is at work in his shop, probably on a figurehead; the cooper is making barrels, and the ship's chandler is ready to outfit your barque with any manner of equipment and supplies. (Ask him to demonstrate the portable fog horn, taken aboard ships, but you may have to hold your ears when he does. My daughter jumped)! Craftsmen are weaving, printing and sailmaking, while a daily cooking demonstration, usually of a fish dish (I remember cod fish cakes), is being held over the open hearth in the kitchen of the 18th century Buckingham House.

There's more than the *Morgan* to climb aboard. Try the *Joseph Conrad*, one of the smallest full-rigged ships built in modern times (1882) and used summers as a training ship for the popular Mystic Mariner program; or the *L.A. Dunton*, a Gloucester fishing schooner impeccably restored. For an additional fee, you can take a ride aboard the *Sabino*, the last remaining coal-fired steam-powered ferry in operation in the country. She once ferried passengers between the coast of Maine and some of its islands; the ride these days is up the Mystic River and takes about a half hour (adults $1.75, kids $1).

If you're the type who has stars in your eyes, you'll want to visit the planetarium, which schedules shows daily and which is worth the additional 25 cents admission, even though I find "extras," after buying a ticket at the gate, annoying. This is a most interesting lesson in how navigators used the skies, and a

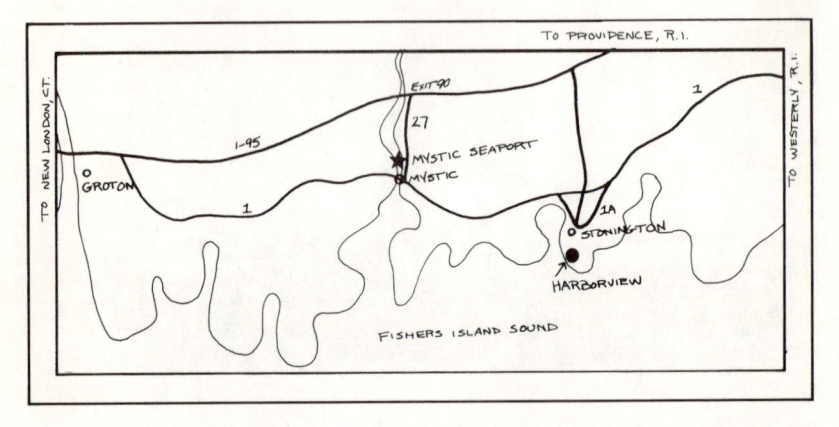

Location: Route 27 south of the Connecticut Turnpike in Mystic, Conn. Take Exit 90 from Connecticut Turnpike (I-95).

Open: Year-round except for Christmas Day and New Year's Day. Summer hours, April through November, 9 a.m. to 5 p.m.; winter hours, December through March, 10 a.m. to 4 p.m.

Admission: Summer, $5 adults, $2.50 children; winter, $4.50 adults, $2.25 children. Senior citizens and older (through college) students with identification, $3.50. Special 2-day ticket available during summer: $6 adults; $2.75 children. Must be used on consecutive days.

Special Events: Band concerts, Tuesday evenings in the summer, and other events ranging from courses to sailing races are scheduled. Check at the gate or call ahead for schedule. Sunday before Christmas is traditionally the annual Free Day with carol sings and other holiday events, very popular.

Picnicking: At tables outside The Galley restaurant, on the seaport grounds, or anywhere else that is not designated "off limits." Eat your sandwiches on the pier, if you'd like.

Telephone: (203) 536-2631.

general astronomy lesson as well, geared toward the sky at the time of year you visit.

Static exhibits there are, too, which you can choose according to your interests. Boatsmen will not want to miss seeing some of the more than 200 small craft owned by the seaport, a number of which are regularly on display in the North Boat Shed or at the Small Craft Exhibit in the Spar Shed.

A recently completed and truly outstanding exhibit is the *Benjamin F. Packard* cabin exhibit, the restored cabins of a large "downeaster" cargo ship, salvaged and at the seaport nearly forty years until the magnificent restoration of a couple of years ago. The cabin boy on this ship also slept in a gimballed bed, you'll note.

The recreated 19th century village along the waterfront happens to be a popular part of the seaport, especially with children, although it's a bit contrived. Less so is the shipyard near the south end, where visitors may stop in the 100-foot-long main shop to observe restoration work going on from a second-floor balcony.

And for the person who wants to put it all into perspective, leave some time for the new and permanent exhibit, "New England and the Sea," in the Stillman building.

Other popular exhibits are the Mystic River diorama, which shows Mystic much as it looked in 1853; the Plymouth Cordage Co. ropewalk; the Charles Mallory Sail Loft, and the tiny Children's Museum with an exhibit about children who went to sea.

If you have your own children along, bring a backpack or stroller for the very young.

You'll build up an appetite, which can be satisfied at the fast-food restaurant, the Galley, or the more formal Seaman's Inne, both run by Mystic Seaport, or by picnicking at tables near the Galley or indeed at any of a number of spots throughout the grounds. You'll be impressed with the fact that, generally, everything is "shipshape."

Don't worry about finding your way around. At the gates where you purchase your tickets you'll also receive a marvelous three-color map of the seaport, which is indispensable, and a schedule of daily events, which frequently change. Thorough types also will want to purchase the official seaport guide for 75 cents, containing detailed descriptions of each exhibit (I recommend it).

Also in the Area

Mystic Marine Life Aquarium, a short distance from Mystic Seaport (just follow the signs), has more than 30 living exhibits indoors plus sea lions and seals in a special outdoor area. Demonstrations with dolphins, a Beluga whale and sea lions occur every hour on the hour. Open every day of the year except Thanksgiving, Christmas and New Year's Day from 9 a.m. to 4:45 p.m. Admission: Adults $4; children 5 to 14 $1.75; children under 5 free. (203) 536-3323.

Stonington. A charming and historic village located just east of Mystic on Route 1A, the state's most picturesque seaside community is a treasure out of the past. Be sure to walk its narrow main streets to savor its sights and sounds. **The Old Lighthouse Museum** at The Point in Stonington is said to be the first government lighthouse in Connecticut (1823). Displays of 19th century portraits, whaling and fishing gear, etc. July-Labor Day, Tuesday-Sunday, 11 a.m. to 4:30 p.m. Adults, 75 cents; under 12, 25 cents. Tel. (203) 535-1440.

Dining 15

Harborview/Stonington, Conn.

Heavy, ornate wooden doors open up on the Harborview Restaurant, an unlikely mecca for connoisseurs of fine food in out-of-the-way Stonington, Connecticut's quaintest coastal village.

Inside is a charming quasi-Victorian atmosphere of dark-panelled drawing room by the sea. The French menu is ambitious and the food superb, amply and expertly served.

The result is one of Connecticut's finest restaurants, a tribute attested to by the crowds which turn over twice in the 200-seat dining room on weekday evenings and three times on weekends in summer.

Owner Jerry Turner, serving drinks in the bar, said "we're even filled at lunch." The reason is obvious: The finest haute cuisine on the shore between Westport and Newport — with New York style at Stonington prices.

Before the Harborview started accepting reservations, lines often were long so we chose the time for our first visit carefully. Arriving at 6:35 on a Thursday night, we were seated immediately. Within five minutes, all the tables were filled and the bar started absorbing the overflow. That situation continued until 9, when latecomers could get right in.

The crevettes Remoulade and Billi-Bi soup were the first indications that an exceptional feast was in store.

The Billi-Bi, of which the New York Times Cookbook says "this may well be the most elegant and delicious soup ever created," was sensational, and a bargain for a large bowl at $1.50. The combination of mussels, shallots, wine, butter, cream and herbs was rich and heavenly.

We also loved the crevettes Remoulade for $2.95 — a dinnerplate full of five huge shrimp on a bed of tender lettuce, covered with a fine and piquant sauce, although I couldn't detect any capers in it. This was a meal in itself. A woman at the next table had the right idea; she ordered an appetizer and a salad, and skipped the entree.

Other appetizers include canapes varies, scallops en brochette Hollandaise, moules grillees and clams naturel, all $2.50; terrine du chef, $1.50; quiche du jour, $1.75, and saumon fume, $3.25. Soups (onion, du jour and Madrilene) are all $1.50, and you can have fettucine Alfredo or with mussels for $3.50.

House salad (greens, beets, croutons, cherry tomatoes and extraordinary house dressing of sour cream, mustard seed and garlic) comes with entrees. My mushroom and watercress vinaigrette for $2 had lots of sliced raw mushrooms and crisp watercress, but was overpowered by so much dressing that it pooled on the bottom of the plate.

Before all this, we had ample drinks (a Lillet and a Manhattan) served in ice-cold stemmed glasses. From the smallish wine list we chose a crisp Muscadet for $6. Most wines are in the $6 to $10 range, but you can splurge on Chateau Mouton Rothschild 1967 for $45.

For entrees, seafood and veal dishes abound, plus three poultry and five hearty meat offerings. Turner and his wife Ainslie, who does some of the cooking for the evening meal, are inspired by the cuisine of Brittany, which they visit every year in the late fall.

Prices range from $7.50 for coq au vin to $24 for chateaubriand bouqetiere and rack of lamb for two. Most are in the $7.95 to $8.95 range. Specials of the day are offered, some depending on local catches — scrod for $7.50 the night we dined.

Although almost sated after the generous appetizers and salads, we enjoyed a lovely sole Marguery, poached with shrimps, mushrooms and mussels and a sauce of egg yolks and butter, $7.95. Veal scallops a la creme were served with sauteed mushrooms, cream and a touch of cognac, a portion large enough to feed two, with outstandingly good veal, $8.50. There was a choice of potatoes, baked or parsleyed, which were divine, tiny new potatoes in their jackets, swimming in butter.

After this, dessert was impossible, and the choices recited by the waiter seemed rather mundane. We did enjoy cups of strong coffee and then a walk around the lovely village to work off some of the calories.

Space prevents listing the nearly two dozen entrees but all sound wonderful, and it is really hard to choose between filet en croute, bouillabaisse a la Marseillaise, crevettes au Pernod or timbale de moules Melanie.

Many of the same dishes are served at lunch time, with the addition of three egg dishes. Prices for the entrees are in the $4.25 to $5.95 range, while prices for the appetizers, soups and salads remain the same as at night.

The decor at Harborview is handsome but unobtrusive. Paned windows along the back of the dining room give a fine view of picturesque Stonington harbor, and one can watch the sun go down over the water while the room darkens. Flowers, candles in hurricane lamps, and handsome pewter cutlery are on each blue-clothed table.

You'd expect diners at such a select spot would be dressed in best bib and tucker but not so — many patrons dock their boats in the harbor and come ashore, so you see elegantes flanked by informal outfits, including a man in orange short shorts and a woman of certain age, who shouldn't have been, in white shorts and halter.

As the efficient waiters in black bow ties and white shirts and waitresses in black scurry by, the effect is one of organized chaos. But the only time we had to wait was for the bill!

Harborview Restaurant, Cannon Square, 60 Water St., Stonington, Conn. 06378. Tel. (203) 535-2720. Reservations recommended. Major credit cards. Lunch: noon to 3 p.m. daily except Tuesday. Dinner: 5 to 10 p.m. daily except Tuesday, 4 to 9 p.m. Sunday. Open Tuesday July and August.

Also in the Area

Sandy's, 66 Water St., Stonington, Conn. (203) 535-9335. If you're feeling a bit more informal and in the mood for what Sandy MacKay, the young proprietor, calls the "New England Experience," head for Sandy's, a glorified fish shack just behind the Harborview. Place your order for lobster, steamers, steamed fish of the day (flounder, swordfish, sole or scallops) at the counter and pick raw clams from a clam bar for 25 cents each. You dine at picnic tables, and you can bring your own wine or whatever. A lobster, served with corn, cole slaw and bread, is $4.95. Sometimes there's a smoked bluefish and always, New England chowder. Sen. Lowell Weicker likes to eat here when he's in town. Sandy's is also retail, and we have fond memories of a gigantic bluefish we bought there once and cooked on our barbecue with Sandy's personal recipe. It opens around Memorial Day and closes in September, serves dinner seven nights and lunch on Saturday and Sunday.

Abbott's Lobster in the Rough, Pearl Street, Noank, Conn. (203) 536-7719. We bring visiting relatives and friends to Abbott's for a lobster feed, partly because of the delectable lobsters, partly because of the view of Fishers Island and Long Island Sound, with a constant stream of interesting craft parading back and forth into Mystic Harbor. Here we prefer to eat outside at gaily colored picnic tables on ground covered with mashed-up clam shells, and the kids can scamper around the rocks, finding jelly fish and snails. Again, you order at a counter and get a number (usually about a 40-minute wait) and you bring your own beverage and appetizers. Lobster, last we knew, was $4.95 for 1 1/4 pounds, and comes with bags of potato chips, small containers of home-made coleslaw and melted butter, plus a bib! You can also get terrific clam chowder, steamers, baked stuffed clams, shrimp roll, lobster roll and crab roll. Abbott's has a retail outlet where cans of its own clam bisque and chowder, lobster bisque and other items are sold. It's open from about May 1 through Labor Day, 11 a.m. to 9 p.m.

Poor Richard's, 49 Boston Post Rd. (Route 1), Waterford, Conn. (203)443-1813. A new restaurant in an old house, Poor Richard's has an English Tavern atmosphere (copper tables) downstairs and is elegant Victorian upstairs. The menu offers continental and French specialties, and always lots of seafood, bouillabaisse, scallops prepared three different ways and lobster. A house specialty is veal cooked in parchment paper with prosciutto and mozzarella cheese. Businessman's lunch is served in the tavern for $2.95 (25 cents extra for a glass of wine or beer) and is understandably popular. Dinner entrees are $7.50 to $9.75, and a Sunday brunch at $5.75 features omelets and crepes. A carafe of the house wine, Pastine, is only $3.25. It's open seven days, Monday to Saturday for lunch and dinner; Sunday brunch is 11:30 a.m. to 2:30 p.m. and dinner from 4 to 9 p.m.

Daytrip 16

River View; Castle, Too
Gillette Castle/Hadlyme, Conn.

The way to approach Gillette Castle in Hadlyme, Connecticut, is as its owner first did, via the Connecticut River. It's possible, too — aboard the tiny ferry that plies its way between Hadlyme and Chester "on demand," carrying six cars and several foot passengers.

The ferry is fun and just a five-minute ride, but from the river you get a magnificent aspect of green hills with the castle nestled among them, a view that first enchanted the Connecticut actor, William Gillette. The Hartford-born Gillette wasn't on the ferry, but aboard his houseboat on a leisurely cruise up the river when he discovered the site. He was returning from Greenport, Long Island, where he had all but decided to build the home of his dreams, and had anchored for the night close to the spot where the Chester-Hadlyme ferry now docks.

Gillette woke up the next morning to a view that held him captive for a few extra days, long enough to abandon plans for the Long Island site in favor of this verdant spot on the banks of the river. There he purchased 122 acres of land with nearly a mile of shorefront. And in the next five years, between 1914 and 1919, he had a "castle" built to his exacting specifications. Gillette never called it one, but that's what it is, a massive stone building atop the southernmost hill in a series along the river known as the Seven Sisters. Gillette simply called it the "Seventh Sister."

For an actor it was a terrific stage set. No copy of a castle in Spain or England, Gillette's castle came from his own fertile and inventive mind. The aging actor, who was in his 60s at the time, drew all the architectural plans himself. And not only the castle, with its four-to-five-foot thick granite walls, 24 oddly shaped rooms and marvelous stone terraces (wait till you view the river from them), but the furniture, too, was designed by Gillette.

95

Most of it is heavy, of hand-hewn oak. The dining room table moves along on metal tracks on the floor (I first saw it at age 8 and never forgot that table); some of the bedroom furniture is built into the structural frame of the castle itself; even the lights were designed by the actor. Stout oaken doors are fastened by intricate wooden locks reminiscent of Rube Goldberg; at every turn there is another stamp of Gillette's own unique personality.

But the actor-architect undoubtedly had the most fun creating a railroad on the castle grounds, which was a reflection of his favorite hobby, trains and locomotives. (Already at the age of 16 in his home in Hartford's Nook Farm area he had built a stationary steam engine).

The train in Hadlyme not only ran but accommodated passengers, and was in fact Gillette's favorite way to entertain his many visitors. They boarded at "Grand Central," a depot closest to the castle itself, which survives as a picnicking site in today's park. With Gillette at the throttle (and we are told he was no overly cautious engineer), the group would travel through forest and glen to "125th Street Station," then to the east end of the property, back to Castle Oak near the present entrance and finally around to Grand Central again. It was a three-mile ride.

The train has long since gone to Lake Compounce Amusement Park in Bristol, Conn., (where visitors may still ride it around the small lake) and most of the tracks have been dismantled, although there are persistent rumors, some of them quite serious, that it will be rebuilt.

But even without it, the castle attracts more than 100,000 visitors a year under the auspices of Connecticut's state park system. It is probably as Gillette would have wished. The forthright actor, who wrote his will just months before his death at the age of 87, wanted his executors to see "that the property did not fall into the hands of some blithering saphead who has no conception of where he is or with what surrounded."

That didn't happen, for the state acquired the property back in 1943, just six years after the actor's death. Inside the castle, in addition to the unusual inventions and furnishings, are the rich mementos of William Gillette's long and successful stage career. He was known best for his creation of the role of Sherlock Holmes in a play which he wrote himself as an adaptation of the Arthur Conan Doyle character, and was honored in his own day. He actually performed the role more than 13,000 times all across the country.

(Just a few years back, Gillette's script was successfully revived on Broadway and the entire cast trooped up to Hadlyme for a visit to the castle in Gillette's memory).

Theater buffs will enjoy all the stage memorabilia — in particular the room which is almost an exact replica of the stage set for the play in which Gillette starred. That room is on the third floor of the castle, approached by narrow staircases from the second floor balcony which overlooks the grand living room and massive fireplace.

There's an art gallery on the third floor, too, where Gillette displayed his fine collection of paintings on walls hung with Javanese raffia mats made to his order. Everything was his own idea, from the design of a "bar" which transforms into a simple cupboard on the spot to bubbling fountains in mini-greenhouses off the living room.

But the castle proper is not all there is to the state park. It serves as the focal point, but there are also views of river and woods, and trails leading through a dark and lush pine forest. A variety of spots are perfect for picnics and there is a snack bar for those who haven't brought along their own.

On our most recent visit, we arrived just before noon via the Chester-

Location: Route 148. Exit at 68-69 from Connecticut Thruway to Route 9. Exit 6 from Route 9 to take the Chester-Hadlyme ferry; Exit 7 to take Route 82 and the bridge to East Haddam; follow 82 south to 148.

Open: Daily, Memorial Day to Columbus Day, 11 a.m. to 5 p.m.

Admission: Park is free; to tour castle, adults pay 50 cents apiece; children under 12 are free.

Telephone: (203) 526-2336.

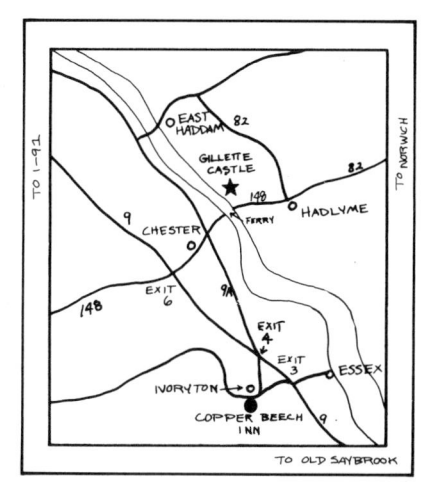

Hadlyme ferry and went through the castle (it takes about a half hour) before spreading out lunch on a table in Grand Central Station. It sits nearest the river of any picnic spot and its thick stone walls make it welcomingly cool on hot summer days. After lunch we spotted signs for the "Loop Trail" promising a river vista and we hiked down the walkway to get closer to the water. It was not a strenuous walk — just about a half mile — and rewarded us with its natural loveliness.

Other trails wander through the park; there are also open meadows and a lily pond. Gillette himself is not buried on the property he loved, but in Farmington, Conn., next to his wife of six years, Helen Nickles Gillette, whose early death caused him great sadness.

A visit to Gillette Castle can be happily combined with a stop at East Haddam, just a few miles to the northwest, where the presence of the Goodspeed Opera House has encouraged the arrival of fine small shops and some good restaurants, too.

Also in the Area

Chester-Hadlyme Ferry. Route 148 (either direction). Daily, April 1 to November 1, 7 a.m. to 8 p.m. 25 cents for car and driver; 5 cents for each additional passenger.

Goodspeed Opera House, East Haddam, Conn. (203) 873-8668. Overlooking the Connecticut River, this Victorian opera house is enjoying a revival — of musicals, of interest, of enthusiasm. Three shows, all musical, are presented each season, which now extends from mid-April to early November. Two are revivals and one is always an original. The Goodspeed's track record is fine in sending its productions on to Broadway, including "Man of LaMancha," "Shenandoah" and "Annie." You can attend the Goodspeed Tuesday through Friday evenings at 8:30 p.m.; Wednesday matinee at 2:30 p.m.; two shows Saturday at 5 and 9 p.m. and an early evening performance on Sunday at 5 p.m. The house is dark Mondays. The smell of popcorn, from an old-fashioned popcorn wagon, fills the lobby, and cocktails or champagne can be sipped during intermission on the porch which overlooks the river. Reservations are usually a must.

Dining 16

Copper Beech Inn/Ivoryton, Conn.

Copper Beech Inn

In the guest book just ahead of our entry, someone had written, "If there is a heaven, it must be like the Copper Beech!" The accolade may be exaggerated, but dining at the Copper Beech comes close to bordering on the heavenly.

The beautifully restored 19th century inn in Ivoryton, once the residence of the Comstock family in this center of the ivory trade, has been open since 1973 and has gained a reputation as one of the finest restaurants in New England (four stars recently in the Mobil Guide).

Framed by the burnished leaves of supposedly the oldest copper beech in Connecticut, the big white house with its porches and trellises is a most inviting sight. Soft light from the many brass chandeliers spills over the green lawn on a summer night, welcoming you inside. In the winter, a beautifully decorated Christmas tree glows on the front porch, and around it are fascinating dolls at least three feet high from the owner's collection, clad in Victorian costumes that were made by her mother in Halifax. The house cat, Mr. Bombay, surveys the scene from his wicker basket.

Robert and Jo McKenzie (she's finance chairman for the state Republican party as well) bought the abandoned Johnny-Cake Inn when it was little more than a shell filled with mildew. It took nearly eight months of back-breaking work to achieve what they have now — a warm, serene and elegant inn, with several dining areas and a menu featuring country French classical cuisine.

We've dined twice in the Georgian Room, reminiscent of Williamsburg, with its many chandeliers, wall sconces, subdued but tasteful decor and dignified white-jacketed waiters. Lighting is dim and romantic, handsome silver and china gleam on the pristine white cloths, and napkins folded strikingly to look like long crooked candles are tucked into tall stemmed water goblets. Candles in hurricane lamps center the tables, which in winter are adorned with Christmas greens and white rosebuds.

A stunning lithograph of the copper beech is superimposed on the menu, written in dark blue script on a pale blue background. It offers an amazingly varied selection of appetizers and entrees.

Nineteen appetizers range from $1.50 for marinated artichoke hearts mimosa to $3.75 for a house specialty, shrimp in beer batter with fruit sauce, and iced shrimp cocktail. Then there's a sharp jump to caviar Romanoff, $22.

Of the appetizers we've tried, we loved an avocado half filled with scallops and shrimp on tender lettuce, and a lobster cocktail Louis, a large serving of lobster meat in a piquant mayonnaise-based sauce. The specialty shrimp, plump and firm in their crisp beer batter, are fantastic with the mustardy fruit sauce. Mussels mariniere are served in a heady wine, parsley and shallot-laden broth, their blue-black shells gleaming and their insides sweeter than clams (and a finger bowl follows). The hot country pate in a Madeira-based truffle sauce is a hearty dish, almost a meal — the large slice of veal and pork meat wrapped in bacon and served en croute.

The seafood crepe Bonne Femme (shrimps, scallops, crab and lobsters) was good although it was served lukewarm, but the special soup of the day, a Back Bay clam chowder, was piping hot and the hearty broth base a welcome change from the usual cream. Other soups are French onion soup gratinee, $1.50; chilled crabmeat bisque, $1.25, and lobster bisque, $1.75.

The house salad, served on crystal plates, is a refreshingly crisp mixture of greens garnished with green pepper, black olives, hard-cooked egg, tomatoes and onions, with a choice of the excellent house dressing, creamy garlic with herbs, or Russian, French or Roquefort. Big, crusty homemade French rolls and sweet butter are also served.

There's a huge wine list, with many extremely expensive bottles (Chateau Latour $150 and seven reds over $50) but good bargains as well for around $6, a Graves and a California Gamay Beaujolais, for example. All wines are served impeccably, the reds in large globe-shaped glasses and the whites, properly chilled, in pretty fluted glasses. A small carafe of the house wine, Martini Vineyards, is $2.50. Cocktails are perfectly made and there's a good selection of aperitifs.

Twenty-three entrees include three house specialties, glazed boneless game hen with country sauce, crabmeat Tetrazzini and veal maison with noodles Romanoff. The Tetrazzini is an extravagant affair with delicate strands of pasta, mushrooms, a creamy sauce flecked with herbs, and plenty of crabmeat.

We've tried the veal maison twice — once it was tender and in a delicate batter; another time very heavily breaded and disappointing, as was the veal in the veal Oscar (served under glass)! The sauce with it is nice, lemony and tomato flecked, and the noodles Romanoff richly covered with cream and cheese.

Entrees start at $5.95 for fish of the day, then jump to $7.50 to $11.95 with roast lamb persille for two, $26. The day's fish was sole, done quite simply in butter and crumbs. Other entrees from the really ambitious selection include roast stuffed brace of royal quail with sauce grand veneur, coquille of lobster maison, sauteed sweetbreads, beef Wellington with Madeira sauce, sirloin steak with green peppercorns and roast stuffed duckling with wild rice and a brandied peach sauce.

Vegetables of the day change constantly — we've had zucchini and broccoli, both cooked al dente.

We're impressed with the highly professional and unobtrusive service at

Copper Beech. Dishes are presented superbly and the table is even cleaned of crumbs between courses.

Also impressive are the 18 choices on the dessert list, all $1.50. The inn's own velvet cake is so dark and rich it could be fudge, and the lime daiquiri chiffon pie is a delicate treasure. A deep dish cheese pie comes with brandied raspberry sauce and you can have Grand Marnier mousse en swans, brandied peach trifle Anglaise or pistachio nut parfait with caramel sauce.

Fine coffee, 50 cents, is served in individual silver pots. Espresso is $1, and Irish coffee and cafe Chantilly, a house specialty, are $2.50 and $2.75, respectively.

At luncheon, the same appetizers and desserts at the same prices are available; entrees, some of which are the same as at night, with additions of more lunchy things such as quiche Lorraine, omelets, eggs Benedict and a couple of sandwiches, go from $2.95 for club sandwich of the day to $4.95 for shrimp scampi, Bercy butter.

Other dining areas include a charming small porch with white Parsons tables and white wicker chairs, and the Comstock Room, with dark oak panelling, named after the original owner. The Greenhouse, a new lounge in back, is open every night in summer, Friday and Saturday in winter, usually with entertainment by a pianist. Five spacious guest rooms, decorated elegantly with period pieces, and with private bath, are $30 a night double.

Many customers here are regulars, devotees who return time after time to sample the imaginative offerings of chef Raymond Terrill, who's only 27. You have to reserve days (sometimes weeks) ahead for Friday and Saturday nights. Despite the full house, a calm and unruffled atmosphere prevails, a tribute to the McKenzies, who keep everything running like exquisite clockwork.

Copper Beech Inn, Main Street, Ivoryton, Conn. Tel. (203) 767-0330. At east edge of Ivoryton along Ivoryton-Centerbrook Road. Exits 3 or 4 off Route 9 near Essex. Reservations recommended. Major credit cards. Luncheon, noon to 2 p.m. Tuesday to Friday; dinner, 6 to 9 p.m. Tuesday to Thursday, to 10 p.m. Friday and Saturday. Sunday dinner, 1 to 8 p.m. Closed Monday.

Also in the Area

Gelston House, Goodspeed Landing, East Haddam, Conn. (203) 873-9300. There's been an inn on this site in picturesque East Haddam since 1736, and the early Victorian architecture of the Gelston House blends beautifully with the landmark Goodpseed Opera House next door. The Gelston House does a booming business in the summer when the Opera House is open, and the outdoor Beer Garden is an especially delightful place for a light meal (hot dogs, hamburgers, grinders, steamers, etc.) and/or a drink or beer. Inside, dinner entrees are $6.25 to $10.50 (filet mignon with mushrooms and onion rings,) and you can choose from all kinds of seafood, veal, mixed grill, calves liver with bacon, and lamb shish kebab. The Beer Garden opens at noon and closes at 11 or later, depending on the weather. Lunch is served inside from 11:30 a.m. to 2:30 p.m., noon to 2 on Saturday. Dinner hours are 5:30 to 9 p.m. and Sunday, noon to 8 p.m.

Old Lyme Inn, Lyme Street, Old Lyme, Conn. (203) 434-2600. A sophisticated and formal restaurant in an 1850 Victorian house redone in the French Empire style, the Old Lyme Inn offers classic and country French dining, a pretty blue and gold color scheme, and a "candlelight and roses" romantic atmosphere. The menu changes every two months or so, but there's usually fresh salmon with different sauces, veal, roast game hen, Chateaubriand and rack of lamb. Prices at night are $7.50 to $25 (rack of lamb for two) for entrees; at noon, $3 to $6. Bouillabaisse with clams, mussels, scallops and the day's catch is $5. Lunch, noon to 2:30 p.m. Tuesday to Friday, noon to 2 p.m. Saturday; dinner, 6 to 9 p.m. Tuesday to Saturday, 1 to 9 p.m. Sunday.

The Gull, Dauntless Boat Yard, Essex, Conn. (203) 767-0916. Owner Lu Lockwood's soups are renowned, and she has recently published a cookbook with her recipes. Her handsome restaurant, with its view of the Connecticut River and amusing paintings of gulls, offers a wide selection of knife and fork sandwiches ($1.75 to $4) at lunch. The menu changes seasonally, with some lovely cold dishes in summer at dinner (chicken breast poached in wine with tarragon dressing, for instance) and Athol Brose, a Scottish dessert made with heavy cream, honey and Scotch whiskey, has been the subject of a small controversy in *Gourmet* magazine. A mushroom roll with Hollandaise sauce is one of the splendid appetizers. Dinner entree prices range from $5.95 to $9.95. A popular Sunday brunch, $5.50 including a drink, has such exotic items as the "Far East," ground lamb in puff pastry with a curry sauce and peach chutney. Lunch, 11:30 a.m. to 3 p.m.; Sunday brunch, noon to 4 p.m.; dinner, 5:30 to 9:30 p.m. The Gull is especially delightful on a summer evening.

The Griswold Inn, Main Street, Essex, Conn. (203) 767-0991. The "Gris" opened for business in 1776 and has been nurturing travelers and diners ever since. In the Tap Room, built in 1738 as the first schoolhouse in Essex, there's usually a crowd enjoying the ample drinks or English beer on draft, and hot buttered popcorn from an antique machine. The four dining rooms are nearly always full — you really need reservations here, especially in summer. The food is New England fare with lots of seafood (bluefish, scrod and sole are favorites) and prime ribs, and the menu is extensive. A hunt breakfast from noon to 2:30 on Sundays is especially popular at $4.75. Dinner entrees are $5.95 to $9.95; at lunch $2.95 to $4.95, and there's a sandwich list, too. Check out the steamboat prints by Currier & Ives, and the Antonio Jacobsen collection of marine oils, as well as a collection of firearms in the Gun Room. Lunch, noon to 2 p.m. Monday to Saturday; dinner, 6 to 9 on weeknights, to 10 p.m. on summer weekends, and 5 to 9 p.m. Sundays.

Daytrip 17

Society for the Preservation of New England Antiquities photo

In the Pink
Roseland Cottage/Woodstock, Conn.

Driving through the center of lovely old Woodstock, Conn., you cannot miss the place. The locals call it the "pink house" and that's the color it is: A rather bright pink with dark green and red trim, reminiscent of the flower its owner loved.

Roses and the Fourth of July were his passions and Henry Chandler Bowen indulged them both. He planted a rose garden outside the house, had much of the furniture upholstered in pink and then, in case you didn't get the point, he named it "Roseland Cottage." A cottage it was not, but more a mansion in the Gothic Revival style (familiarly known as Gingerbread), used for summers only by Bowen and his family. Actually, it was probably not pink to begin with, either, but a purplish gray until the turn of the century. It's just that it's been pink as long as anyone around Woodstock can remember.

To his summer place Bowen invited prominent figures of the day to celebrate the Fourth of July, and the celebrations were famous. The "day" was the mid to late 19th century and no fewer than four United States Presidents (Ulysses S. Grant and Benjamin Harrison while in office; Rutherford B. Hayes and William

McKinley while Congressmen) made the trek to the little town in northeastern Connecticut for Bowen's celebration.

The guests usually arrived by train in neighboring Putnam the day before, and were transported by carriage to Woodstock, where they gathered the evening of July 3 for a reception at which reportedly nothing stronger than pink lemonade was served.

The Fourth was the big day. A huge American flag, each stripe of which is about a foot in width, fluttered from the wing of the house facing Woodstock Common and the guests would march down Route 169 in a parade. Their destination was Roseland Park (a gift of Bowen to his children for public use) where they regaled one another with pompous speeches; afterward, they returned to the "cottage" for more festivities and more pink lemonade. It was probably an appropriate beverage for reasons other than color — Bowen was at the time the publisher of an anti-slavery, temperance newspaper in New York, where he resided most of the year. He returned to Woodstock summers because he had grown up there, a descendant of one of the town's founders.

The house remained in the Bowen family from the time it was built for $10,000 in 1846 until 1968, when the last of the family to live there, Bowen's granddaughter, Constance Holt, died. Shortly afterward the house was acquired by the Society for the Preservation of New England Antiquities and opened to the public.

The rose garden is still there. So are the flag (folded on one of the chairs in the parlor when I visited, but hung outside each year on the Fourth), the barn with its bowling alley and, best of all as far as some visitors are concerned, much of the original Gothic Revival furniture made especially for the house. Twelve pieces of that ornate furniture were shown at the first exhibition of Gothic Revival Furniture in America in 1976 in Houston, Tex.

The house itself is of board and batten construction with the fancy scroll-work and trellis detail that gives it its Victorian look, and with dark green shutters which, it is said, were often closed in the 1800s "to keep the heat out." Joseph C. Wells, a New York architect, was the designer. He also did churches (one is First Presbyterian Church on New York's Fifth Avenue between 11th and 12th streets) and the ecclesiastical influence is apparent. Note the cathedral window in the writing room.

The ornate iron fence which surrounds the place is the original, but the garden house in the style of a pedimented Greek temple to the left was a later addition. The visitor approaches via a circular drive, with the house to the right, the gardens to the left and the barns and other outbuildings, which also may be visited, straight ahead. Virtually nothing is off limits.

I started outdoors on a June day in the garden. There are not only the roses, but a clever arrangement of boxwood hedges, which form something of a maze. Take time to stroll around the grounds and view the house from different angles before you go inside. Camera buffs and artists may be particularly inspired.

Resident caretakers of the house have acted as guides in the past and will probably continue to do so. My guide, who was caretaker at the time, took pains to explain that the house is meant to show how a particular family lived in the period, not how all people lived at that time. That becomes abundantly clear by the very personal nature of the collection; basically, the visitor sees the house as it was between the years 1875 to 1900, which is when all those Fourth of July parties were held.

The dining room is first, where a set of Limoges china, designed especially for Bowen, tops the table, and where a portrait of Bowen himself is displayed on one wall. The furniture in this room is actually thought not to be original to the house, possibly from the Bowens' Brooklyn, N.Y., home instead.

But almost everything else is. In the double parlor, just beyond, is the Gothic Revival furniture which is original to Roseland. Here are the pink chairs and settees with their ornately carved details in black walnut.

It is in that front writing room just beyond that you find the marvelous cathedral window, and also the original guest book for the house, displayed on the desk. Look not only for the names of Presidents who visited but of other notables of the day, like Henry Ward Beecher, who apparently came out from Hartford. Civil War period historians could have a heyday.

Upstairs you may be intrigued by the amount of wicker furniture in the bedrooms, but you have to remember this was a summer house only. Some of the furniture is heavy, but often it has been painted a brighter color — green or red, for example — in keeping with the house's more casual use. One rather valuable piece in an upstairs bedroom is a Thonet chair, an original bentwood piece, from Vienna.

On the bed in what is thought to be the upstairs master bedroom is the wedding dress worn by Henry Bowen's second wife, Ellen Holt of Pomfret, Conn., whom he married as a widower in 1865. His first wife, Lucy Tappan, had died two years earlier.

There is also a child's bedroom with a darling window seat and an interesting collection of toy soldiers.

Final stop on the tour is the large carriage horse-barn with stalls for five horses and the original carriage used to transport those very important people from the Putnam railroad station.

The bowling alley in the barn, as old as the house itself, is delightful. With its original wooden pins, it is thought to be the oldest bowling alley in a private residence in the country. There is a story that President Grant bowled one ball

Location: Center of Woodstock, Ct., on Route 169. May be reached via Route 44 or I-86.

Open: June 1 to Sept. 30, Tuesday, Thursday and Sunday, 1 to 5 p.m.

Admission: Adults $1; (Connecticut residents, 50 cents); children under 12, free.

Telephone: (203) 928-4896.

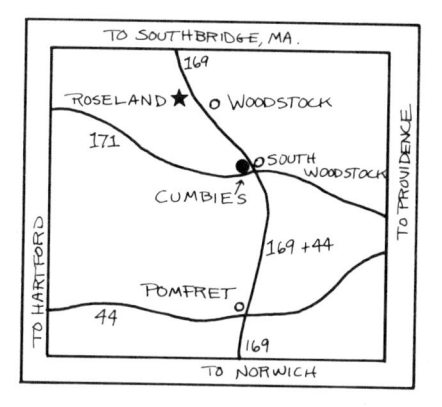

there, while visiting for the Fourth of July, and made a strike. He declined an offer to try again.

Roseland is a good day trip destination not only for the house itself, but for the town, which is reminiscent of comfortable old New England places and quite lovely. It even has a preparatory school, one of the many in Connecticut, Woodstock Academy. Don't leave until you've prowled around a bit, perhaps picnicking in Roseland Park just down the road, where swimming is also possible.

Also in the Area

Roseland Park, Route 169, Woodstock, Conn. (203) 928-4130. An appropriate place to visit in conjunction with Roseland Cottage, it was donated to his children by Henry C. Bowen in 1876 for public use. Picnicking. Swimming.

Wolf Den State Park, Pomfret, Conn., Route 44 near junction of 169 and 101. Marked trail leads to woodland cave where the young Israel Putnam in 1742 slew a great wolf that had been preying on sheep in the area.

New England Center for Contemporary Art, Route 169, Brooklyn, Conn. (203) 774-8899. About three miles south of intersection with Route 101 are four galleries in a gigantic barn on the property of a former Cornish game hen farm. Exhibits of work by contemporary artists change monthly. Open seven days a week, 1 to 5 p.m. Downstairs is a **Children's Museum,** opened in Spring 1978, with work by and for children. Open daily from 10 a.m. to 4 p.m. and Sundays, 1 to 4 p.m.

Caprilands, Silver Street, Coventry, Conn. (203) 742-7244. Adelma Grenier Simmons, an indomitable herbalist, horticulturist, writer and cook, runs this marvelous herb farm off Route 44A in the rural town of Coventry. The herb gardens stretch over the hillside behind an ancient brown colonial house, where an imcomparable luncheon of herb-flavored dishes is served Monday through Friday from mid-April to mid-December for $6.95. Luncheon guests must reserve in advance, and arrive by 12:30 for Mrs. Simmons's personally conducted tour of the gardens, after which they sit down to an unusual and always delectable meal, along with a talk on herb lore. Caprilands is open seven days a week from 9 a.m. to 5 p.m. and visitors may tour the gardens on their own. Herbs as well as books and herb products are for sale.

Dining 17

Cumbie's/South Woodstock, Conn.

"Would you like to sit under the Warhol?" asked our bearded host, Jim, as he led us into the pretty dining room at Cumbie's. A strange question, perhaps, but not when the restaurant's owner is a former curator at the Worcester Art Museum. Wylie Cumbie opened his establishment in a restored barn in the unlikely town of South Woodstock in June 1976, and his artistic eye is evident in the decor and the food.

As in a private home, our coats were taken by the host and put in a closet behind louvred doors (no coat racks here). Then we settled in beneath the Warhol print of huge red, yellow and orange poppies.

Our eyes feasted on the art works from Mr. Cumbie's collection, subtly lit by track lighting; dark stained walls on which were displayed copper pots, molds and pewter plates, tables with crisp white linen topped with spring-like green placemats and napkins printed with colorful flowers. Beautiful arrangements of dried flowers in wicker baskets on each table are exchanged for fresh flowers in the summer. Chairs are cane, modern, handsome and comfortable, and tables spacious and spaced a reasonable distance apart.

None of the fine details is overlooked here. Drinks are most ample and served in good-looking glasses, water is poured into fragile wine goblets with plenty of ice, candles flicker on each table and the atmosphere is unhurried and gracious. Even though the aforementioned Jim did all the bartending, waiting on tables and changing the records for the whole dining room (it was an off night and only a few of the 15 tables were occupied), he remained amazingly calm and unruffled!

We were served some of the best rolls we've had, too hot to eat at first, with parsley and onion baked in the center.

A garlic soup was simply sensational, with many herbs, a half onion roll sprinkled with fresh Parmesan cheese, and not too overpowering a garlic flavor. The fine mild house pate ($2) of goose livers was beautifully presented with triangles of pumpernickel bread, tomato, cucumber and gherkins.

The day's menu is written on a blackboard, brought to the table and propped on a nearby chair. From it we chose filet au poivre ($9.95), two thin pieces of filet, cooked rare, in a cream sauce that was flavored just right and a sultan's curry ($6.50) of beef and lamb in a heavenly sauce, which stayed piping hot throughout the meal. This came with a sensational rice pilaf that had nuts in it.

The menu changes daily. Other items that come and go are creamed ham and mushrooms on herbed rice, chicken imperial, filet of sole, prime ribs with

Yorkshire pudding, duck a l'orange, fresh swordfish, roast lamb with horseradish sauce and lobster crepes. They range from $5.50 to $9.95.

The soups are inventive here, and other possibilities are black bean with sherry, lemon dill, curried cream of chicken, Scotch broth and mulligatawny, and cheddar cheese with pimento. They're always made from scratch, and most cost $1. Escargots and shrimp cocktail are sometimes available, $2.95 and $2 respectively.

Vegetables of the day (creditable peas and carrots when we were there) and salad are served with entrees. The salad was mostly iceberg and fairly undistinguished; one imagines that in the summer other greens are used. The house dressing is an interesting and quite garlicky cream dressing.

White wines and desserts are kept in a big glass refrigerator just inside the front entrance (the old red barn was formerly a nursery).

There's an intelligent selection of wines. Villa Banfi, a straightforward Italian wine and one of our favorites, is the house wine ($4.50 and $2.25 for full and half carafes). We passed it up for a Chateau Senejac Haut Medoc for $6 that was rich and full-bodied. Wines are sensibly priced with a chablis from Concannon in California for $4.25, Louis Martini Burgundy, $4.25 as well, Gamay Beaujolais $5.50 and Graves $5.25. Chateau Mouton Rothschild is $39.

Desserts of the day were apple and mince pies, glaceed oranges and ice cream with chocolate sauce, as well as a large piece of pineapple raspberry cake that we tried — very moist, loaded with fruit and with a thick and creamy vanilla icing. Coffee from a silver pot was hot and fragrant.

In the summer, we hear, Cumbie's cream of vegetable soup is unsurpassed. All the fresh vegetables come from a garden plot behind the barn, where broccoli, tomatoes, zucchini, cauliflower, lettuce, tons of parsley for garnishes and lots more are grown. Also, in summer, all the entrees are garnished with flowers — black-eyed Susans on the duck, for instance, and gladioli on the filet au poivre! These are charming touches, ones that would appeal to anyone with an artist's eye.

There are many wedding receptions here in summer and, twice a year when conductor Sarah Caldwell visits nearby Annhurst College, opera parties.

At lunch time such things as cheese omelet, eggs Benedict, spaghetti carbonara and chef's salad are offered in the $2 to $3.50 range.

The little kitchen is gleamingly clean, efficient and open to partial view near the entrance. There's a bit of a whimsical attitude about the cooking. "What's in the seafood Newburg?" we asked. "We don't really know," was the answer, "the chef who made it went off duty this afternoon without telling us. But it's probably shrimp and crab!"

Cumbie's, Routes 171 and 169, South Woodstock, Conn. Tel. (203) 974-0531. Just west of main intersection in South Woodstock. Reservations recommended on weekends. Masterchage and American Express. Luncheon, noon to 3 p.m. Wednesday to Saturday; dinner, 6 to 10 p.m. Wednesday to Saturday. Hunt breakfast, noon to 2:30 p.m. Sunday. Closed Monday and Tuesday and, in winter, Wednesday.

Also in the Area

The Golden Lamb Buttery, Hill and Dale Farm, Bush Hill Road, off Route 169, Brooklyn, Conn. (203) 774-4423. In an atmospheric barn dating from 1890 (once the writing studio of a well-known New Yorker) filled with early primitive antiques, you can lunch on the chicken salad that travelers come from across the U.S. to eat, innovative hot or cold soups, homemade bread and special sauces topping the famous University of Connecticut ice cream. A feature is a healthful, high-protein but slimming luncheon choice every day, as the owners are keen on organic and no-preservatives-used foods. Dinner, served Friday and Saturday nights only, changes nightly and the three or four entrees can include pork Normandy (poached in bourbon for four hours, with a sour cream sauce), bird of paradise (chicken stuffed with fruit), or crab in heavy cream and brandy. Vegetables from the farm are featured — as many as eight at a single meal. The atmosphere is almost that of a private club, and reservations are imperative. The barn also includes an antique shop and art gallery, and at night there's live chamber or piano music. Complete dinners are $12 to $15; lunch salads in the $3.95 range. There's only one sitting at night; patrons start cocktails around 6:30 p.m. and the main course is served by 9 p.m. Lunch, noon to 3 p.m. Monday to Saturday. Closed end of December to Memorial Day.

General Lyon Inn, Route 198, Eastford, Conn. (203) 974-1380. This inn, dating from 1776, is laden with antiques, some of which it sells in the Sign of the Silver Stag, and also has an herb shop, featuring items from the extensive herb garden. Yankee pot roast and roast lamb are perennial favorites, but the fresh seafood includes a marvelous baked stuffed flounder filled with clams and lobster, baked in sherry lemon butter and topped with Newburg sauce. Red flannel hash, baked beans and ham and Indian pudding are good old New England fare, and on Friday, at noon there are Yankee clam cakes and at night, a fisherman's platter. Special gourmet dinner forums are offered on some Wednesday and Thursday evenings, with meals and entertainment (talks on herbs, antiques or witchcraft, or musical divertissements) at a bargain $6.95. At Christmas, English medieval dinners are served with appropriate musical background. Since Eastford is dry, you may bring your own bottle (setups provided). Lunch, noon to 2 p.m. daily except Monday; dinner, 6 to 8:30 p.m. Tuesday to Saturday, noon to 5 p.m. Sunday; winter, only on Friday, Saturday and Sunday.

Old Putt Tavern, Berris Motor Inn, Route 6, Brooklyn, Conn. (203) 774-9644. Honest country cooking (nothing frozen or pre-packaged) is featured in the Old Putt Tavern. A special Greek dinner for two, $20, includes stuffed grape leaves, salad with feta cheese, Greek cheeses, sausage and olives, broiled lamb chops with pasta Greek style, five pastries and a carafe of Retsina wine. Armenian shish kebab is another speciality, as are various seafood dishes. The walls, covered with antique farm tools and lovely prints, are made of real barn planks — some from Teddy Roosevelt's summer home, Mortlake Manor, in Brooklyn. The homemade pies (especially lemon meringue) have been written up from San Francisco to Paris! Lunch entrees range from $1.50 (oyster stew in season) to $7.75, and dinner from $4.75 to $8.95. Hours, 11:30 a.m. to 2 p.m. and 5 to 9:30 p.m. daily.

Daytrip 18

"Huck" Finn's Birthplace
Mark Twain Memorial/Hartford, Conn.

Go to the Mark Twain House in Hartford at Christmastime, if you can.

Go when it's snowing and you'll see what Twain meant about the window over the dining room fireplace, where he loved to watch the snowflakes fall to meet the rising flames of the fire. But go in order to see the house decorated for the holidays — the wreaths on the windows and the doors, the yards of roping up the center staircase, the stockings hung by the fireplace in the children's schoolroom, the masses of poinsettias in the conservatory, even the partly wrapped packages in the mahogany guest room. Best of all perhaps is the Victorian Christmas tree in the library, one of Twain's favorite rooms, lovingly decorated by the active Women's Committee members who string cranberries and popcorn themselves to achieve the proper effect.

It's not just for the visitor. It's done to approximate the very steps Olivia Langdon Clemens might have taken to prepare for the holidays a hundred years ago, and we're told she didn't scrimp (substantial bills from local florists are verification). So popular is visiting at this time of year that the house remains open Mondays in December (a day it's normally closed in winter) and the decorations are up from the Sunday following Thanksgiving to the Sunday after Twelfth Night (Jan. 6).

Authenticity at Christmas is no different from the prevailing mood at the home of the popular American author, where an exacting restoration has just been completed. The house appears as it did in 1881, the year Twain and his wife had the place redecorated by Louis Comfort Tiffany and his firm of Associated Artists in New York. (They also did the White House).

That was seven years after the house was completed in 1874, when Twain and his young wife had moved into the unusual 19-room mansion. Part medieval

109

fortress, part Mississippi riverboat, part cuckoo clock is one way the house has been described and it's about as good as any.

Rising as it does from its knoll above Hartford's busy Farmington Avenue, the rambling Victorian edifice is a sight to behold. Huge chimneys (there *were* 18 fireplaces) and gables poke upward from a three-colored Vermont slate roof; the red brick exterior is painted with black and Chinese red stripes and a deeper red trim; bays and angles and a huge rounded back porch, like the back of a Mississippi showboat, all catch the eye.

The house was designed by Edward Tuckerman Potter, a New York architect, but Mark Twain had his hand in all the way. There are riverboat doors and intercom system, those fireplace windows (one in the front hall, too) and other features which delighted the writer who delighted the world. To the house he and his wife invited a constant stream of visitors, for dinner, for overnight, for days, even for months on end.

Samuel Langhorne Clemens, as Mark Twain was born, grew up in Missouri, we know, but became enamored of the Connecticut capital after a visit in 1868 to his publisher, Elisha Bliss of the American Publishing Co. He stayed then with prominent Hartfordites, Isabella and John Hooker, who were living on part of a 140-acre tract of land west of the city proper known as Nook Farm.

Twain came back in 1871 after a short residency in Buffalo, N.Y. with his bride of one year, Olivia Langdon Clemens. He decided to build a home in Nook Farm, where he was not the only prominent resident. The area developed as an intellectual and literary community and was the home of many well-known people including Harriet Beecher Stowe, author of *Uncle Tom's Cabin,* whose house

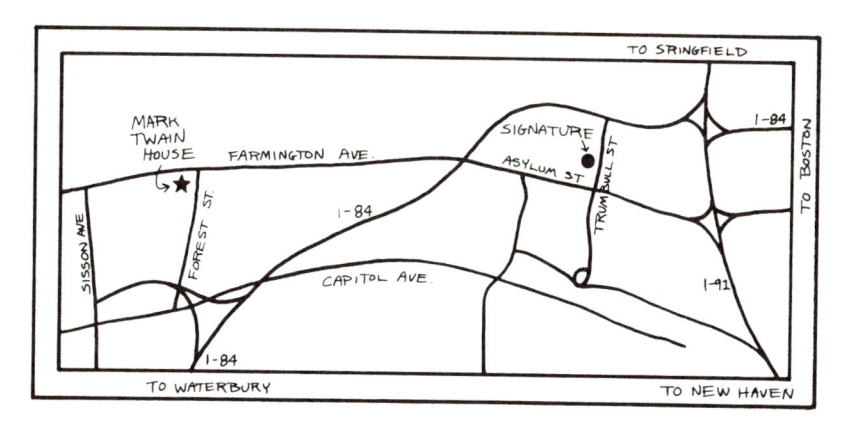

Location: 351 Farmington Ave., corner Forest Street, Hartford, Conn. Exit 46 (Sisson Avenue) from I-84.

Open: September through May, Tuesday through Saturday, 9:30 a.m. to 4 p.m.; Sunday, 1 to 4 p.m.; closed Monday except December; June through August, daily, 10 a.m. to 4:30 p.m. Closed Jan. 1, Easter, Labor Day, Thanksgiving, Christmas.

Admission: Adults $1.50; 16 and under, 75 cents; pre-schoolers free. A combination ticket for both Mark Twain and Harriet Beecher Stowe houses available for $3, adults; $1.75, children 16 and under.

Special Events: Annual "Jumping Frog Contest" co-sponsored by Mark Twain Memorial and the Children's Museum of Hartford, second Saturday in June, 2 p.m. Open to boys and girls between the ages of 6 and 16 who vie for prizes including copies of Twain's favorite books. A popular, fun event on the grounds of the Mark Twain House.

Telephone: (203) 525-9317.

Twain could see from his own (it is now also open to the public); the actor, William Gillette (see chapter on "Gillette Castle" in this book) who was born in Nook Farm, and other intellectual and religious leaders of the day.

The house was completed in 1874 and from then until 1891, Mark Twain lived happy, contented years, surrounded by friends and family, which consisted of three lively young daughters and assorted dogs and cats and servants. It was his most fertile period; from Twain's pen came several major books including *The Adventures of Tom Sawyer, Adventures of Huckleberry Finn, Life on the Mississippi, The Prince and the Pauper* and *A Connecticut Yankee in King Arthur's Court.*

Your guided tour begins in the magnificent front hall where the Clemenses welcomed their many guests. It is just an aperitif to the house as a whole: Warm, deep Venetian red walls with geometric hand-stencilled designs in black and silver; heavy hand-hewn oak beams and a hand-carved wooden staircase rising to the floors beyond. In the corner is a bust of Mark Twain which was there originally; in the center, the circular tufted sofa on which guests sat. There is the fireplace with the window above it (the flue is to the side) and underneath it all, a wonderful marble floor.

If it sounds extravagant and a little crazy, it is, and so is the house. Twain would have had it no other way. He delighted in the unusal and condemned the banal; it is wonderful to picture the bushy-haired author striding through these rooms with a cat perched on his shoulder, as we're told he did.

Every room in the Twain house is a treat, and the chief reason is the philosophy followed by the trustees since they voted in 1955 to restore the house to the 1881 period. Without hurrying, and with painstaking research and devotion, these men and women oversaw a restoration to the original which is so exact that it can serve as a model. (A recent book by former curator, Wilson H. Faude, *The Renaissance of Mark Twain's House,* details the effort step by step).

And while it's a common joke that New Yorkers never go to the Empire State Building or Washingtonians to the Washington Monument, Hartfordites I know not only visit the Mark Twain House but go back repeatedly. Everyone has his favorite room; one friend likes to poke her head into the conservatory on one of those dog-days of late winter to be renewed by the greenery and flowers and the Japanese lanterns that hang from above, just as they did when Twain was there.

My husband likes the billiard room on the top floor, where Twain retreated to write from late morning to mid-afternoon, to smoke cigars and indulge his passion for the game in the evening with his men friends and members of the Monday Evening Club, a literary group. The room was "off limits" during the day to all but his "Livy," whom Twain adored.

My favorite is Twain's bedroom with the massive carved Venetian bed where the Clemenses slept, their heads against the footboard so they could see the intricate carving of the headboard. The little girls, Susy, Clara and Jean, were permitted to climb into the bed on days when they were sick, and they would unscrew the cherubs from the bedposts and play with them like baby dolls.

The nursery is also a delight, with its charming wallpaper, a hand-crafted copy of the original Walter Crane nursery rhyme paper from England. So is the library, with the massive fireplace mantel which the Clemenses purchased in Scotland, and which was found years after the house had been sold in a barn in Redding, Conn., a town in which Twain later lived. The marvelous dining room, with the deep red and gold hand-embossed wallpaper (the story of its recreation is another tale) and that favorite windowed fireplace was the scene of many parties, including one where the guests solemnly voted not to leave the house until morning had arrived.

The only sad place in the house, really, the mahogany guest room off the library, which accommodated many visitors, was the place where Livy Clemens wrapped her Christmas packages. The marvelous big bed of African mahogany and adjoining bathroom complete with sinks, toilet, tub and shower, and the intercom (which is a "speaking tube" system like that on riverboats) are extravagant and delightful, but it was to this same room and this big bed that Susy Clemens, the eldest and favorite daughter, was brought with spinal meningitis in 1896 to die.

That was after Twain and his wife had left the house to embark on a lecture tour in Europe with which they hoped to pay off massive debts, partly incurred by his investing in the Paige typesetting machine, an invention which was a commercial failure. They planned to return to Hartford and Nook Farm, but following Susy's death were so bereft they were unable to.

The house was sold and the contents auctioned in 1903. But the devoted members of the Mark Twain Memorial have tracked down fully 40 percent of the original furnishings and don't plan to stop yet.

There is a new museum exhibit area in the basement of the house, worth a visit; and a carriage house exhibit nearby. The gift shop is fun: Books by Twain and Harriet Beecher Stowe, Victorian toys and puzzles, and some frog-related items to recall Twain's popular little book, *The Notorious Jumping Frog of Calaveras County.*

Also in the Area

Picnicking is not allowed on the grounds of Mark Twain House but can be enjoyed in two nearby parks. ELIZABETH PARK, 915 Prospect Ave., on the Hartford-West Hartford line, has more than 100 acres including the first municipally owned rose garden in the country with 14,000 plants, 1,100 varieties. Greenhouses are open free. BUSHNELL PARK, in the shadow of the State Capitol in downtown Hartford, is a popular lunchtime spot with office workers in nice weather.

Old State House, 800 Main St., Hartford, Conn. (203) 522-6766. Designed by Charles Bullfinch, the building was the State Capitol from 1796 to 1878. The chambers have been restored with many original furnishings. National Historic Landmark is reopening Fall of 1978 after extensive renovation. Usually open daily.

Hill-Stead Museum, Farmington Avenue, Farmington, Conn. (203) 677-9064. A gem of a house museum, this was built in 1901 for Mr. and Mrs. Alfred Atmore Pope from designs by Stanford White. The house, in neo-Colonial style, was built to house Pope's collection of French Impressionist paintings and other objects. Bequeathed by his daughter as a museum, it is open year-round, Wednesday through Sunday, 2 to 5 p.m. Adults, $1; children under 12, 50 cents.

Wadsworth Atheneum, 600 Main St., Hartford, Conn. (203) 278-2670. In this nationally ranked art museum, the Nutting collection of Early American furniture is outstanding. The annual Christmas tree exhibit is a highlight early in December. Open year-round, Tuesday through Friday, 11 a.m. to 3 p.m.; Saturday and Sunday, 11 a.m. to 5 p.m. Voluntary donations of $1 suggested.

Bushnell Park Carrousel, Bushnell Park, Hartford, Conn. (203) 525-1618. This antique carrousel with its individually and artistically repainted horses, housed in a marvelous wooden building, is open from April to December. It's just 10 cents a ride, and the old popcorn wagon is usually dispensing goodies inside the building. The ride is a generous one, and Hartford's businessmen sometimes take one after work, briefcases in hand. Open "weekends" only in April and October through December, Friday, Saturday and Sunday from 11 a.m. to 5 p.m.; May through September, open Tuesday through Sunday, 11 a.m. to 5 p.m. Closed Monday.

Dining 18

Signature/Hartford, Conn.

Mark Twain left his mark on the literary scene in Hartford, and the Signature, Hartford's swankiest restaurant, is leaving its mark on the dining scene.

Businessmen with expense accounts, those who live high on the hog and local celebrants crowd the Signature, drawn by the exotic American cuisine carried out with a flair unrivaled in the area and a Windows-on-the-World type of setting over Hartford's Civic Center.

Signature

Never mind that the windows look out on Trumbull Street, a mere one story below rather than 50 miles away over New Jersey and Long Island. The Signature definitely has a "top of the something" New Yorkish flavor about it.

Opened in 1975 as the luxury restaurant of Hartford's new Civic Center, the Signature is a Holiday Award-winning member of the national Davre's restaurant chain, known for the Crown Room in Kansas City and the Carnelian Room in San Francisco, among others.

The decor is strikingly modern (with a touch of art deco) and even theatrical, but not obtrusive, although the windowless cocktail lounge is somewhat claustrophobic and some liken the place to an airport VIP lounge. It's urbane and elegant, with the prevailing golden beige and warm cream colors lit by banks of tiny golden bulbs behind smoked glass panels. The main accents come from the comfortable upholstered chairs in deep red and burgundy flanking the tables, which are well-spaced and unusually large. The dining levels are separated by handsome cane and gold metal dividers.

American regional specialties are featured on the substantial leather menu. Including a large selection of game, the choices range across the country from Montana elk to Long Island duckling, South Dakota pheasant to southern seafood pie with bourbon. All are cooked imaginatively — the venison sauteed in brandy, with baked apple and cranberry, for example.

We imagine Mark Twain would enjoy as we have the New Orleans Carpetbagger steak, a house specialty that presents a nice thick and tender filet mignon stuffed with fried oysters ($12.50).

The San Francisco cioppino here is as attractive to look at as it is to taste — a careful selection of available fresh fish and shellfish, gleaming in a delicate, wine-based broth.

Prices are steep (entrees from $8.50 to $12.50, with appetizers proportionately costly), but you can order a table d'hote "American Dinner" featuring a selection of appetizers, soups or salads, entrees and desserts for $11 to $14.50.

Drinks also are expensive and not particularly generous at $2 apiece. With them comes a woven basket with hot nut bread, dense rye rolls and amusingly shaped white rolls, served with iced butter curls.

On one recent evening we chose the American Dinner, starting with Alaska shrimp Boreal, a thin-stemmed goblet lined with butter lettuce and filled with the tiny cold-water shrimp, bathed in a zesty Russian dressing. Oysters Bienville, breaded and served on rock salt, also were excellent.

Other appetizers you could order for the American Dinner are oysters Rockefeller, Kentucky spiced ham, clams on the half shell or pate of wild game. We've tried the pate on another occasion and it's delicious, coarse-textured and hearty. Smoked salmon is superb, too, but it's $4.75 extra.

Salads were perfectly adequate if unexciting, the mixed greens and the heart of lettuce garnished with crisp watercress and served with a creamy sage dressing.

For entrees we tried braised veal sweetbreads with mushrooms and — touching off an event that will forever be chronicled in our memories of culinary excursions as the hare and the tortoise — the snow hare in casserole, sealed with a fluffy crust. We waited a long, long time for the entree to arrive, nibbling on rolls and trying not to drink all our wine. Then, with a flourish, the hare was wheeled to the table on a serving cart (every entree is heated for a moment on a huge chafing dish before it is served).

With an equal flourish, the captain started to unseal the flaky crust. But it wouldn't unseal, having been baked too long. After a slight struggle, the whole thing was whisked away to the kitchen to have another crust put on, and the other dinner, which already had been served, also vanished. Another twenty minutes passed, while a solicitous waiter put a new basket of rolls and bread in front of us. Finally out came the hare, with a proper crust this time, and we started our main course some 2 1/2 hours after we arrived.

The hare, beautifully served inside its ill-fated ring of bread, was most flavorful, slightly chewier and stronger-flavored than chicken and in a nice spicy sauce, but it was rather bony. The sweetbreads were so tender they almost melted in the mouth, but the sauce was a bit bland. We were served roast potatoes and crisp yellow squash with the entrees.

It's the mark of a suave restaurant to carry off a near-disaster with aplomb, and this the Signature did by offering a special dessert, compliments of the house. It was fun to watch the special flambe man Andre create a masterpiece of a dish — first came cognac and triple sec in the chafing dish, lemon rind and juice, orange rind and juice, and sugar. This mixture was flamed and then poured over tall goblets of ice cream studded with huge strawberries, where it hardened almost like a praline. Stupendous!

Cafe filtre that came in its own little machine and was served in a tiny black and gold cup put a finishing touch to this happy ending.

The wine list at Signature carries an astonishing 171 selections, 59 of which are Californian. Prices are not bargains; Soave is the cheapest at $7, Muscadet is $9.25 and Cote du Rhone $9.75, and they go up sharply from there.

The service here is really professional and attentive (when you first arrive almost too attentive, with about four different people pouring water, getting rolls, serving drinks and taking orders). But one wonders why all these people disappear for such long intervals and why it sometimes takes so long between courses.

In any event, the Signature is well worth a try for a special night. Just make sure you have time for a leisurely evening, for that's what it is — an event!

The Signature, Hartford Civic Center, Hartford, Conn. Tel. (203) 249-1629. Downtown Hartford, at Trumbull and Asylum streets, on second floor of Civic Center shopping mall. Reservations recommended. Major credit cards. Luncheon, 11:30 a.m. to 2 p.m. Monday to Saturday; dinner, 5:30 to 10 p.m. Monday to Friday, to 11 p.m. Saturday. Sunday dinner, 5:30 to 9 p.m. Sunday brunch (seasonal), 11 a.m. to 5 p.m.

It doesn't have to cost an arm and a leg to eat at the Civic Center, and it's lots of fun to try the Promenade, six restaurants in one, cafeteria style, on the main level.

Also operated by Davre's, the six different stations offer a choice of Mexican, Chinese, Greek, Italian, Deli-style and southern type food. We like the egg rolls at Hung Hing, moussaka at Skouro's, and guacamole and taco chips at Rivera's. Prices are reasonable, the atmosphere is attractive, with modern fixtures and lots of plants, and you can order drinks, wine or beer.

Also at the Civic Center you can have a choice of dozens of crepes at La Crepe and some terrific tempura at the Rising Sun, or you can eat at any time of the day or night at Rein's Deli, a real New York deli with sour pickles on every table.

Also in the Area

The Reading Room, Helen Winter's Grist Mill, Farmington, Conn. (203) 677-7997. In the elegant town of Farmington, almost a museum of 19th century life in itself, is Helen Winter's Grist Mill complex on the banks of the Farmington River. Here you'll find a fine small art gallery, antique and artisan shops, one of the best book stores we have found, and the Reading Room, a really fun restaurant with a great view of the wide curving river and good honest food, opened in 1976 by the owner of the book store. Lunch entrees are $2.95 to $3.95, and dinner, $5.95 to $6.95. Usually specialties are listed on the blackboard as well as in the menu, and the soups and quiches and salads are always interesting. We like to eat basket after basket of the garlic bread, it is so outstanding. Fish comes in fresh daily from the Bostonian Fish Market in Hartford, and the desserts change almost every day and are super rich (we have memories of a dreamy mocha almond pie). You bring your own wine (there's a corkage charge) and some regulars leave their bottles of Old Granddad or whatever there for $1 a month storage! In the summer, you can eat on the lawn that slopes down to the river. There are two sittings for lunch, starting at between 11:45 a.m. and noon, and 1 to 1:30 p.m. Dinner is served from 6 to 8:15 p.m. Tuesday to Thursday; Friday and Saturday the sittings start at 6 to 6:45 p.m. and 8:15 to 9 p.m. Sunday brunch is 10:30 a.m. to 1:30 p.m. and the Reading Room is closed Sunday nights and Monday.

Chez Serge, Avon Park North, Route 44, Avon, Conn. (203) 678-0175. Serge Backes, who when 18 was the youngest graduate of the Cordon Bleu School in Paris, runs a strictly classical French kitchen in this modern chalet-style building with high vaulted ceilings in the Farmington Valley Arts Center complex. His food is beautifully seasoned, imaginative, fresh, abundant and pure, and if you ask for ketchup or mint jelly, you will not be accommodated! Great French bread, fantastic onion soup, superb sweetbreads, veal and seafood, and patisserie (the mocha whipped cream here is too much) add up to sensational dining. Wines are carefully chosen and a house Vouvray served en carafe is delightful. Most entrees are in the $9 to $15 range, with beef dishes particularly on the high side. At lunch prices are about half those at dinner. Service here is exceptionally informed. Lunch is served from 11:30 a.m. to 2 p.m., dinner begins at 5:30 p.m., and Chez Serge is closed Sunday and Monday.

The Aetna Restaurant, 267 Farmington Ave., Hartford, Conn. (203) 522-7488. If you want some interesting Greek food, in a really fantastic art deco "diner," the Aetna is for you. It also has good seafood dishes (poached salmon with avgolemono sauce is great), crusty and rich Greek bread, a lovely rice pilaf, a fine seafood souvlaki and thick Greek coffee. Try a glass of Rodytis, a dry rose, or get a bottle of Demestica white, not exactly subtle, but with character! The diner, built to order for the lot in the 1940s for the Greek owners who took over the Aetna in 1935, is gaily decorated in reds and oranges with lots of glass. Entrees here range from $4.25 to $7.95, and there's always a sandwich menu as well. Baklava and other super-sweet Greek desserts are made on the premises. The Aetna opens at 11 a.m., serves lunch until 3:30 p.m., and then dinner until 12:30 a.m. weekdays, 1:30 a.m. Friday and Saturday. The lounge downstairs is open until 2 a.m.

Daytrip 19

Island Hopping, More or Less
Thimble Islands/Off Stony Creek, Conn.

Vacation islands with pirate treasure? Yes, and you don't have to go to the West Indies to find them.

Right off the coast of Connecticut, so close in fact that one of them can be reached on foot at low tide, are the Thimble Islands, which legend says may be the hiding place for the treasure of that pirate extraordinaire, Captain William Kidd.

No one has found it yet. But the kids on Money Island spend hours and hours every summer searching in a cave on that island. And on High Island, which residents have renamed Kidd's Island, they paint their cottages black and fly the Jolly Roger in the pirate tradition. All in fun, of course.

There's a lot of that out on the Thimbles, which have been used as a summer resort since the Indians first paddled out in canoes and camped on Governor's Island.

The compact archipelago, which legend says number 365 in all (one for every day of the year), lies within a radius of five miles off the shore at Stony Creek, east of New Haven. There are probably nowhere near 365 islands, even if you count every rock that raises its head above water level at low tide, but the 32 inhabited Thimbles, ranging from three-quarter-acre Dogfish Rock to 17-acre Horse Island, represent nearly as many islands as can be found all along the rest of Connecticut's shore.

Like other islands off New England, the Thimbles are a gift of the glacial age, formed after the great ice cap melted and "drowned" huge portions of shoreline. From shore they look like great stone masses rising from the sea; for centuries, their very nearness has intrigued mainlanders, who could see them but for the

117

most part couldn't quite reach them. It's that "couldn't quite" that makes the difference. Thimble Islanders are enamored of their world apart and fiercely protective of their privacy.

For the 90 or so cottage owners — one cottage is actually a 27-room mansion, but most are much smaller — the Thimbles provide a way of life that is much simpler than the hustle and bustle of ordinary living. They have no electricity, no roads, few telephones, no stores. While a few people use generators to recharge batteries or run vacuum cleaners and irons, most are content with gas and kerosene lights and doing without television until the season is over.

Just last year, islanders defeated yet another petition to install electricity, and while one summer resident says "I know it's coming eventually," she, like the others, will put it off as long as possible.

Actually, when you think about it, the Thimbles (named for a wild thimbleberry which grew there) are much less commercial today than they once were. Their heyday was late in the 19th century when the islands boasted two hotels and there were at least five more in Stony Creek. Regular excursion boats made the run from New Haven, and from then until the First World War the islands enjoyed real prosperity.

Now they're all owned privately. The hotels have become private residences, and other than invited guests, non-residents are clearly unwelcome.

But while tourists aren't free to walk (or more aptly, climb) around on the Thimbles, they can sail through them, and if they don't have their own boat, they can hitch a ride on a small ferry which wends its way among the islands, taking the islanders back and forth to Stony Creek and delivering groceries, messages, mail and other links with the mainland — sometimes even furniture.

The regular service is now provided by Dwight H. Carter, who says he's a descendant of one of the oldest island families (seven generations), and for a price he'll take tourists along for the ride. This is island-hopping in the truest sense of the word as the "Volsunga III," with its 33-passenger capacity, putts its way from island to island.

You can sit back in the boat, enjoy the breeze, and listen to the "yarn" that Captain Carter spins about the islands as he goes. The story, since it's live each trip, is apt to change a bit from one time to the next, but some of the facts and fancies are bound to be the same.

You're likely to hear, of course, about Captain Kidd. Even though the infamous pirate's visit to the Thimbles has never been verified, it is known he sailed around Long Island Sound in 1699, after his return from the Indies and before his capture, and the Thimbles, some people think, would have been a great place to hide treasure. The Buccaneers (as they call themselves) on High Island even point to a hidden harbor between the island's two halves and ask if that might not have been the spot.

You'll learn that Governor's Island, to which the Indians first went, has 16 cottages and 40 varieties of trees, thanks to a botanist who once summered there and planted them as a hobby.

Money Island is actually the most densely populated of the Thimbles, with all 30 cottages clinging precariously to the granite that makes up the island. Because of all that granite (the base of the Statue of Liberty is Thimble Islands granite), the islands have never been much good for farming or grazing, which is why they developed the only way they could — as resorts.

The 27-room mansion on Rogers or Phelps Island is the most elaborate of the

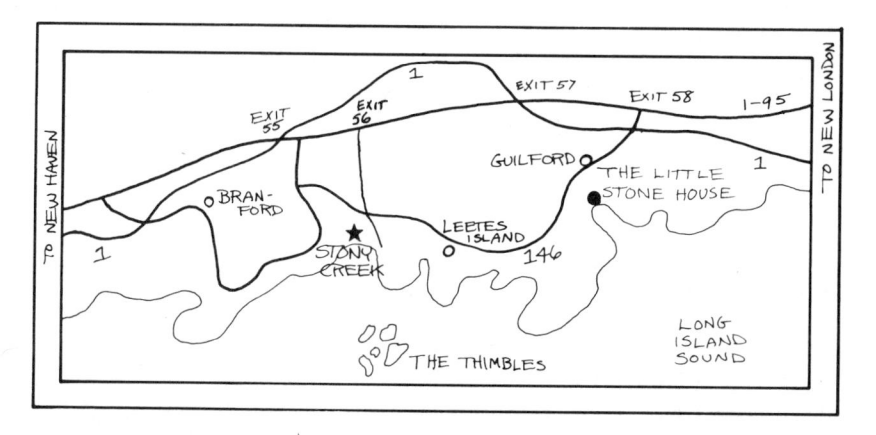

Location: Stony Creek, Conn., is east of New Haven, south of Connecticut Turnpike (I-95). Take Exit 56 from turnpike and head south.

Boat trips around Thimbles are provided by two sources. Dwight Carter and his "Volsunga III" give regular daily service from Memorial Day through Labor Day, and weekend service only from mid-April to Memorial Day and Labor Day to Columbus Day. His boat leaves on the hour between 8 a.m. and 9 p.m. Sightseers pay $1.50 (adults) and 75 cents (children) and are not permitted to get off at any of the islands which are strictly private. Commentary is live and usually given on trips from noon to 5 and 7 to 9 p.m. Duration of trip: about 40 minutes. Telephone: (203) 488-9978. Matt Infantino with the "Sea Mist" runs weekend sightseeing service only from 11 a.m. to 6 p.m. Saturdays and Sundays. Adults $1.50; children 50 cents. Taped commentary about the islands. Telephone: (203) 488-2490.

summer homes, complete with tennis courts and a six-hole golf course. But on Wheeler Island there is an old Victorian place which locals refer to as "the ghost house" (it looks like one) and on West Crib a low contemporary structure. You'll see them all as you sail by.

Horse Island, now owned by Yale University as a research station, was so named because some horses were found there long ago, presumably after they swam ashore from a nearby ship.

And there's a good story about Mother-in-Law's Island. A young couple from one of the other islands was married and decided to begin their honeymoon on this island, which was at the time deserted. They pitched a tent and settled down for their first night of wedded bliss. The girl's mother, concerned about her daughter, rowed over to the island to see how things were going. The irate son-in-law took his bride and rowed ashore, taking the mother-in-law's boat as well. Islanders who were sympathetic with young love didn't rescue the mother-in-law for three full days.

It's that kind of story — and more — that you'll hear out on the boat with Dwight Carter or, on weekends, with Matt Infantino, who runs "Sea Mist" for sightseers only.

Parking is tight in Stony Creek (all islanders must leave their cars on shore), so you may have to park some distance from the dock and walk the rest of the way. It is a fun walk along the waterfront, and you may stop to watch the traffic in the harbor if you have the inclination and the time.

Picnicking is possible on a small slice of land right on the water's edge, complete with benches for relaxing. If you've no picnic, a snack bar at the Town Dock, where you get the ferry, is usually in business, dispensing hamburgers, fried clams and the like.

The entire circuit of the islands takes no more than 30 to 40 minutes, but there is more to do in the area. The lovely old town of Guilford, just up Route 146 a bit, has some fine historic homes and a wonderful system of hiking trails known as Westwoods. And, if you have your own boat, you might drag it along and explore the Thimbles and the nearby shoreline on your own.

Also in the Area

The Puppet Theatre, 128 Thimble Islands Road, Stony Creek, Conn. (203) 488-8511 or 488-5089. Jimmy Weil, owner and chief puppeteer, and Sal Macri give puppet shows on the Crusades and Middle Ages with unusual Sicilian puppets. The theater also presents other entertainment, children's shows, and usually a Thursday evening "hootenanny."

Westwoods Trail System, Guilford, Conn. One and a half miles west of the Guilford Green off Boston Post Road (Route 1) via Dunk Rock Road is this open space area of 2,000 acres in all. Part is owned by State of Connecticut; part by Guilford Land Conservation Trust; a small portion by Town of Guilford; other, privately owned. Six marked hiking trails and a bridle trail traverse land that ranges from low and marshy to high and rugged. A map is available from Guilford Conservation Commission, Town Hall, Guilford 06437.

Whitfield House Museum, Whitfield Street, Guilford, Conn. (203) 453-2457. New England's oldest stone house (1639-40) was originally a parsonage, fort and community hall. Beautifully furnished, it is open from April to November, Wednesday to Sunday, 10 a.m. to 5 p.m.; November to April, 10 to 4. Adults, 50 cents; children 6-17, 25 cents.

Dining 19

The Little Stone House/Guilford, Conn.

After a trip on the water, it's fun to continue that nautical feeling by eating some fresh seafood beside the shore. The Little Stone House, by the town dock in Guilford, fills the bill.

In fact, the man who runs the Thimble Island boat tours dines there fairly often, as do the tourists who come to see charming Guilford and the oldest stone house in America, the Whitfield House, just up the street. The place is crowded with women and elderly couples at luncheon. The regulars like the good food and wholesome atmosphere and don't seem to be thwarted by the rather steep prices. At night, the clientele is a bit more sophisticated, perhaps, but families and tourists are still welcome.

The nautical atmosphere is enhanced by captains' chairs, nice placemats with birds, and duck decoys adorning the plain wooden walls which are also lined with hurricane lamps. The windows provide a fine view of stone walls, old wooden piers and Long Island Sound, with lights flickering at night on yachts and far islands.

As the waitress took our cocktail order, she served a relish tray with watermelon rind pickle, cottage cheese and a red onion pepper relish. With ample drinks she brought a basket of cranberry-nut bread, white rolls and muffins, all excellent, served with plenty of butter on ice.

The menu is very straightforward — no fancy continental entrees here, just good plain seafood and lots of it. Those who won't eat seafood can get boneless chicken breast, sirloin steak or the roast of the day.

Full dinners cost $7.95 to $9.95 and for seafood lovers, there's a fine choice of lobster, haddock, sole, crabmeat, shrimp, scallops and oysters prepared in various ways.

You can order the same entrees a la carte for $6.95 to $8.95, including salad, potato and vegetables.

Starters are a choice of soups or juices. The soup of the day was a real Jewish mother's chicken soup, guaranteed to cure what ails you, thick with rice and big hunks of chicken meat. A lobster bisque was creamy and loaded with the delicacy. The clam chowder had a broth base (like that called Back Bay Chowder at the Copper Beech) with many clams, diced potatoes and herbs; a bit of milk was added just before serving. All the soups were excellent.

Salads of crunchy mixed greens are also generous, topped with tomato and cucumber and with a choice of thick blue cheese, Russian or French dressing.

The baked stuffed shrimp at Little Stone House is justly famed, and for $9.50 you get six large shrimp with a bowl of melted butter and a heap of savory crumb stuffing. It is a delectable dish.

The fresh poached filet of sole ($8.75) was perfect, with a generous helping of a Newburg-like sauce. Crabmeat warmed in butter ($9.50) couldn't have been simpler or better, just a huge helping of delicate meat unadorned by anything except the melted butter.

Roast of the day was a tender pot roast with a hearty and well-flavored gravy and came with a big plate of excellent French fries. We also had a choice of baked or mashed potatoes, and mashed turnips, succotash and peas.

The clientele here is not particularly partial to wine, and the choice is rather limited. We sipped from a bottle of most pleasant Graves, Chateau Piron, for $5.75. Prices go from $4.75 to $9.75 for a Pouilly Fuisse St. Vincent.

Desserts also come with the meal. You won't be very hungry by now, but you should try one of the chiffon pies, made on the premises — mile-high and cloudlike! We sampled strawberry chiffon and lemon chiffon, both wonderful, and the chocolate parfait was nice.

You also can get liqueur parfaits, $1.45, and Irish or Jamaican coffee is $1.75.

Nearly all the same entrees are available in the full-course luncheon, quite a bit less expensive ($4.20 to $6.50), with the addition of crabmeat salad and broiled chicken lobster.

A well-stocked gift shop occupies a nearby building on the premises (another reason why ladies' groups are attracted here?) and at the adjacent fish market, you can buy the makings for your own seafood dinner at home. The market is open all year, though Little Stone House closes following Thanksgiving weekend until spring.

Little Stone House, Lower Whitfield Street, Town Dock, Guilford, Conn. Tel. (203) 453-2566. South toward harbor off Guilford Green. Reservations recommended in summer and on weekends. Major credit cards. Luncheon, noon to 3 p.m. Tuesday to Saturday; dinner, noon to 8:30 p.m. Tuesday to Thursday, to 9 p.m. Saturday, to 8 p.m. Sunday. Closed Monday and from Thanksgiving weekend to mid-March.

Also in the Area

Cap'n Nick's, Hemingway Avenue, East Haven, Conn. (203) 469-2397. Cap'n Nick moved inland a couple of years ago from his waterfront location in Branford and now has a liquor license. Otherwise, he is still serving up the same marvelous seafood, including the popular Cap'n's platter ($6.95), piled high with deep-fried seafood. House specialties are bouillabaisse and salsa di mara, pasta with a spicy sauce of shrimp, clams, king crab and blue shell crab, both $10.95. Entrees start at $4.95 and there are several veal and beef dishes. Children's plates are $1.95. The old Nick's had the best onion-rings ever, and you can still order them specially, although they aren't on the menu. Lunch entrees (burgers, stuffed clams, lobster salad sandwich, etc.) are $2.50 to $4.95, and Nick's wine list includes nice California whites and reds, $4.50 to $12. Open every day for lunch, 11:30 a.m. to 2 p.m.; dinner from 4:30 p.m. Monday to Saturday, from 1 p.m. Sunday.

Top of the Dock, Cedar Island Marina, Clinton, Conn. (203) 669-7808. A splendid view of Long Island Sound is obtained from the Top of the Dock, situated right on the water with a glass-enclosed porch, used in the summer, wrapping around on three sides. Among many seafood specialties is Seafood Top of the Dock ($9.50), a tasty combination of shrimp, clams, mussels, lobster tail and crab legs in a white clam sauce over linguini. There's piano entertainment Wednesday through Saturday nights in the Fantail Lounge. Entrees at lunch are $1.50 to $4.50; at dinner $5.95 to $9.50, and include roast duckling, veal and steak au poivre. Open seven days from noon to 3 p.m. for lunch; 5:30 to 11 p.m. for dinner; closed Monday in winter.

Dock n' Dine, Saybrook Point, Route 154, Old Saybrook, Conn. (203) 388-4665. The Dock n' Dine is a large and very popular restaurant with a magnificent waterside setting at the mouth of the Connecticut River on Long Island Sound, and you can dine on good seafood while watching the river traffic and the gulls through large picture windows. We sat next to travelers who drove 150 miles for the fisherman's platter — a veritable ton of shrimp, scallops, clams and sole for $7.25. Entrees range from $5.50 to $10.95 (for a 1 1/4-pound lobster) at dinner and we can recommend the Boston scrod and crabmeat au gratin. Children's plates are $3.75. There are four dining rooms, a cocktail lounge, and the Captain's Lounge with dancing to live bands. It's open from 11:30 a.m. to 9 p.m., to 9:30 p.m. Friday, to 10 p.m. Saturday (later every night in summer) and serves right through — lunch until 4 p.m., and the dinner menu is available all day. Closed Monday in winter.

Daytrip 20

Books in a Barn
Whitlock Farm/Bethany, Conn.

If you're one of those people who can't pass a bookstore without going in and can't seem to leave once you're there, heaven is waiting for you in Bethany, Conn. Off a winding country road in the pleasurable ambience of old red New England barns, you can browse, and buy, books to your heart's delight.

Whitlock Farm is the name of the place, and it doesn't look like a bookseller's at all — at least not on the outside. That's because it was and still is a working farm presided over by John Whitlock, whose brothers, Gilbert and Everett, run the book business.

Gilbert was the farmer when he started his book buying — and selling — back in the late 1940s; nobody is quite sure when. It was just that following the Depression, the farm wasn't doing as well as it might, and Gilbert began to do the only other thing he knew how: Buy books. First he filled his bedroom and the adjoining rooms on the third floor of the family homestead with books; gradually he filled the rooms downstairs, one after the other. And all the time he was developing a thriving business, selling books to other booksellers, mostly by mail.

When the house was nearly filled with 10,000 books, Gilbert moved some of his inventory across the road to the hayloft of a large barn. And the decision was made to "go public."

In those days the barn was left unmanned, open 24 hours a day, and people

Location: 20 Sperry Road, Bethany, Conn. Exit 59 from Wilbur Cross Parkway (Route 15); take Route 69 north four miles. Left onto Morris Road to Sperry Road. Right on Sperry Road. Farm is a short distance on right.

Open: Year-round, 9 a.m. to 5 p.m. Tuesday through Sunday. Closed Monday. Print loft open 1 to 5 p.m. weekends.

Telephone: (203) 393-1240.

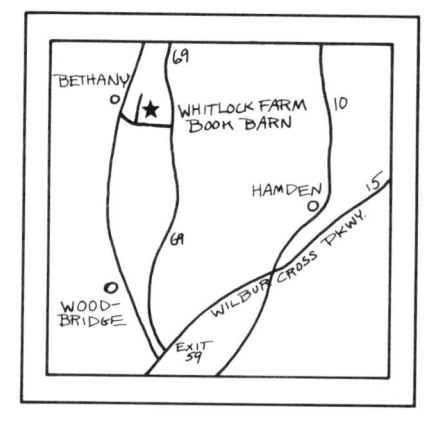

were on the honor system to pay for their books by leaving money in an open cigar box on the counter at the top of the stairs. Most of the books cost five to 50 cents then and it was paradise for insomniacs who would, indeed, arrive in the middle of the night and read away their sleepless hours.

Now Whitlock Farm Booksellers is a full-scale operation — the largest used and rare bookseller in the state, one of the largest in the country, one of the best-known in the world. There are 14 employes, full and part-time, and normal working hours, 9 to 5. But it hasn't lost much of the old flavor, and Gilbert and Everett Whitlock, the soft-spoken brothers who run the business, are seeing that it doesn't.

To the average customer, not understanding or being able to afford rare books doesn't make a lot of difference. Everyone is welcome in the barns, where the good smell of hay still lingers a bit, where there's usually a dish of candy to munch and lately some for sale, and where nobody, but nobody, will tell you to hurry up — even if you've got kids.

A new sideline has even made its appearance: The sale of young houseplants grown by Everett Whitlock as his hobby.

All of that takes place in the lower barn, the turkey barn, which is the main office and sales desk of Whitlock Farm. The older, rarer and more expensive books are shelved here. Up in the sheep barn, just a few steps up the hill, are the less expensive books (generally $5 and under), and upstairs a print loft with old maps, children's book illustrations, calendars and prints of hundreds of subjects. It's a place to sit down on the floor and pore over the treasures (which is what some of the customers do and no one tells them not to).

Deidre Caproni, who runs the upper barn with quick bird-like gestures and dark flashing eyes, says of the place, "Let's face it, I'm an indentured servant." Like that of other book lovers, her joy is in the product itself, and she says there are many weeks when she owes more than she is due in pay.

The feeling at the barn is almost spartan: Just books and more books, filling the shelves from floor to ceiling and lighted only by bare lightbulbs which hang from cords. Deidre is compulsively neat though, and everything is arranged quite systematically, according to subject matter, and then alphabetically by author within each section, so it's easy to find something special, if you're looking for that. More often people are just apt to walk up and down in the barn, which seems amazingly spacious even though you know it's not, until something happens to catch the eye.

125

While the Whitlocks will buy almost everything — Gilbert says that's his weakness — what is selling fastest these days, he says, are travel books with color plates. Whitlock Farm is known to be a bargain hunter's paradise, and while most customers don't come away, as one did, with an edition of Goethe in which some marginal notes turned out to have been made by Goethe himself (he realized a profit of thousands), there are always bargains to be had.

Gilbert and Everett Whitlock know books because they more or less grew up in the business. Their father, Clifford, now in his 90s, operates Whitlock's Inc., a bookstore in downtown New Haven, a few miles away, and it was from experience with their father's store that the men were able to get into the book business themselves. But there's still a lot of farmer in Gilbert, and he talks with just a touch of wistfulness about the Herefords that his brother is raising outside his windows. At least he can look across the fields and feel at home.

In good weather, some of the paperbacks and less expensive books are displayed in outdoor stalls and tables, lending an almost carnival atmosphere to the spot. Picnic tables are placed nearby, and anyone is welcome to spread out his lunch and enjoy it in the shade of the big old trees around the barn. In rainy weather it all moves inside and then, in the warmth of the barns, with the patter of raindrops on the roof, there is a different, no less wonderful, experience.

Of the Whitlocks' regular customers, a favorite is the retired postal worker who visits two or three times a week, taking a bus part of the way, walking the rest, and toting home a few books each time in a bag he carries with him. He is a shy, quiet man, who has been known to return books to the shelves when he's through with them, refusing to take any money, just because he's so grateful to be able to visit at all.

It's no wonder. While the atmosphere is simple, there's a musty warmth about it all, and on Saturdays and Sundays the place is so popular that Gilbert Whitlock says "you can't even get in here on weekends." I can only speak for weekdays when it isn't nearly that crowded.

Best-sellers are not the Whitlocks' stock-in-trade, although some can be found, after a year, for 50 per cent or more off the original price. Better to look for old, less known books; better to browse and see what you come up with.

Actually the biggest portion of their business is not to the Sunday book lovers, but to other booksellers and a few collectors (although Gilbert says "there aren't any book collectors any more the way there used to be"). Much of it is mail order. When he comes up with a really rare book, Gilbert usually offers it first to nearby Yale University, with which the family has strong ties. Professors and students also have long been customers.

But people who visit Whitlock Farm are just as likely to be from far away. A recent entry in the guest book — yes, there's a guest book to sign if you want — was from visitors from Australia with the notation "we finally found you again after many years."

If you haven't found Whitlock Farm yet, you'll discover that the ride itself through the roads of rural Connecticut adds to the experience and like most people before you, you'll probably be back.

Also in the Area

Walking Tours, Yale University. Meet at University Information Office, Phelps Gate, 344 College St., New Haven, Conn. (203) 436-8330 — Tours are offered year-round of this famous school. Tour A is the central campus including the Beinecke Rare Book Library and other well-known places. Tour B is of the North

Campus, including science facilities. Each takes a bit over an hour. Summer hours, end of May to early September: Tour A, M-Sat., 9:15; 1:30 and 3 p.m.; Sunday, 1:30 and 3 p.m.; Tour B, M-F, 10:30 a.m. School-year schedule: Tour A, M-F 10 and 2; Saturday, 11 and 2; Sunday, 1:30 and 3; Tour B, M-F, 11:30. All tours guided and free.

Yale University Art Gallery, 1111 Chapel St., New Haven, and **British Art Institute,** 1080 Chapel St., New Haven, Conn. (203) 436-8330. These fine art collections, a part of Yale, are just across the street from each other so you can do them both. The hours are the same: year-round, 10 a.m. to 5 p.m. Tuesday to Saturday; 2 to 5 p.m. Sunday. Free, although voluntary donations are accepted.

Dining 20

Poor Lads/New Haven, Conn.

One of the great things about Poor Lads in New Haven is that all the patrons there seem to be regulars, with their own favorite waiters and tables, thus giving it almost the feel of a private club.

Another great thing is the food, billed as French country dining, but to my mind more classical French. Not the great steaming ragouts or cassoulets dot this formal parchment-type menu, but such dishes as rack of lamb persillee, roast duckling flambe with sauce Montmorency, and filet of sole Dieppoise.

Yet another plus is the price of entrees, ranging from $6.25 for Delmonico steak through boneless chicken Kiev and saddle of lamb Poor Lads for $7.50, to several veal dishes in the $8 range, and sliced filet mignon saute with fresh mushrooms for $9.50. Chateaubriand flambe au cognac is $22 for two, highest on the menu. Even though nothing accompanies these entrees except vegetables of the day, it's still quite a bargain for a really suave city restaurant.

With our ample drinks ($1.50), a Dubonnet blonde served in a stemmed goblet and a Manhattan, came crusty French rolls and foil-wrapped squares of sweet butter.

For appetizers we couldn't resist trying cold mussels Parisienne ($2.75) and smoked salmon for $3.75. The mussels were plump, tender and bathed in a subtle vinaigrette, nestled in a cup of lettuce, and were truly outstanding. The smoked salmon, cut properly thin and served with large capers and lemon, was a very generous portion and equally delicious.

One may also have escargots de Bourgogne, clams casino or crabmeat cocktail for $3.50, pate maison or quiche Lorraine for $2, or fresh fruit cup for $1.25.

Several soups are offered, ranging in price from soup du jour for 95 cents to Saint Germain aux croutons, cold vichyssoise or cold consomme Madrilene, all $1.25, or, for $2, lobster bisque or French onion soup gratinee.

Specials of the day were broiled swordfish, poached halibut with Hollandaise sauce (pronounced 'alibut by our charming French waiter) and veal Oscar ($8.50), which I tried, a marvelous dish of veal scallops topped with firm pink crabmeat and a rich Bearnaise sauce, heavily flavored with shallots.

We also tried the tournedos Rossini ($9.50) and were pleased with the large portion of tender fillet, wrapped in a crouton, topped with foie gras and swathed in a flavorful sauce made with Madeira.

Vegetables of the day (always changing) were nicely crisp green beans drenched in butter and Duchesse potatoes topped with cheese. Both were perfect accompaniments to the very fine entrees.

One of those glamorous wine lists with all the labels enshrined between sheets of plastic offered a nice selection, with several bottles for $6 and under, rising to Chateau Lafite Rothschild 1964 for $75. We had an excellent Chateau de Lachaize 1976 for $7.50, a fresh and almost sparkling Beaujolais. The huge wine glasses were balloon-shaped for red and large thistle-shaped for white, and the waiter even swirled ice in the glasses before he poured the white wine for the diners at the next table.

Because it was late at this point, we missed out on the French pastries and the chocolate mousse, both of which were gone — just as well! Other desserts are cherries jubilee, $3.25; crepes for two, $4.50, and strawberries Romanoff, $2.75. We settled for coffee, the Poor Lads special blend, for 50 cents. I always wonder why coffee in good restaurants tastes so much better than at home.

Decor at Poor Lads is another plus — it's on the ground floor of a deep, narrow building (like a New York brownstone) and it's a very pretty room, with spacious tables, pale pink cloths and napkins, fresh flowers on every table, subtle and soft lighting, paintings for sale by local artists, and a fantastic pink and green wallpaper festooned with exotic birds in full plumage.

A cozy little bar is just to the right of the main entrance and on one brick wall beyond, a mantelpiece is covered with wine bottles.

Waiters, decked out in gold-trimmed navy uniforms (just as on an ocean

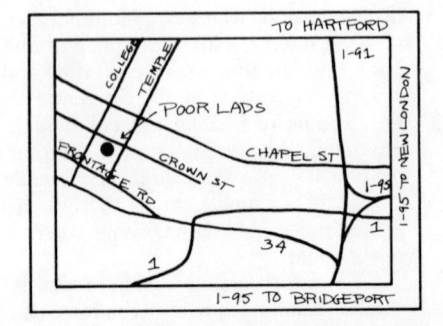

Poor Lads, 204 Crown St., New Haven, Conn. Tel. (203) 624-3163. On Crown Street between Temple and College streets, downtown New Haven. Reservations recommended. Major credit cards. Luncheon, noon to 3 p.m.; dinner, 6 to 10 p.m. Closed Sunday.

liner!) are most efficient and courteous, although we found the service a trifle slow. We didn't mind, but if you had a post-dinner engagement, it could be annoying.

Poor Lads serves complete lunches from $3.25 to $4.95, and also offers a little nightclub upstairs, the Greenhouse, where there is live music after 9:30 p.m.

Why the name? Poor Lads was opened a few years ago by two "poor" young men. One of them, Ernest Nejame — poor no longer, we assume — is the sole owner now.

Also in the Area

Curious Jane's, 9 Elm St., New Haven, Conn. (203) 562-6010. Colorful and with a San Francisco aura is Curious Jane's (the name taken from *Curious George*, which owners Jane and Peter Tracy read to their children). The walls are decorated with Jane's batik hangings and other crafts, and the seats are church chairs from Hartford's Trinity Episcopal Church. The menu is international, and luncheon abounds in crepes, omelets, quiches, pates, chicken enchiladas and such. A Sunday brunch includes huevos rancheros, bagels and lox, and eggs Benedict. A specialty at night is duckling with a choice of cherry, currant or orange sauce. There is an exceptionally wide selection of good California wines at modest prices in the $4.50 to $8 range. Our newspaper drama critic proclaims the puree of Swiss cheese and bacon soup delicious! Prices at lunch are in the $2 to $5 range; at night $4 to $9. Lunch, 11:30 a.m. to 2:30 p.m.; dinner, 5:30 to 9:30 or 10 p.m. Sunday, brunch from noon to 2, dinner 2 to 8 p.m. Closed Monday.

Pippins, 1995 Whitney St., Hamden, Conn. (203) 281-1514. We hear lots of nice things about this new and interesting small restaurant, done in a British Victorian oak-panelled style. At lunch (price range: $2.50 to $7) you can choose from a dozen omelets, quiches, a great baconburger, and whopping salads of crab or shrimp Louis. At dinner prices start at $5.50, rising to $28.50 for rack of lamb for two. Specialties are paella ($8.95) and bouillabaisse ($9.95), and many entrees and desserts are flamed at tableside. The house cheesecake made with brown sugar and pecans is super, and there's a pastry cart with Italian pastries. The wine list has 130 selections. You should make dinner reservations well in advance for weekends. Lunch, 11:30 a.m. to 3 p.m. Monday to Friday, to 2:30 p.m. Saturday, and Sunday brunch, noon to 3. Dinner, 5 to 10 p.m. Monday to Thursday, to about midnight on Friday and Saturday, 4 to 8:30 p.m. Sunday.

Blessings, 45 Howe St., New Haven. (203) 624-3557. The decor is plain but the food isn't; when we first moved to this area we were told that Blessings is the finest Chinese restaurant on the East Coast! The cuisine is in the Peking style, and outstanding are the moo-chi pork and the Peking duck. Lunch, noon to 2:30 p.m.; dinner, 5 to 9:30 or 10 p.m. Closed Sunday.

Daytrip 21

Come to the Circus
Barnum Museum/Bridgeport, Conn.

All Egyptian mummies are not the same. The one housed in Bridgeport's Barnum Museum has a name, Pay-yeb, and an occupation, third priest, and something is even known of his father (thanks to a Yale graduate student who translated the hieroglyphics from the coffin). Moreover, Pay-yeb is unwrapped (thanks to a group of Bridgeport physicians who apparently got curious some years back).

But kids love skeletons, and so the 3,000-year-old skeleton of Pay-yeb — in remarkably good condition, by the way — has proved repeatedly to be one of the most popular exhibits at the museum. When I was a kid in Bridgeport, I thought it was the only one worth seeing.

But when I was a kid, the Barnum museum wasn't what it is today. At that time it had been all pushed upstairs into the third floor of the unusual looking building, while city offices occupied the lower two floors. I remember the must and dust and clutter of trinkets and treasures, little of which made a lasting impression.

All that has changed since the late '60s when the City of Bridgeport coughed up the shekels to clean, renovate and expand the museum to the three floors that are, in fact, its rightful domain. Now the Barnum Museum is a light, bright, fun spot quite in keeping with the spirit of the man for whom it is named and who provided for its construction, Phineas Taylor Barnum himself.

It was Barnum's last gift to the city he loved. Just a week before his death in 1891, in a final codicil to his will, the famed circus impresario provided $100,000 for the construction of a building to be known as the Barnum Institute of Science and History. The quarters were shared by the Bridgeport Scientific Society, the Fairfield County Historical Society and the Bridgeport Medical Society. The Wright Brothers even came with their "flying machine" on one occasion and Thomas A. Edison with his "talking machine" on another.

But the city took over the building in 1934 in lieu of back taxes, and nothing much was done until Bridgeport realized it might, in fact, have something good on its hands.

It does. And in keeping with the spirit of P.T. Barnum himself, whose famous Barnum & Bailey Circus wintered for years in Bridgeport, the place has become more a circus museum and less an historical one. Oh, there are some exhibits of objects from early Bridgeport and the second floor was supposed to be devoted to the history of the city, even after the renovation, but jovial curator Robert S. Pelton agrees that "Tom Thumb and P.T. Barnum are taking over the place." As well they should.

Location: 820 Main St., Bridgeport, Conn. Corner Gilbert Street. Exit 27 north from Connecticut Turnpike (I-95).

Open: Year-round, noon to 5 p.m. Tuesday to Saturday, 2 to 5 p.m. Sunday.

Admission: Free.

Telephone: (203) 576-7320.

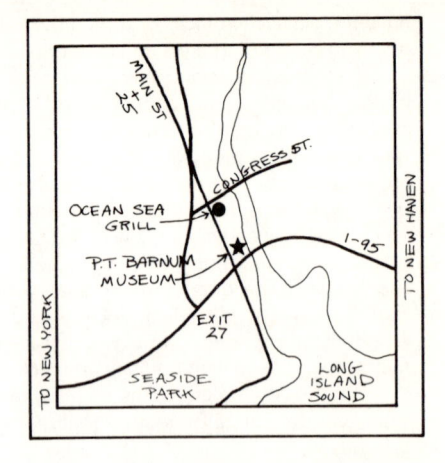

Barnum wasn't a native of Bridgeport, but you'd never know it. He came from nearby Bethel but spent the better part of his life in Bridgeport, even serving as the city's mayor (1875) and representing it in the State Legislature, and somehow also being the showman for which he is remembered.

Tom Thumb *was* from Bridgeport. He was born Charles Sherwood Stratton, and he was a midget. He was also one of the great showman's greatest showpieces. The tiny man — about 35 inches when full grown — was signed by Barnum at the age of 5; under Barnum's tutelage he toured the world and when a member of Barnum's American Museum in New York, he met, loved and married another midget, Lavinia Warren.

So when you visit the Barnum Museum, it's a little like going to Barnum's own circus. Even the exterior of the building is showy. A contemporary newspaper account touted it as "pure Romanesque in style;" we'd probably call it eclectic. It has almost everything: A round dome and a square tower, arches and friezes, pillars and windows, all done up in red sandstone and heavy rock.

The circus motif is apparent from the moment you step into the bright, welcoming lobby, where you'll probably be snagged by Miller B. Ross, a former newsstand operator in Bridgeport, who serves as one of the museum's more loquacious and enthusiastic guides. Tours don't cost a thing, but if you prefer you can wander on your own.

In the lobby are some antique circus posters from Barnum's day, a miniature circus done by Bridgeport resident Bruce Hawley (this is just a teaser; wait 'til you see the one on the third floor), clown costumes and props. There is also "Baby Bridgeport," the stuffed and mounted four-year-old elephant which was born in Barnum's circus and was only the second elephant ever born in captivity in the world. He's been painted and he doesn't look real, but he is.

Given the spot of honor in the adjoining first-floor room is the brown velvet suit worn by the midget Tom Thumb when he was presented to Queen Victoria in England at age 5. It is displayed in its own glass case. This is real showmanship stuff: Think of Barnum having had the suit whipped up for the tiny child, whom he promoted, exploited and even named General Tom Thumb.

In this room you will also see some of the furniture from Barnum's Oriental villa, "Iranistan," which was one of three homes he built in Bridgeport (it burned down but lives on in a street name); memorabilia from Jenny Lind, the Swedish nightingale brought to America and toured by Barnum, and the head of Tom

Thumb from a grave figure made for his final resting place in Bridgeport's Mountain Grove cemetery (Barnum is buried nearby).

Stop at the landing between first floor and second to see the tiny carved rosewood bed Tom Thumb used as an adult (your kids will be enchanted by the miniscule proportions) and then go to the second floor for more fun. A fairly recent addition to the collection is tiny coaches used by Tom Thumb and another of Barnum's midgets — "Commodore" George Washington Morrison Nutt. Commodore Nutt's coach is shaped like a nut — a walnut, believe it or not.

Kids like to honk the horn on the unusual bicycle-built-for-two that is part of the historic Bridgeport collection — and Curator Pelton encourages them to — but once they spot the signs leading to the Egyptian mummy, all else will be secondary. "Do Not View the Mummy If You Scare Easily," warns one placard nearby, and Pelton tells of two young teenage girls who left the museum after one quick look, at a very quick pace, never to return again.

(It's not *that* scary).

There's more for the circus fan on the third floor, the *piece de resistance* being the "William R. Brinley Miniature Circus," which takes up most of the room. Brinley, of Meriden, Connecticut, started at age nine and hasn't yet finished the circus, a three-quarter inch scale model of the real thing. With five rings rather than three, it has many workable parts, like the cook tent where a chef flips pancakes, the ring where trapeze artists fly back and forth, and the like. More amazing still, the entire circus — tents and wagons, animals and performers — can be moved into the circus wagons and then rolled aboard the circus train which sits at its siding. Brinley makes regular visits to check on, repair, add to (and play with) his circus.

The third floor is also the setting for the Swiss Alpine Village, a miniature Swiss town with 22,000 working parts, when they all work, which Barnum himself displayed in his museum in New York. There's an old-fashioned beer garden, fountains playing water, a shoe shop with cobblers working away and more.

"Clown Alley," donated by a California clown named "Popo," is another exhibit; it shows his costumes, souvenirs and so forth. At this point you may spy the sign that asks, as did Barnum, "Have you seen the egress?" If you haven't, now's the time, with a possible stop at the sales desk in the lobby for appropriate mementos of your visit.

Also in the Area

Beardsley Zoological Gardens, Beardsley Park, Noble Avenue at White Plains Road, Bridgeport, Conn. (203) 576-8082. Main zoo has tigers, elephants, bears and other large animals and is open free daily year-round, 10 a.m. to 4:30 p.m. Oct. 15 to March 15 and 10 a.m. to 6 p.m. March to October. Children's zoo with "contact area" where children may pet animals is open March to October only, 10 a.m. to 6 p.m., adults 35 cents and children 25 cents. Snack bar and gift shop. **Picnicking** in park.

Museum of Art, Science and Industry, 4450 Park Ave., Bridgeport, Conn. (203) 372-3521. Circus gallery has memorabilia of Tom Thumb (mason's uniform), Jenny Lind (parasol, jewelry, etc.), and P.T. Barnum (furniture). There's a line on the wall where kids can compare themselves to the height of midget Tom Thumb. Open year-round from 2 to 5 p.m. every day except Monday or national holidays; admission by voluntary donation. Planetarium shows Tuesday and Thursday at 3:30 p.m.; Saturdays and Sundays, 2, 3 and 4 p.m.; adults $1; children 50 cents.

Dining 21

Ocean Sea Grill/Bridgeport, Conn.

"Our customers expect quality, but they don't want a lot of frills," said the longtime waiter at the Ocean Sea Grill in downtown Bridgeport. And that's what they get — good fresh seafood, generous portions and reasonable prices, in a fine, solid, downtown dining room of the old school.

No "with-it" decor or fancy names on the menu here — the big square dining room has brick walls interspersed with barnwood panelling. Booths lining the sides of the room are the popular places in which to sit. Soft nondescript music, hanging brass lamps, and gold colored cloths on the tables add to a pleasant if not exciting atmosphere.

Mimeographed lists of the day's choices are inserted every day into the lunch and dinner menus, which are decorated with a most unlikely, hideously crimson lobster. Anywhere from 10 to 15 special items are offered at lunch, with about 20 at dinner, and the fish and seafood are obtained fresh from the establishment's own fish market, just a block away.

Sandwiches, seafood stews, salads and omelets are offered as well, and there is always a handful of meat or poultry dishes such as broiled pork chops, chopped tenderloin or boneless breast of chicken for the uninitiated. But it's seafood most patrons are after, and rightly so.

At lunch, the entrees range from $3.75 to $6.75, with most in the $4.50 range. A choice of Manhattan clam chowder, lobster bisque, tomato juice or fruit cup is included, as are vegetables and beverage.

There is no wine list and most customers order wine by the glass (75 cents) or carafe ($4.50) or beer (several imported brands are available). The house wine is Paul Masson, and our carafe of chablis was just fine, although a Bloody Mary was not as spicy as I like.

The crusty rolls (in a basket that was generously refilled) were followed by a lobster bisque, a thinnish but richly flavored golden pink soup with a few pieces of lobster floating about. Since it was oyster season, we tried the oysters on the half shell, big beautiful plump oysters served on ice, with tabasco, horseradish, cocktail sauce and lemon juice to use at will, plus oyster crackers. Impeccable, they were six for $2.50.

A specialty here is lobster, offered at a price more reasonable than at many establishments — at lunch a broiled chicken lobster was $6.75, and at night $7.50, medium lobster $11.95, and large $13.95. I tried the lobster thermidor ($7.95), served not in the usual lobster shell but en coquille. Huge and tender chunks of lobster meat and mushrooms in what tasted like a Mornay sauce made an elegant dish, but not what you'd call a classic Thermidor with its hint of English mustard. At any event, it was delicious.

Also a great favorite with the regular customers — of which there are many — is the broiled fish, scrod, lemon sole or whole flounder, $4.50 at lunch and $7.50 at dinner. Broiled fish would seem the simplest of dishes, but somehow it is the hardest to get just right, since the fish, undisguised with sauce, should be freshly caught and broiled to perfection. This the Ocean Sea Grill accomplishes, with the outer edge golden with butter and a dusting of crumbs, the interior moist and firm.

Served with the meal were crisp and tasty French fries or undistinguished baked potatoes wrapped in foil, as well as a choice of creamy coleslaw or string beans.

For entrees you can also have sole, clams, oysters or scallops fried, large smelts sauteed and, at night, frogs legs with garlic sauce. Sirloin or tenderloin steak are always available.

Other appetizers are cherrystone or littleneck clams, clams casino, and a fresh seafood cocktail that seems a bit steep at $4.

For dessert (the owners formerly did all the baking but now baked goods and rolls come from New York), we tried the boysenberry pie, a generous portion which, if not the greatest homemade pie ever, was fresh, filling and reasonable. The fairly standard desserts are only 35 or 50 cents at lunch; at dinner they are included in the price of the meal.

Living up to its name, this is a masculine place, almost clubby in feeling, with considerable jollity between red-jacketed waiters and regular customers. But many women eat here, too.

Three generations of the Rolleri family have been operating Ocean Sea Grill since 1936, and the inside exudes a sense of permanence, even though it's at the edge of downtown Bridgeport and does not have a spiffy facade. It's less than a mile from the Barnum Museum, but better to take the car than walk.

Ocean Sea Grill, 1328 Main St., Bridgeport, Conn. Tel. (203) 336-2132. One-half mile north of Connecticut Turnpike Exit 27 at northern edge of downtown Bridgeport. Major credit cards. Open noon to 10:30 p.m. Tuesday to Sunday. Closed Monday.

Also in the Area

Pjura's. Also in the heart of Bridgeport, some four blocks from Ocean Sea Grill, this is another family-owned (since 1926), city-type restaurant with reasonable prices, lots of seafood and sandwiches and salads at noon from $2.25 to $3.75. Some of the entree favorites are sauteed liver with bacon, corned beef and cabbage, and chocolate nut mousse. Don't miss the beautiful art deco mirrors over the bar, and the paintings of Bridgeport buildings. No dinner entrees are over $7.95, and baked stuffed lobster with crabmeat dressing is only $6.95.

Pjura's, 121 Wall St., Bridgeport. 1-203-333-0759. 11 a.m. to 10 p.m. Monday to Saturday. Closed Sundays. Mastercharge and Visa.

Barnaby's and **The Gazebo** are two new places to eat at University Square, that complex of factory outlets on Atlantic Street. Barnaby's, a casual but pretty restaurant with red curtains on brass rings and green shaded lamps, is in an old warehouse and features live music and dancing on weekends. It has burgers ($1.75 to $2.95), salads in the $2.50 range, sandwiches from $1.35 for grilled cheese to $3.25 for open steak sandwich, and omelets for $2.75. Specials of the day are written on a blackboard and usually include a steak (New York strip is $6.95). A liter of wine is $3.50. Meals are served 11:30 a.m. to 10 p.m. and it's closed Sundays.

The Gazebo, an ice cream parlor on the first level of the complex, serves a mighty banana split for $1.75, and cones for 50 or 65 cents. Eleven flavors of ice cream and 13 toppings for sundaes let you indulge your sweet tooth — sundaes are $1.50. It's open every day from 10 a.m. to 11 p.m. and serves mid-morning snacks, items from the grill, and sandwiches and grinders. If the kids can't get through lunch without a peanut butter and jelly sandwich, you can get one here for 65 cents.

Daytrip 22

They Really Dig Indians Here
American Indian Archaeological Institute/Washington, Conn.

Grab your cigar box full of arrowheads and head for the American Indian Archaeological Institute (AIAI) in Connecticut's western hills. There in the lovely old town of Washington the group at AIAI is delving into the prehistoric period of New England Indians and there's usually somebody on hand who can look over a few arrowheads. Besides, you never know what might turn up in a cigar box.

You never know what might be lying around in the nearby hills, either, which is what a group of archaeologists from AIAI discovered during the summer of 1977. The group of mostly tyros, led by Dr. Roger W. Moeller, director of research at the institute, unearthed a fluted "clovis type" spear point, typical of those used by hunters who followed the glaciers north at the end of the last Ice Age. That was about 10,000 years ago. Even more exciting, the point was found *in situ* or at the actual place it was used, marking it as the first such Paleo-Indian site ever discovered in Connecticut, and the oldest in New England.

For a fledgling group, and the AIAI is barely five years old, that was a heady discovery. And for a state like Connecticut, which doesn't have much of a reputation in archaeological circles, it was real news. Newspapers around the world reported the discovery.

If you visit the institute's small but exciting museum-center just outside Washington you won't get to view the Paleo-Indian site explored by Dr. Moeller and his team (even though it is just three miles away), but you will be able to see the actual clovis spear point that caused all the excitement. Also found were two miniature points, the use of which is still a mystery.

These rare artifacts are among the Indian items displayed at the two-year-old contemporary building which houses the institute, albeit snugly. (A new wing, the second addition in as many years, is under construction to help accommodate a growing staff and program).

No ordinary Indian museum, that of the AIAI is devoted to the period of Indian life long before the white man ever set foot on the North American continent. Thousands of years before the Indians were grinding corn and growing pumpkins they were hunting huge ancient animals like the mastodon, a prehistoric elephant, and just to show you what that was like, the skeleton of one of those huge beasts, about 12,000 years old, is on display.

The mastodon, the only one of its kind unearthed in Connecticut, was found on the grounds of the Hill-Stead Museum in Farmington in 1913 but had been wasting in storage at Yale's Peabody Museum. It is displayed at the museum in a dismembered state — with all the parts numbered and a key mounted nearby — to emphasize the institute's major thrust, archaeology, and to show the public how archaeologists find, deal with and examine artifacts.

Mastodon may be the largest single exhibit, but this small and brightly lit building, which fairly hums with activity, is full of other gratifying surprises.

Arrowheads there are, from all over Connecticut, but you will also view an unusual birdstone in striped slate (which has become the museum symbol and dates from about 1,000 B.C.), very early Indian pottery, sandstone dishes, the reconstruction of an ancient Indian firepit also unearthed in Connecticut and dioramas of early Indian life. All the displays are neat, effective and well-marked, so the visitor can get a genuine sense of Indian life many centuries ago. It is a bit staggering to think about.

Also on the premises is an Indian longhouse, reconstructed by local school students under the watchful eye of an Onondaga Indian woman from New York State. This is particularly fun for children who will see clothing, animal skins, birchbark and log carriers, early pottery and deerskin in various stages of curing — all planned to give an idea of what life was like for Indians hundreds of years ago.

That appreciation can be expanded by taking a walk on the habitat trail just outside the museum, for which a mimeographed guide is available free. The short (20 to 30-minute) walk takes the visitor through various stages of life in Connecticut by showing the geological formations and botanical growth that would have been predominant at various times.

The habitat trail is a creation of the museum's president, Edward N. Swigart, one of the founders and something of a guiding spirit. A professional ecologist and for more than 20 years an instructor at the Gunnery, well-known preparatory school in Washington, Swigart and five amateur archaeologist friends banded together in the early '70s to form the Shepaug Valley Archaeological Society. AIAI grew out of that organization.

Researching prehistoric woodland Indians and educating the public to what is known about them is the main point of the activity in Washington. To this end archaeological digs are conducted each summer (amateurs are welcome if they commit themselves to a minimum of one or two weeks — write AIAI for information).

For those who don't have to go the whole route but want to see what it's like, a simulated dig site is also on the museum's grounds and used to explain the group's work. Classroom groups get regular instruction in this, but anyone can check it out.

One of the delights of a visit to the archaeological institute is a stop at the tiny

Location: Route 199, Washington, Conn., between towns of Roxbury and Washington.

Open: Year-round, 10 a.m. to 4:30 p.m. Tuesday through Saturday, 1 to 4:30 p.m. Sunday. Closed Jan. 1, Thanksgiving Day and Dec. 25.

Admission: Adults $1; children 50 cents.

Telephone: (203) 868-0518.

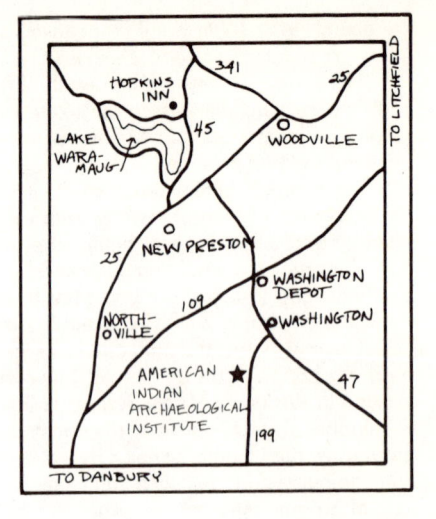

but very specialized museum shop near the entrance. In an age when many musuem shops are beginning to look like each other, AIAI has preferred to do its own thing.

Most articles are handcrafted by friends of the institute and are copies of items in the collection. You will find pewter pendants which are reproductions of the clovis spear point, fused glass ashtrays with the birdstone design, enamelled pendants on leather with hand-done Indian motifs and a cookbook of Indian recipes by a local Indian woman.

A visit to the AIAI will probably take one-and-a-half to two hours, after which there is the marvelous town of Washington to explore and, nearby, Litchfield with its outstanding examples of colonial architecture, fine shops and restaurants. Any time of year is lovely in western Connecticut but especially fine and appropriate might be: Indian summer.

Also in the Area

White Flower Farm, Route 63, Morris, Conn. (203) 567-9415. South of Litchfield, one of the country's more unusual nurseries grows and sells the less common varieties of perennials (and some other specialty horticulture items), usually to the most dedicated and knowledgable of gardeners. Their own gardens, which bloom from mid-May to mid-September, are wonderful to visit and you are welcome to do so, free of charge from Spring to Fall. If you want to visit the greenhouses or production block, you can, but it costs 50 cents extra. White Flower Farm has a new owner, Eliot Wadsworth, who promises to keep the place much as it was under the management of William B. Harris, its founder.

Litchfield — This town is one of Connecticut's great prides, with many marvelous old colonial homes and an honest-to-goodness New England green in the center of town. Each year, in July, some of these homes are open to the public to benefit the Connecticut Junior Republic.

Tapping Reeve House & Law School — South Street, Litchfield, Conn. (203) 567-8919. America's first law school (1784), it numbers among its graduates Aaron Burr and many other distinguished lawyers. The house has finely furnished period rooms. Open mid-May to mid-October, 11 a.m. to 5 p.m. Tuesday to Saturday. Adults $1.50; children, 50 cents.

Gunn Historical Museum, On the Green, Washington, Conn. (203) 868-7756. Less than three miles from the American Indian Archaeological Institute is this establishment in a 1781 house in the center of Washington. It offers a fine thimble collection, dollhouses and western Indian baskets collected by an early U.S. senator, Orville Platt of Washington. Open free year-round, 2 to 5 p.m. Tuesdays and Thursdays, 1 to 4 p.m. Saturdays. Closed holidays.

Dining 22

Hopkins Inn/New Preston, Conn.

Beautiful Lake Waramaug sparkles below the terrace, with the Litchfield Hills rising around it. With a little imagination, you could imagine yourself on one of the lovely lakes in the European Alps.

The Hopkins Inn, owned for 15 years by Swiss-born Margrit and Ruedy Hilfiker, was taken over recently by Beth and Franz Schober. Mr. Schober, who is Austrian, must feel quite at home.

With 11 guest rooms, it's a rambling old New England inn, established in 1872, painted a soft yellow with white trim, set high on a hill overlooking the lake. Porches and terraces abound, to take full advantage of the view. On a summer's night while sitting on an outdoor terrace and sipping a pre-dinner drink, the air is still — only faint sounds of neighing horses disturb the calm, plus a putt-putt from a motor boat towing water skiers below.

Tables are set on a large outdoor patio, under a gigantic horse chestnut tree strewn with pretty yellow lights, and lunch and dinner are served here on warm days.

Inside, one is struck by a Victorian feeling, mixed with a bit of Colonial. It's the kind of place where, on a rainy day, you would be happy taking an old book out of the bookcase and curling up in one of the comfy overstuffed chairs in front of the parlor fireplace.

On a pegboard in the entrance hall are an amazing variety of old hats (one is reminiscent of the Teddy Roosevelt character in "Arsenic and Old Lace," charging up the stairs). Some came with the inn; some were acquired at a rummage sale in New Milford.

Two dining rooms stretch around the lakeview side of the inn. They are decorated in keeping with the period — one small room sporting a sprigged pink and red paper, soft green wood trim and a dark panelled fireplace. The other has rough wooden walls lined with figureheads. A huge fireplace in the corner has glazed raised tiles depicting, among other things, Rip Van Winkle. Its history seems to have been lost.

Some appetizers and soups are included in the price of the meal and gazpacho and vichyssoise are always featured in the summer — the gazpacho is highly seasoned and very good. A pate maison is creditable, and we also liked eggs a la Jacques, served with a Russian dressing. Salad was a simple mixture of greens with a tart vinaigrette, mixed in the dining room in a huge bowl.

Melon and prosciutto is $2.25, and a special Swiss appetizer, bundnerteller, consists of air dried beef and Swiss cheese, served on a cutting board, $1.75.

Most entrees are $7.50 to $8.75 and there are often seasonal changes on the blackboard menu. They include broiled salmon, Wiener schnitzel, sweetbreads, roast duck, veal piccata Milanese, calves' brains, chicken cordon bleu, beef Bourguignon and filet of sole amandine. Sirloin steak is $10.50 Prices include soup, salad, vegetables, potato and coffee.

The broiled sweetbreads were really special, a large serving of the tender delicacies under a superb light Hollandaise-type sauce. The veal piccata and Wiener schnitzel, sauteed with cheese and breading, had veal almost as good as the European.

With dinner we shared a bottle of Pouilly-Fuisse for $10.25, the soft dry wine blending well with all the entrees. The wines are well chosen and quite fairly priced, starting at $4.75 and going up to $54 for Chateau Lafite Rothschild, 1967. Five Swiss wines (rarely seen in this country) are offered, four whites and one red, from $9.75 to $12.50. A quart carafe of the imported house wine is $5.50.

Served family-style with our meal were fresh carrots, delicately roasted potatoes, and something new to us, braised Romaine lettuce, absolutely delicious.

The Hopkins Inn always offers a great selection of desserts and most are 75 cents or $1. Their white chocolate mousse is renowned, and customers also love the pecan pie and coupe aux marrons. The baba au rhum is rich, moist and very rummy, and the Irish coffee, $1.75, is luscious.

Entrees at lunchtime are in the $3 to $5 range and include Swiss bratwurst, chef's salad, omelet du jour, crepes a la Reine, and broiled scrod.

The inn boasts a steady clientele and has to turn people away on Saturdays. Open from Easter to the beginning of January, it has a private beach on the lake.

We've known a lot of friends over the years who've taken visiting mothers-in-law, aunts and friends from other parts of the country to the Hopkins Inn, and they always come away charmed by the combination of location and food.

Hopkins Inn on Lake Waramaug, Hopkins Road, New Preston, Conn. Tel. (203) 868-7295. North end of lake, follow signs off Route 45. Reservations recommended at night and on weekends. No credit cards. Luncheon, noon to 1:30 p.m. Tuesday to Saturday, early May through summer; dinner, 6 to 9 p.m. Tuesday to Saturday. Sunday dinner, 1 to 3 p.m. and 5 to 8 p.m. Closed Mondays except holidays. Closed from beginning of January to Easter.

Also in the Area

Meetinghouse Inn, West Street, Litchfield, Conn. (203) 567-8744. An historic home (circa 1760) with a beautiful pillared facade houses the Meetinghouse Inn. You can dine in the Blue Room, the library with its book-lined walls or the porch, with sunny yellow tablecloths and filled with hanging plants. In the summer there's also a canopied terrace. The varied menu has New England seafood, beef and international specialties including veal Saltimbocca, coquille St. Jacques and roast duckling a l'Orange, in the $6.95 to $9.95 range. A carefully chosen wine list and some rich desserts are other pluses. Lunch, noon to 2:30 p.m. Monday to Friday, to 3 p.m. Saturday; champagne brunch, noon to 2 p.m. Sunday. Dinner, 6 to 9 p.m. Monday to Thursday, to 10 p.m. Friday and Saturday, noon to 4 and 5 to 9 p.m. Sunday.

Today's, Washington Depot, Conn. (203) 868-7670. In a Victorian house moved by horse and cart to its present location, two young men are dishing up fantastic soups like Boola-Boola, pear-leek, chilled avocado and watercress-almond, and imaginative entrees ($8 to $11), including French, Chinese and American cuisines. Breast of chicken stuffed with chicken mousse and lobster, tangerine squab, medallions of pork in a fennel butter sauce and sauteed veal with artichoke puree are some. Lunch prices range from $2.50 to $4.50, and include cassoulet and salad, sweet and sour sole, tarragon cheese souffle and many omelets. Lunch, noon to 2:30 p.m.; dinner, 6 to 8 or 9 p.m. Closed Wednesday, and Monday and Tuesday in winter.

Le Bon Coin, Route 202, Woodville, Conn. (203) 868-7763. This nice little family-owned French restaurant has two pleasant dining rooms in a small house where food is lovingly prepared. Dinner is table d'hote (Dover sole at $10.25 is the most expensive entree) with appetizer and dessert included, although some items are extra. The special cream of watercress soup is superb, as are mussels Provencales with fragrant garlic butter. We still remember the veal kidneys flamed in cognac and bathed in a marchand de vin sauce, served with a thyme and onion flecked rice pilaf. The owners are especially proud of their two veal dishes and their salad has an excellent vinaigrette. Afterward try cafe Le Bon Coin, with Grand Marnier, Kahlua and filtered coffee, served with whipped cream and cognac floated on the top — don't think of the calories! Dinner only, from 5:30 to 9:30 p.m. Monday to Saturday, 1 to 9 p.m. Sunday. Closed Monday from November to mid-April.

The Golden Bough, Route 45, Warren, Conn. (203) 868-2355. Lovers of fine French cuisine mourned the passing of L'Ermitage, but were heartened by the reopening of the lovely 200-year-old building, where one can still dine in summer on the terrace beneath the huge old maple tree strung with handsome globe lamps. The entree offerings are international now, with the specialties of many countries, Dutch, German, Russian, Chinese and French. From a repertoire of more than 150 entrees, 12 to 15 are listed each day on the blackboard menu. Chicken Kiev, ballotine of duck, Danish roast pork, shrimp in beer batter range in price from $6.95 to $11.95. On the walls are paintings by local artists, and there's an extensive wine cellar. Lunch, noon to 2:30 p.m., Sunday brunch, noon to 3 p.m. Dinner, 6 to 8:30 p.m., to 9:45 p.m. Friday and Saturday, and 5 to 8:30 p.m. Sunday. Closed Tuesday; also Wednesday in winter.

Daytrip 23

Contemporary Art; Colonial Setting
Aldrich Museum/Ridgefield, Conn.

Contemporary art is served up in a colonial setting at the Aldrich Museum in Ridgefield, Conn., and it's the setting that gets you at first. Driving along the conservative old town's gracious Main Street, with its colonial homes, churches and ancient trees, you don't quite expect to be confronted with Robert Morris's L-beams or Sheldon Machlin's "Great Red Ring."

And you aren't — not exactly. First you must pull to the side of the 1783 landmark building, with its demure white clapboard and black shutters and its history, and you have to walk out back to see the enormous pieces of contemporary sculpture that sit on the great expanse of lawn as it slopes away from the building. There are thirty of them, mostly massive, and they provide a startling and stunning contrast to the building itself, which is not permitted to alter its exterior and so blends with the rest of Ridgefield's Main Street.

By this time everyone has gotten over the inhibiting idea that antiques have to be exhibited in old houses, or contemporary art in glass and steel buildings, so the mix at the Aldrich is better the way it is. And the local kids who cavort in front of the Eduardo Paolozzi stainless steel sculpture, which acts like a mirror in an amusement park "Fun House," have a good time even if it's taken awhile for the rest of the local populace to accept. And it has.

When the Aldrich Museum opened in 1964 under the private ownership of Mr. and Mrs. Larry Aldrich (he is a well-known dress manufacturer), its patrons tended to be the cognoscenti from New York who would tool out to the country on nice weekends from Spring until Fall to view the art. In those days the museum closed during the winter.

But gradually the reputation of the Aldrich grew, it went public in 1969, began to open year-round in the mid-1970s, and now gets support from the entire area. The focus has changed, too, from strictly paintings and sculpture to include photography, drawings, and, in the form of special events, contemporary music and films. Says curator of education Jacqueline Moss: "We're making an effort to present a broader aspect of contemporary art."

Still, the Aldrich is best known for its three major exhibitions, where the paintings and sculpture of contemporary artists are displayed. Probably the most exciting of the three is the annual summer exhibition, "Contemporary Reflections," which opens in April each year and is on view until September, presenting artists who are not yet represented by an important gallery or who have not yet had their own one-man shows. It is a valuable exposure for them and they know it, sending hundreds of slides to museum director Carlus Dyer each year in the hopes of being represented in this show. The museum's track record is good in terms of helping the artists to connect with galleries.

Larry Aldrich himself has been strongly committed to young, little-known artists, from the days when he personally selected the works for "Contemporary Reflections" by tramping through lofts in Manhattan and elsewhere. Now he has removed himself from much of the day-to-day operation of the museum, but his commitment to those artists is kept in a variety of ways; one is the refusal of the museum to take a commission when works exhibited in "Contemporary Reflections" are sold.

The summer show serves as a good way to get in touch with the experiments of young American artists, a time to see what new movements are being pursued, what new directions taken. But the other two major exhibitions are also important in the contemporary art world, in which the Aldrich is managing to make a real name for itself. Recently Dyer put together an exhibition of art from the private collections of people in the area around Ridgefield. It was a fine representation of work since the late 1950s and included such names as Louise Nevelson, Willem de Kooning, Andy Warhol, Helen Frankenthaler and Robert Motherwell.

In conjunction with that exhibit, a smaller "Showcase" exhibit was shown in the ground-floor gallery. In this case drawings by Richard Lindner, who was also represented in the major show, were on display. On other occasions the Showcase gallery has been used to display photography or other media which are generally not given major shows in the upstairs galleries.

The Aldrich is an exciting place to visit, mostly because of the art that's on

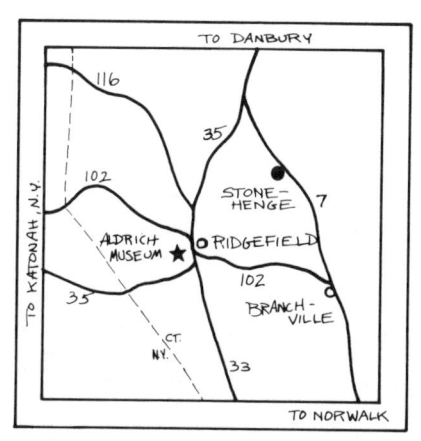

Location: 258 Main St. (Route 35) Ridgefield, Conn. Reached via Merritt Parkway or I-84, then Route 7 to Route 35.

Open: Year-round, 1 to 5 p.m. Wednesday, Saturday and Sunday. Group tours by appointment.

Admission: Adults $1; children, students and senior citizens, 50 cents.

Special Events: Gallery tours at 2:30 p.m. Saturday.

Telephone: (203) 438-4519.

display, but also because of the way it is done. The interior of the old building has been pretty much gutted to allow for broad expanses of white walls where the canvasses (many of them huge) of contemporary artists can be shown to fine advantage. The polished wood floors and good lighting add to the general pleasure.

Outside, the sculpture garden is a place to walk, to chat and finally to sit at wrought-iron chairs and tables thoughtfully provided by the museum. Picnicking is welcomed, and it's a glorious spot, on a terrace just behind the building where you can enjoy the sculpture as you have your lunch or supper. The sculpture garden is always open, so if you're in the area at a time when the rest of the musuem is not, you can stop to view the sculpture alone, and I think it's worth it.

As you might expect, children tend to enjoy this museum, for they have a grand time playing on the grass around all those "funny shapes" and are inclined to respond, too, to the contemporary work that is displayed inside. Your trip to the Aldrich makes a good focal point for a day which might also include shopping in Ridgefield's splendid little stores, and a meal at any of the many outstanding restaurants in the area.

Also in the Area

Keeler Tavern, 132 Main St., Ridgefield, Conn. (203) 438-5485. A short and pleasant walk from the Aldrich Museum, this colonial tavern was operated as an inn from 1772 to 1907. A British cannonball remains imbedded in the wall of the building from the Revolutionary War. Furnishings are largely original. Open 2 to 5 p.m. Wednesday, Saturday and Sunday. Adults $1; children 25 cents.

Putnam Memorial State Park, Route 58, Redding, Conn. Site of the winter encampment of the right wing of the Continental Army under General Israel Putnam, the historical area recreates area of encampment, with some buildings reconstructed. A map is available which may be followed. A small museum contains collection of relics of the Revolutionary War. Museum is open noon to 4 p.m. daily from Memorial Day to Labor Day. Park has picnicking area, closes at sunset.

Ridgefield is a prosperous suburban town from which executives commute to New York, Stamford, Norwalk or Danbury. Center of town has many boutiques and shops and fine restaurants. Gold's Delicatessen in the Ridgefield Shopping Center next to Ballard Park sells sandwiches; food for picnics may also be purchased at Brunetti's Market, Main Street.

Dining 23

Stonehenge/Ridgefield, Conn.

Connecticut's most famed inn, perhaps, is Stonehenge in Ridgefield. In an early 19th century colonial-style white building, it is enhanced by its surroundings of towering trees, spacious lawns and a lake where swans, ducks and even a gaggle of Canada geese carry on their affairs.

Judging from the bits of conversation overheard inside the dining rooms, one wouldn't be surprised if a few affairs were being carried on there as well! Stonehenge has that kind of romantic atmosphere.

At night, dining in the dark-panelled cozy and intimate bar is especially romantic, when red shaded candles inside glass lamps cast a seductive glow on the tables elegant with cream cloths and red napkins.

In the daytime in the large and airy main dining room, the lovely grounds can be viewed from three sides through the sparkling windows. Handsome heavy draperies add a luxurious note, as do the wood panelling and corner cases filled with rare china and silver pieces. Fresh flowers are on every table, and the same red lamps enhance the red and cream color scheme as at night.

Stonehenge has been known for its distinguished cuisine since the famed Swiss chef, Albert Stockli of Restaurant Associates in New York, became co-owner in 1965, and has consistently won Holiday awards as well as four stars in the Mobil Guide. Although Stockli died in 1972 and the inn's reputation dipped for awhile, present owners David Davis and Douglas Seville are doing a grand job in keeping up the traditionally elegant food and service.

We've had lunch and dinner here, and can't figure out which we enjoy more. Although less expensive than dinner, lunch is certainly not inexpensive, with entrees costing from $4.95 for cheese quiche to $7.50 for either roast baby rack of lamb, bratwurst with onion rings or Stonehenge's own sausage with champagne kraut.

The menu changes seasonally, and at lunch we've sampled the famous and hearty Stonehenge barley soup, the marvelous shrimp in beer batter with pungent fruit sauce, a fabulous chef's salad and a beautifully arranged seafood salad in an avocado shell. Country pate is rough textured and delicious, and chicken livers in an excellent sauce are served on crisp toast.

At dinner the cost is a prix fixe $15.95, with some items carrying a surcharge. Or one can order a la carte — entrees $11.95 to $14.50, desserts at least $2 and coffee $1.

Drinks are large (as they should be at $2.25 each) and served in pretty long-stemmed goblets. The wine list is extensive and expensive, with Soave the cheapest at $7 and nothing else much below $9. You can get a carafe of the house wine, Almaden, for about $6.50. We've had a lovely Alsatian Riesling, fragrant and fruity, and, with a recent dinner, Vouvray for $9.50, soft yet vibrant and served in large hurricane-lamp shaped glasses.

At dinner, our appetizers were simply superb. Mushroom crepes with a Mornay sauce in which was Gruyere cheese were truly out of this world, rich, yet a delicate preamble to the meal. Since Stonehenge smokes its own sausage, the sausage with a mustard wine sauce is well worth a try, garnished with grapes and served sizzling, the edges slightly curled from the broiler. The sauce is extraordinary.

Stonehenge also has its own trout tanks, and its live brook trout poached blue is its most famous dish. For blue trout, the fish must be killed by a blow to the head just before being cleaned and plunged into boiling court bouillon. After this indignity, it curls up and turns a bright blue, almost a cobalt. When it is brought to the table, with glaring eyes, one wonders if one should eat it! But after being skinned and boned by the waiter and adorned with a mousseline sauce (Hollandaise made lighter by whipped cream), the trout is just fantastic, with the most clean, fresh taste imaginable.

A whole roasted squab chicken Grandmere was a tasty if formidable dish, garnished with mushrooms and carrots, and swathed in a rich brown sauce. The meat was moist and tender. Vegetables of the day were carrots, glazed to a candy-like perfection, and a discreet small boiled potato with the trout, dusted with parsley.

The house salad was a nice mixture of greens, gleaming with its coat of a mustardy vinaigrette.

There is a luscious selection of desserts, although we thought the Black Forest cake rather ordinary. A strawberry tart was really special, with an abundance of fresh fruit on a shortcake crust, topped with a deep and shiny glaze. Chocolate mousse, coupe aux marrons and selections from the cheese tray are some other choices.

Service here is distinguished, quiet and efficient, with many dishes heated on and served from a rolling cart.

And if you think you are spending a bundle on your meal, consider the tale of the group of eight who flew in two helicopters from New York, landed in Danbury since Stonehenge wouldn't grant landing privileges, hired a limousine to the inn, entered holding their glasses full of Dom Perignon, and ordered three bottles of the $175 wine. It was a birthday party for the manager of a noted rock group, and the bill came to more than $700!

Stonehenge, Route 7 (Danbury-Norwalk Road), Ridgefield. Tel. (203) 438-6511. Stonehenge Road, west side of Route 7, south of Route 35 junction. Reservations recommended. Major credit cards. Luncheon, noon to 2:30 p.m.; dinner, 5:30 to 9 p.m., to 10 p.m. Friday and Saturday. Sunday dinner, noon to 8 p.m. Closed Tuesday.

Also in the Area

Fat Tuesday, 105 Elm St., New Canaan, Conn. (203) 972-0445. Southern comfort is the word in this New Orleans-style restaurant in downtown New Canaan. The tile floors, brick walls, stained glass panels lit from behind and skylight filtering the sun to the thriving hanging plants make a most attractive dining spot. The menu combines French and Italian delights with broiled fish and several veal dishes, and especially good is the shrimp flamed at tableside in apricot brandy and served on saffron rice. Entrees are $4.75 for pasta dishes to $24 for chateaubriand for two. At lunch, hamburgers, omelets, salads and fish are $2.50 to $5.75. At the Sunday brunch, fresh mussels ravigote are $3.25 and eggs Benedict $3.75. Open seven days, lunch, noon to 3 p.m.; dinner 6 to 10 p.m., and Sunday brunch, noon to 5 p.m. Light food is served in the handsome bar from noon to 10 p.m.

The Inn at Ridgefield, 20 West Lane, Route 35, Ridgefield, Conn. (203) 438-8282. This Holiday Award-winning inn has a cozy and friendly feeling (a high proportion of the customers are regulars), a nice piano bar and distinctive French cuisine. There are different specialties every day, game and fish in season like soft-shelled crab. A prix fixe dinner is $15.75, except $17.95 on Saturdays when beef Wellington is featured, but you can order a la carte as well (entrees $8.75 to $26 for rack of lamb for two). Luncheon entrees are $3.75 to $9.75 and Sunday brunch, $6.75. Next door an old white clapboard house has just been renovated into an inn with 14 rooms, available at $65 per night. Lunch, noon to 2:30 p.m.; Sunday brunch, noon to 2:30 p.m. Dinner, 6 to 9:30 p.m., to 10:30 p.m. Friday and Saturday, to 8:30 p.m. Sunday. Closed Monday and Tuesday.

The Elms Inn, 500 Main St., Route 35, Ridgefield, Conn. (203) 438-2541. This charming inn, built in 1760, is said to be the oldest continuously functioning inn in Connecticut (1799). You can eat in either of two delightful dining rooms, with their corner cabinets of rare old china, or in the cozy grill and taproom. Table d'hote dinner is $8 to $15 with a wide selection (eggs Benedict to broiled English lamb chop with kidney and bacon), but you can order a la carte as well. The house pate, a specialty, is packaged to sell. Lunch, noon to 2:30 p.m.; dinner, 6 to 9:30 p.m. weeknights, to 10 p.m. Saturday. Sunday brunch, 12:30 to 2:30 p.m.; dinner 12:30 to 8:30 p.m. Closed Wednesday.

Daytrip 24

A Place to Stop and Think
Hammond Museum/North Salem, N.Y.

When you are seated on one of the small Oriental benches in the gardens and you find your mind wandering from your usual concerns, you will discover for yourself the secret of the Hammond Museum. Its vibrant founder-director Natalie Hays Hammond understood all that, and so she admitted on our first trip to this very personal museum, "we built the gardens first to make friends."

That was back in 1959 and make friends they did, and do, for the Oriental Stroll Gardens of the Hammond are a find. They are 15 or so individual landscapes, each leading naturally and unhurriedly into the next, and arranged to represent points of contemplation in the Eastern mood. They're a world apart — not only from the pace of everyday life, but from the rest of the museum as well.

Only a flagstone courtyard separates the two, it's true, but the philosophical distance is admirably achieved. Once in the gardens, the call of a bird or a bullfrog is the most likely interruption. Even other strollers manage not to intrude, which is just what Miss Hammond had in mind.

While their creator describes the gardens as a "free translation" of those to be found in the Far East, all are based on authentic Eastern symbols and the last of the gardens, the Zen Garden, is said by Miss Hammond to be "authentically correct." She knows because she studied gardens in Japan when she lived there for a while prior to World War II, profoundly affected by the experience. You will note that things Oriental are given a certain prominence at this museum.

But that's not all there is. There's the Guildhall, in which a wide range of exhibitions is regularly mounted. And there's that flagstone courtyard, on which al fresco luncheons are served to satisfy the most discriminating of palates.

It's a lovely mix, reflecting the varied interests of its founder, who is an artist in her own right and who traveled all over the world, partly as a result of being the daughter of a world-famous mining engineer, John Hays Hammond.

When she decided to found her own "museum of the humanities," Miss Hammond and her cousin, Mrs. E.H. Taylor, who lives with her on the grounds and is the museum's associate director, searched the Northeast for the perfect rural setting within access of a large metropolitan area. They found it in the hilltop site in North Salem, tucked into the northernmost corner of Westchester County, and from which on a clear day you can see farmland, lakes and Bear Mountain in the distance.

That's an added attraction of the stroll gardens, for they provide not only their own finite points for contemplation, but the vast expanse of the world around, so that you may, in fact, find yourself looking off into the distance when you're not contemplating the shrubs, rocks or lily-bedecked pond that make up the gardens proper.

Gardeners, nature lovers and those in search of peaceful moments will find the gardens alone worth a visit to this museum. Many people do, and for that reason admission is charged separately to gardens and Guildhall.

With your ticket to the gardens you'll receive a mimeographed sheet describing the more than 100 varieties of shrubs and trees (many of them Western) All are neatly numbered and you'll have no trouble making identifications.

For an added 25 cents you should purchase the green garden booklet, which gives the meanings of the symbols in each garden. They range from the Garden of the Rakan (the sixteen disciples of Buddha who forfeited Nirvana to remain on Earth and uphold the Buddhist law) to the Sundial Garden (where a weathered tree trunk serves as the sundial) to the Katsura Walk from which you can look down on the garden of the "I Ching."

One of the most charming spots is the island of the Bodhisattva in the pond, or "reflecting pool" as it is called, which can be reached by a natural stone bridge. And a favorite of mine is the dry landscape garden, which features a dry waterfall delineated by tiny white alyssum, leading into a dry stream of blue lava stones which wind through a miniature landscape. Rock and moss are placed to suggest the cliffs and damp banks of a natural watercourse.

It can take as little as a half hour or as long as you want to stroll from one garden to the next along neat stone and gravel pathways, but whatever your pace, go in good weather and without toddlers or small children who might disturb the tranquility.

The museum members have taken the gardens so much to heart that they annually hold a "Moon Viewing Party" in August when, to the accompaniment of soft koto and flute music, they sip plum wine and watch the moon rise. It's a 10th century Japanese custom.

After the gardens, the Guildhall may be less impressive (especially on a balmy summer day) but is usually worth a visit. Exhibits change two or three times a season and will influence your enthusiasm. The building itself, given by Joseph Mullen, a former president of the American Institute of Interior Designers, in memory of his wife Joanna, is built in the manner of Georgian — a gray building

Location: Off Route 124 on Deveau Road, just north of the intersection with Route 116, North Salem, N.Y. Drive to the top of the hill.

Open: Wednesday through Sunday from 11 a.m. to 5 p.m., mid-May to late November. Stroll Gardens close end of October.

Admission: Adults $1.50; children $1 (for each, the Stroll Gardens or the Guildhall).

Special Events: "Blessing of the Animals and the Land," an interfaith service annually on the Sunday before the museum opens.

Telephone: (914) 669-5033.

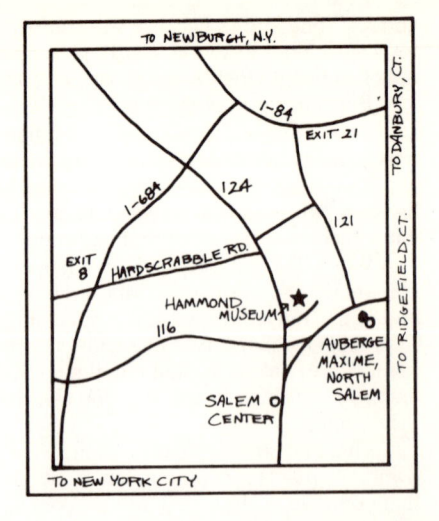

with white columns and a surprising departure from the Oriental mood of the gardens. It contains six galleries and a large main hall, in which luncheon is served in inclement weather, often to the crackling of a roaring fire.

Exhibits since the Guildhall's opening in 1965 have touched a wide spectrum of subjects, reflecting Miss Hammond's equally wide range of interests. Her specialty is an ability to place exhibitions in their context and so, for example, broad topics such as "Faiths" or "Contemporary American Realism" have been chosen and then approached from a number of angles.

Through them all, a strong interest in the Far East, in Great Britain, in drama, painting, photography and needlepoint can be observed. Miss Hammond has established for herself a reputation in the creation of needlepoint designs, and has written a book on the subject. She is rather likely to be found intently working on the latest, in fact, at the museum entrance by the small shop, where she loves to chat with visitors.

Inside the shop you'll find some of the Hammond needlepoint designs, crafts done by area craftsmen, a few Oriental items, attractive note cards, books, etc.

Mrs. Taylor is always on hand, too, and the cleanliness and professional running of the place are no accidents, for both women keep it firmly in control.

Finally, but by no means the least of the pleasures at the Hammond, luncheon is served from noon to 1:30 p.m. (on days the museum is open) on that flagstone courtyard, which is banked with flowers for the occasion and where you will find cozy tables dressed in red cloths. (Everything is moved inside when the weather dictates). I remember a choice of jellied madrilene or cream of tomato soup to start, followed by chicken-filled crepes, delicate and tasty. An unusually good "salad buffet" is a feature, and includes such delights as tomatoes vinaigrette, raw onions in sour cream, tender asparagus spears, potato salad and the like. Dessert is included in the one-price meal, but a cocktail or wine is extra.

Reservations are a must for luncheon, although one day when I visited two stragglers who arrived at 1:45 p.m. without reservations were cheerfully accommodated. On days when there are bus tours (the Hammond mercifully accepts no more than one a day), it is more difficult to do this.

The home in which Miss Hammond and her cousin reside is presently off limits, but plans are to turn it over to the museum eventually as a library.

Also in the Area

John Jay Homestead, Route 22 south of Route 35, Katonah, N.Y. (914) 232-5651. The 1787 farmhouse became the retirement home of the first Chief Justice of the United States. John Jay, also a governor of New York State and the author of the controversial Jay Treaty, retired here in 1801, and four more generations of Jays occupied the home into the 1940s. Jay family heirlooms are displayed throughout. Open free 9 a.m. to 5 p.m. Wednesday through Sunday, year-round.

Caramoor, Center for Music and the Arts, Route 137 near Route 22, Katonah, N.Y. (914) 232-4206. Once the country estate of Walter Tower Rosen, a lawyer and investment banker of New York, and his wife Lucie, the 54-room house is styled like an Italian villa. It is crammed with art treasures from the Middle Ages to the 18th century, including whole rooms or parts of rooms removed from European palaces and villas. Outdoors are formal gardens, intricately carved wrought iron gates and the Venetian Theater, site of the annual summer Music Festival. Some experts say the house has the finest collection of Venetian furniture in the world. Open to the public Wednesdays and Saturdays from 10 a.m. to 4 p.m. from April to November 1; on Tuesdays, Thursdays and Fridays by appointment. Adults $2; children 50 cents. Summer music festival runs weekends, includes Sunday afternoon concerts at 5:30.

Picnicking. Pound Ridge Reservation, Katonah, N.Y., intersection of Routes 35 and 121.

Dining 24

Auberge Maxime/North Salem, N.Y.

When two sophisticated and travelled women like the Hammond Museum's Miss Hammond and Mrs. Taylor dine in a favorite restaurant twice a week or so, one must assume it is worthy of their attention. And when they invite the chef to their museum to cook for a special event, you know it's got to be great!

Auberge Maxime, set in a charming Normandy-style house on Ridgefield Road in North Salem, has been open only since summer 1977, but already is garnering a reputation in this corner of New York State that abounds with fascinating (and expensive) restaurants. Its owner, Maxime Ribera, also has the award-winning Auberge Argenteuil in Hartsdale, N.Y., and is former owner of the famed Cafe Argenteuil on East 52nd Street in Manhattan.

In this small and elegant dining room, we had one of our best meals ever. The classic service, exquisite food and welcoming atmosphere combined for a rare dining experience.

Such pleasures do not come cheaply, and the prix fixe dinner here is $15.95, with a few items costing extra. There are no real bargains on the wine list, either.

Drinks are served in the same balloon-shaped glasses that hold the wine, and are most generous. Of course, every aperitif you ever heard of is available.

The pristine tables gleam with polished silver, crystal, shining brown and white service plates, and candles in hurricane lamps. A few oils of fruits and

151

flowers are hung on the walls, and the back wall is an expanse of mirror, visually enlarging the fairly small room.

Crusty French bread wrapped in a linen napkin and a crock of sweet butter accompany the drinks.

The best salmon I ever had, la Barquette de Saumon Fume, arrived on a light pastry oval, covered with creme fraiche. The exceedingly generous portion of smoked salmon was surrounded by small heaps of capers, finely chopped onion and thinly shredded lettuce, and garnished by a fluted half lemon. It almost seemed a shame to cut into this artful arrangement!

Coquilles St. Jacques featured tiny, tender scallops, cooked to a turn and served in a shell with a marvelous sauce laden with herbs, parsley and garlic.

Other hors d'oeuvres are littlenecks baked with garlic and herbs, puff pastry with spinach, melon and smoked ham, and asparagus or leeks vinaigrette. The smooth house pate, combining several kinds of meats plus chicken, is served with cornichons. Escargots de Bourgogne are $1.75 extra.

Next course is a choice of salad or soup — onion soup or the soup of the day. Ours was an excellent potage julienne, a cream of vegetable with leeks and carrots cut in little strips. The house salad was a simple dish of Bibb lettuce dressed with a fine vinaigrette.

The special entree of the night was baby pheasant, sauteed with onions and mushrooms, rather like a coq au vin. It was brought out in its copper pan for us to survey before being taken back into the kitchen to be disjointed, and was a wonderfully moist and flavorful dish. This was served with Chateau potatoes, sauteed in butter until golden, an unusual and nicely textured puree of broccoli, and fresh watercress.

A house specialty, grenadins de veau au poivre vert, consisted of triangles of white veal, cut from the saddle and cooked with butter, mushrooms, shallots, white wine, heavy cream and green peppercorns. The veal was superb, and the sharpness of the peppercorns nicely balanced the creamy sauce. This was also served with the broccoli, watercress, Chateau potatoes and, unexpectedly, rice pilaf as well. This was a bit of overkill on the part of the chef; it reminded us of Portugal where it is common to get huge portions of rice and potatoes on the same dish.

Nine other entrees grace the handsome cream and brown menu. They include roast chicken in cream sauce with champagne, trout with mousse of salmon plus lobster and champagne sauces, red snapper grilled with fennel, filet mignon with cognac and peppercorns, scallopini of veal with herbs, and duck with bigarade sauce and peaches. For $2 extra you can have rack of lamb with garlic cloves, tournedos with Bearnaise sauce, or lobster with mousse in pastry shell.

We chose one of the least expensive wines for our meal, a 1975 Chateau de LaChaize, Brouilly, for $9, recommended by the captain as light enough for both the pheasant and veal. The most costly wine was Chateau Lafite Rothschild, 1967, for $33.

French pastry, chocolate mousse, peach Melba, sherbet, ice cream or strawberries with cream come with the meal; bombe glacee au pralin is $1 extra and souffle Grand Marnier $2.50 extra (you could spend over $22 for your meal by ordering all the extras — those are New York prices, for sure)!

The strawberries were fabulous, large but full of flavor, served in the delicate wine glasses, doused with a shot of Grand Marnier and a dusting of powdered sugar. This really was Nirvana. We also tried a plate with a sampling of the pastries, including a tarte tatin and the mousse. Everything was perfect. Coffee was served in individual pots and my cafe filtre had its own little drip pot.

It was such a great meal that we hated to leave, so we lingered at the bar for a minute enjoying a cognac and talking to the captain who served us, Christian Milonas, who has what must be the world's most charming French accent. The small bar just inside the entrance was accented by a large and tasteful arrangement of dried flowers by Chef Bernard's wife and light fixtures lined with the same material that is used on the handsome draperies in the dining room — an interesting effect.

The cognac, following such attentive service and unforgettable food, provided the finishing touch to an evening long to remember.

Auberge Maxime, Ridgefield Road, North Salem, N.Y. Tel. (914) 669-5450. At junction of Routes 116 and 121, just west of Connecticut state line. Reservations recommended. Major credit cards. Dinner, 6 to 9:30 p.m. Wednesday and Thursday, to 10:30 p.m. Friday and Saturday, 1 to 9 p.m. Sunday. Closed Monday and Tuesday.

Also in the Area

Le Chateau, Junction of Routes 123 and 35, South Salem, N.Y. (914) 533-2122. Drive through the entrance gate and up the winding, dogwood-lined road to the huge baronial stone mansion built by J. Pierpont Morgan in 1907, with its wonderful view across northern Westchester valley. Now owned by Yves and Denise Lozach, former proprietors of the Coq au Vin in New York City, Le Chateau offers meals that are classic and expensive. Dinner entrees are $7.50 for chicken of the day to $26 for rack of lamb or chateaubriand for two, and include only vegetables. Frogs' legs, veal kidneys, sweetbreads and calves' brains are some of the offerings. At noon, entrees are $5.75 for omelet with herbs to $8.50 for bouillabaisse or shrimps. The pastries here are very nice. It's fun in summer to have cocktails on the lawn, enclosed by gray stone walls. As you would imagine, there's a really good wine list. Lunch, noon to 2 p.m.; dinner, 6 to 9 p.m., to 11 p.m. Saturday, 2 to 9 p.m. Sunday. Closed Monday.

Horse and Hound Inn, Spring Street, South Salem, N.Y. (914) 763-3108. A handsome prancing copper horse graces the door of this old (1749), low-ceilinged inn where the floorboards creak as you walk over them and old hunting prints, riding crops, caps and ribbons are on the walls. Game is the specialty here, with pheasant, wild boar with Cumberland sauce, buffalo steak and jugged hare often available. Dinner is price fixe ($15) and can also include lobster crepes and caviar souffle from the blackboard menu. The dessert souffles are extra but highly recommended. A champagne brunch for $8.95 is served on Sunday from noon to 4. Dinner only, 5 to 10 p.m. seven days a week.

Dreamwold Inn, Gypsy Trail Road, Carmel, N.Y. (Exit 19 off I-84, then off Route 301). (914) 225-3500. A 51-room mansion built by a movie tycoon atop a hill and filled with antiques, Dreamwold serves a $16.50 price fixe dinner (with many items extra and a 20% service charge). The fare is classic French in the three beautiful dining rooms. Duckling is a specialty, and the desserts are talked of near and far! Seven thousand bottles of wine are stored in a cave underneath the mansion. It's very formal, and children are not really welcome; reservations are essential. Dinner only, from 5:30 p.m. Wednesday to Saturday, from 2 p.m. Sunday. Closed in winter.

Daytrip 25

The 'Funnies' Find a Home

Museum of Cartoon Art/Port Chester, N.Y.

If you know who "The Yellow Kid" was, then you're a cartoon freak and there's a place for you.

Not only "The Yellow Kid," but all your other favorites: Felix the Cat, Mandrake the Magician, Blondie, Dennis the Menace, The Little King, Alley Oop, Rex Morgan, Prince Valiant, Beetle Bailey, Archie — you name it, you're sure to find it (including original strips of the "Katzenjammer Kids," in German) at the Museum of Cartoon Art in Port Chester, N.Y.

But of all of them, says curator Chuck Green, "The Yellow Kid" is the most valuable single strip — because it's one of only five in existence and because it was the first color comic strip in America. Richard Outcault created the lovable but undisciplined street urchin for the New York World in 1895, but public outcry (the kid was *too* undisciplined) caused him to change the strip fairly early. The replacement: "Buster Brown" in his shiny shoes and nice little suit, with a moral to every story.

You may not realize how much all of this means to you, but comic strips, a strictly American art form, have woven themselves into the very fabric of life, says the ebullient Curator Green. When you visit the museum and view some of the more than 40,000 original cartoons in its collection you will find yourself reading, remembering, chuckling and probably laughing out loud, as were some visitors the day we stopped in.

That's okay. Laughing out loud is encouraged at this new museum which, because of its age or its focus, or probably both, is exceptionally responsive to its fans. And there are a lot of them: Fully 50,000 made their way to the museum in its first three years from 1974 to 1977, when it was leasing quarters in a mansion in neighboring Greenwich, Connecticut.

But now it's found a home of its own just across the Connecticut state line, in a "castle" which Prince Valiant or even the Wizard of Id might be expected to like. Called "Ward's Castle" or even "Ward's Folly" by the locals, after William E. Ward, the man who had it built in 1876, it is noteworthy by itself as the first residence of reinforced concrete in the world. Ward was an inventor and a manufacturer who became fascinated with the properties of concrete.

You won't have any trouble finding the place, even if the town authorities are still having their running battle with the museum over the placement of a sign outside. You can't miss it, for it sits on a scenic knoll on Comly Avenue, quite a thing apart from the little houses with which the street is lined. The gray structure of three floors, with its five-floor turret, has been designated a National Historic Landmark.

That's all well and good, but it is what's inside that matters to the visitors and from the moment you step through the doors and into the bright museum shop (to pay your admission), expect to have a good time.

You'll get to view all your old favorites, of course, displayed in a large room on the museum's main floor (which has wall-to-wall carpeting in a full-color comic strip print). That's what most people expect to find at the museum, and they're not disappointed. But there are special exhibits as well (a holiday one with cartoon Christmas cards when we visited) and a whole wall of Pulitzer Prize-winning cartoons including works from the pens of greats like Pat Oliphant of the Denver Post and the famous Rube Goldberg, who drew for the New York Sun.

A cartoonists' Hall of Fame occupies a separate gallery and displays works from men considered to be the greatest cartoonists of all time. Hal Foster, creator of "Prince Valiant" is the only living member of this group, which also includes Walt Disney, Walt Kelly (Pogo), Billy DeBeck (Barney Google) and other greats.

Around the walls you can read about the origins of cartoon art, which in some senses go back to the days of cave men. Did you know, for example, that Benjamin Franklin was the first political cartoonist in the country? A reproduction of his cartoon of the snake segments with "Join or Die," drawn to urge unification of the young nation, is on display, as is work by Paul Revere and, of course, the famous Thomas Nast.

All of this may sound pretty static, but the museum makes up for that with active auditorium programs where you can see regular showings of — what else? — cartoons. A wide selection is available on request of the visitor — just ask, they'll show it — from "Steamboat Willie," the first sound-synchronized cartoon, to a great variety of others. Among the offerings: "Classic Warner Brothers cartoons," "Porky Pig cartoon," the "Rites of Spring" section of Walt Disney's "Fantasia," a group of cartoons made for television commercials, a selection of Walter Lantz and Walt Disney cartoons and more. Sometimes the cartoons are just run continuously, and then you can wander in and out at will. There's no extra charge; it's included in the price of admission.

Location: Comly Avenue, Town of Rye, Port Chester, N.Y. King Street Exit from Hutchinson River (Merritt) Parkway (Route 15). South on King Street to Comly Avenue. East on Comly Avenue to Ward's Castle.

Open: Year-round, 10 a.m. to 4 p.m. Tuesday through Friday and 1 to 5 p.m. Sunday. Closed Saturday, Monday and holidays.

Admission: Adults $1; children and senior citizens, 50 cents.

Special Events: Visiting cartoonist-lectures held first Sunday of the month. Free with admission to museum.

Telephone: (914) 939-0234.

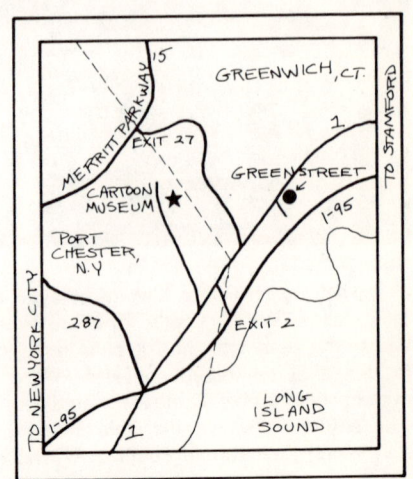

Another special feature of the museum is lectures by visiting cartoonists on the first Sunday of the month. Burne Hogarth, creator of "Tarzan," was due the Sunday after we visited. These lectures are also free to museum visitors, first come, first seated in the 200-person auditorium.

Maybe the reason the museum is so lively and so involved in its work is because the president is Mort Walker, creator of the "Beetle Bailey" strip among others, and the director is Jack Tippit, who does the cartoon panel "Amy." Both past presidents of the National Cartoon Society, they and a few other cartoonists struggled for more than 10 years to make their dream come true, a museum for the cartoon, "whose time has come," says Tippit.

From the response to the Museum of Cartoon Art, the founders did not make a mistake.

After you've wandered around the bright and inviting interior, you will want to spend a few moments in the museum shop, where sale items are strictly in keeping with the museum's focus. For sale are original cartoon strips, the Hyperion Library editions of classic comic strips, paperbacks of cartoons and the like.

The museum publishes a magazine, "Inklings," which keeps patrons up to date on the cartoon world; copies are also for sale.

Picnic tables are set up outside in nice weather so you can tote along your lunch and make a day of it. If you don't, you'll probably want to drive into nearby Greenwich, where there's a whole spectrum of restaurants from which to choose.

Also in the Area

U.S. Tobacco Museum, 100 West Putnam Ave., Greenwich, Conn. (203) 661-1100. This is another new museum, located in an attractive small colonial house on the grounds of U.S. Tobacco's corporate headquarters in the center of Greenwich. The museum is dedicated to collecting, preserving and displaying pipes, tools, packaging, art and advertising that relates to tobacco and it's quite well done. You may be amazed at the Meerschaum pipes, porcelain pipes, Oriental and African pipes on display here. Open daily noon to 5 p.m. except Mondays and holidays. Free.

Dining 25

Greenstreet/Greenwich, Conn.

Snazzy green and white awnings and handsome carriage lanterns set off the white brick facade of Greenstreet, a relatively new restaurant on the Greenwich dining circuit. Near the base of Greenwich Avenue, the town's main shopping street, it's in the 60-year-old former Putnam Bank and Trust Co. building and was, for more than 20 years, the well-known Town House.

Greenstreet is one of the more spectacular restaurants around. The breathtaking interior space and the good — if not as spectacular — food make it well worth a visit.

An old church pew serves as a resting place just inside the front entrance (you can wait and pray at the same time!) and a fine solid mahogany bar with old-fashioned black and white tiles is to the right. A few more steps bring you up the wide, polished oak stairs to the main restaurant, where the recently steam-cleaned, honey-colored brick Romanesque arched and vaulted ceiling soars two stories overhead. Wide oak staircases lined with gleaming brass rails lead up to dining balconies on two sides. The brass is echoed in handsome modern light fixtures with large clear globes. The feeling is light, airy and open, and everywhere there are plants, even a 25-foot-high ficus tree.

Brick pillars reach up to the ceiling, and a pleasing green and white color scheme is obtained with white cloths, green napkins and green carpeting. The walls are brick, painted a hunter green, and fresh flowers bloom on most tables. Chairs are bentwood and cane, and on the walls are hung wonderful antique mirrors, some from Ireland, and bits of old statues.

Altogether a most eclectic feeling pervades the place. On our December visit, red was added to the scheme with magnificent Christmas decorations: Greens draped from one pillar to the next with tiny white lights, banks of poinsettias and trees made of greens on the pillars, studded with tiny foil-wrapped packages.

The clientele is eclectic, too: Tables of cigar-smoking $350-suited New York-type executives, giggling young women home from college and groups of shopping mothers, daughters, and sometimes even grandmothers.

At lunchtime the Bloody Marys are popular, containing a spicy mixture served in huge goblets with a celery stalk stirrer. The house wine is Almaden, and a generous glass of fine chablis is $1.25.

The large luncheon menu offers an extensive choice of appetizers, salads, omelets, soups and cold, hot and club sandwiches. As well, there are luncheon entrees ranging from $2.95 for fish and chips to $5.95 for sirloin steak sandwich or beef brochette.

After being served piping hot rye, pumpernickel and onion rolls in a basket, we started with quiche Lorraine, a nice light quiche with ham and a flaky crust.

Fried Holland (Edam) cheese and parsley was a very interesting though rather heavy dish, but the deep-fried parsley was a welcome taste surprise, simply melting in the mouth. Both appetizers were $1.95 and really could have made a meal.

The spinach, mushroom and bacon salad ($3.75) was served in a gigantic wooden bowl, with generous amounts of sliced fresh mushrooms and bacon, not in bits but in breakfast-sized pieces. The spinach leaves, we felt, had not been sufficiently shredded. The unusual herb dressing, which included bouillion, was a fine complement to the salad.

Steak tartare also comes in a wooden bowl — a more than generous serving of finely ground sirloin. You can mix it yourself with egg yolk, onions and capers, or have it done in the kitchen. Topped with anchovies and served with toasted rye bread, it is a super dish. The salad with it is mostly iceberg, but studded with cherry tomatoes and a zesty creamy Italian dressing.

Other popular appetizers here are French fried zucchini, $1.50; avocado vinaigrette or a la Russe, $1.75, and baked clams or breaded artichoke hearts with garlic butter, $1.95. The chef's salad is $3.95; chicken salad, $3.75, and tuna salad, $3.50. Omelets run from $2.75 for cheese to $3.50 for white asparagus with Hollandaise sauce or the Greenstreet, bacon, tomato and Swiss cheese, and there's a special omelet every day (Italian, on our visit).

Gazpacho and chili are $1.50, cold sandwiches mostly $2.50, and hot sandwiches $2.50 to $3.50. You can have broiled filet of sole or a fantastic looking eggs Benedict for $4.50 on this menu with something for everyone.

A large choice is available at night as well, with 27 entrees from $3.50 for hamburger to $10.95 for sirloin Greenstreet. Many are in the $6.95 to $7.95 range and are served with salad and potato or rice.

The wine list is extensive and expensive with many vintage wines and nothing much under $8.

You also can choose from seventeen appetizers, including most of those at lunch, with such additions as escargots stuffed in mushrooms, $2.95. Crab fingers with mustard sauce are $3.95.

Desserts are fairly straightforward, 75 cents to $1.50. We hear the frozen lemon mousse and carrot cake are standouts, but we really didn't have room left to try. We enjoyed Greenstreet's good coffee as we watched the bustle of Greenwich Avenue from our cozy table on the balcony.

Greenstreet, 253 Greenwich Ave., Greenwich, Conn. Tel. (203) 661-4459. Foot of Greenwich Avenue in downtown Greenwich. No reservations. Major credit cards. Luncheon, 11:30 a.m. to 4 p.m. Monday to Friday; noon to 4 p.m. Saturday. Sunday brunch, noon to 4 p.m. Dinner, 6 to 11 p.m. Monday to Thursday; to midnight Friday and Saturday, 5 to 10 p.m. Sunday.

Also in the Area

Jonathan's Other Brother, 34 East Putnam Ave. (Post Road), Greenwich, Conn. (203) 661-3491. Jonathan's has a blackboard menu, a fun and casual atmosphere, barn siding on the walls, Tiffany lamps and about a million books crammed into shelves and bookcases all over the restaurant. At noon the fare runs to burgers, sandwiches and salads (you can go through the salad bar for $2.25, if you make it your whole lunch, or for $1 with lunch) and the soup bar (75 cents) always has chili and two other soups. Entrees are $2.10 to $4.50. At night, ribs or beef, steak and seafood are featured, $5.75 to $16. Lunch, 11:30 a.m. to 2:30

p.m. Monday to Saturday, Sunday brunch, noon to 3 p.m.; dinner, 5:30 to 10 p.m., to 11 p.m. Friday and Saturday; 5 to 9 p.m. Sunday.

Lewis St. Chowder House, 61 Lewis St., Greenwich, Conn. (203) 622-9827. Despite its downtown Greenwich location, this has the flavor of Nova Scotia or Nantucket about it. Of course, there's chowder: New England clam, Manhattan clam and fish. A cup is 75 cents, bowl $1.25 and meal size $2.50. Mussels, done two ways, are $2.50 a bowl and $4.50 a meal. Fresh fish dishes depend on local catches, including bluefish, swordfish and scallops. Desserts, all homemade, include carrot cake and chocolate chip torte, plus fresh fruit in season. Prices in the $2 to $5.95 range and menus are the same at lunch and dinner, except for the addition of a few sandwiches at lunch (huge ones for $1.75). There's a good selection of white wines to go with the seafood dishes. Children are welcome here. No reservations and no credit cards. Lunch, 11:30 a.m. to 2:30 p.m. weekdays; noon to 3 p.m. Saturday; dinner, 5:30 to 9:30 p.m. Monday to Thursday, to 10 p.m. Friday and Saturday, 5 to 9:30 p.m. Sunday.

Gipfel's, 66 Purchase St., Rye, N.Y. (914) 967-3540. A Swiss restaurant in downtown Rye, Gipfel's has an Alpine flair and a rustic decor, with lots of copper pots on the walls and red and blue checked tablecloths. The menu is Swiss plus international, and there are specials like pot au feu, beef roulade and stuffed veal chops. At lunch, a la carte and table d'hote meals are $3.50 to $4.95, with different quiches, veal bratwurst and chicken breast among favorites. Sauerbraten, veal cordon bleu and emince de veau are popular at dinner, when entrees are $4.25 to $8.75 and daily specials include soup or salad and dessert (Black Forest cake and apple strudel are the most asked for). Cheese fondue and a dessert chocolate fondue ($4.25 for two) are also popular. Four Swiss wines are among the offerings. Lunch, noon to 2:30 p.m. Monday to Friday; dinner, 5:30 to 9:30 p.m. Sunday to Thursday, to 10:30 p.m. Friday and Saturday.

Index

Abbott's Lobster in the Rough 94
Noank, Conn.

The Aetna Restaurant 116
Hartford, Conn.

Aldrich Museum of Contemporary Art 142
Ridgefield, Conn.

Alice's at Avaloch 4
Lenox, Mass.

American Indian Archaeological Institute 136
Washington, Conn.

Anthony's Cummaquid Inn 69
Yarmouthport, Mass.

Anthony's Pier 4 55
Boston, Mass.

Arboretum 75
East Providence, R.I.

Arrowhead 1
Pittsfield, Mass.

Auberge Maxime 151
North Salem, N.Y.

Barnaby's 135
Bridgeport, Conn.

Barnum Museum 130
Bridgeport, Conn.

Bartholomew's Cobble 8
Ashley Falls, Mass.

Beardsley Zoological Gardens 133
Bridgeport, Conn.

Beardsley's 20
Northampton, Mass.

Beauport 47
Gloucester, Mass.

Berkshire Athenaeum 4
Pittsfield, Mass.

The Black Pearl 79
Newport, R.I.

Blantyre Castle 7
Lenox, Mass.

Blessings 129
New Haven, Conn.

Block Island, R.I. 82

Blue Hills Reservation 59
Milton, Mass.

British Art Institute 127
New Haven, Conn.

Bull Run and Sawtelle House 43
North Shirley, Mass.

Burnham's 1742 Manor 37
Ashland, Mass.

Bushnell Park Carrousel 113
Hartford, Conn.

Cafe Budapest 53
Boston, Mass.

Cafe in the Barn 87
Seekonk, Mass.

Cafe L'Orange 43
Concord, Mass.

Cape Ann, Mass. 44

Cape Cod, Mass. 63

Cap'n Nick's 122
East Haven, Conn.

Caprilands 105
Coventry, Conn.

Caramoor 151
Katonah, N.Y.

Chester-Hadlyme Ferry 97
Chester and Hadlyme, Conn.

Chez Claude 41
Acton, Mass.

Chez Serge 116
Avon, Conn.

The Clarke Cooke House 81
Newport, R.I.

Copper Beech Inn 98
Ivoryton, Conn.

Cumbie's 106
South Woodstock, Conn.

Curious Jane's 129
New Haven, Conn.

Custy's 85
North Kingstown, R.I.

Daniel Webster Inn 69
Sandwich, Mass.

161

David's Pot Belly 75
Providence, R.I.
Deerfield Inn 18
Deerfield, Mass.
Deerfield, Mass. 14
Dock n' Dine 123
Old Saybrook, Conn.
Dreamwold Inn 153
Carmel, N.Y.
Eddie Donovan's 49
Rockport, Mass.
El Morocco 32
Worcester, Mass.
Elizabeth Park 113
Hartford, Conn.
Eli's 69
East Sandwich, Mass.
The Elms Inn 147
Ridgefield, Conn.
The Every Day Gourmet 37
Natick, Mass.
Faneuil Hall Marketplace 62
Boston, Mass.
Fat Tuesday 147
New Canaan, Conn.
Fruitlands Museums 38
Harvard, Mass.
Garden in the Woods 33
Framingham, Mass.
Gardner Museum 50
Boston, Mass.
The Gazebo 135
Bridgeport, Conn.
Gelston House 100
East Haddam, Conn.
General Lyon Inn 108
Eastford, Conn.
Gillette Castle 95
Hadlyme, Conn.
Gipfel's 160
Rye, N.Y.
Gloucester, Mass. 44
The Golden Bough 141
Warren, Conn.
The Golden Lamb Buttery 107
Brooklyn, Conn.
Goodspeed Opera House 97
East Haddam, Conn.
Goten of Japan 20
Sunderland, Mass.

Gourmet East 7
Williamstown, Mass.
Green Animals 76
Portsmouth, R.I.
Greenstreet 157
Greenwich, Conn.
The Griswold Inn 101
Essex, Conn.
The Gull 101
Essex, Conn.
Gunn Historical Museum 139
Washington, Conn.
Hahjee's Place 20
Hadley, Mass.
Hammond Castle 47
Gloucester, Mass.
Hammond Museum 148
North Salem, N.Y.
Hancock Shaker Village 4
Hancock, Mass.
Harborview 92
Stonington, Conn.
Heritage Plantation of Sandwich 67
Sandwich, Mass.
The Hermitage 55
Boston, Mass.
Higgins Armory 27
Worcester, Mass.
Hill-Stead Museum 113
Farmington, Conn.
Hopkins Inn 139
New Preston, Conn.
Horse and Hound Inn 153
South Salem, N.Y.
The Inn at Castle Hill 81
Newport, R.I.
The Inn at Ridgefield 147
Ridgefield, Conn.
Institute of Contemporary Art 53
Boston, Mass.
J. Perspico Factor 7
Lenox, Mass.
Jack August's House of Seafoods 20
Northampton, Mass.
John Jay Homestead 151
Katonah, N.Y.
Jonathan's Other Brother 159
Greenwich, Conn.
Joyce Chen 60
Cambridge, Mass.

162

Jury's Tavern   26
South Willington, Conn.
Keeler Tavern   144
Ridgefield, Conn.
Kendall Whaling Museum   59
Sharon, Mass.
La Cipollina   67
Yarmouthport, Mass.
La Cocina   7
Pittsfield, Mass.
La Petite Auberge   81
Newport, R.I.
Laughing Brook   21
Hampden, Mass.
Le Bon Coin   141
Woodville, Conn.
Le Chateau   153
South Salem, N.Y.
The Left Bank   75
Providence, R.I.
Lewis St. Chowder House   160
Greenwich, Conn.
Litchfield, Conn.   138
Little Stone House   121
Guilford, Conn.
The Log Cabin   26
Holyoke, Mass.
Longfellow's Wayside Inn   35
Sudbury, Mass.
Mark Twain Memorial   109
Hartford, Conn.
Meetinghouse Inn   140
Litchfield, Conn.
Memorial Hall   17
Deerfield, Mass.
The Merciful Lion   87
West Kingston, R.I.
The Mileaway   43
Milford, N.H.
Milton Hill Restaurant   62
Milton, Mass.
The Modern Gourmet   55
Newton Center, Mass.
Museum of Art, Science and Industry   133
Bridgeport, Conn.
Museum of Cartoon Art   154
Port Chester, N.Y.

Museum of Fine Arts   53
Boston, Mass.
Museum of the American China Trade   56
Milton, Mass.
Mystic Marine Life Aquarium   91
Mystic, Conn.
Mystic Seaport   88
Mystic, Conn.
Naumkeag   11
Stockbridge, Mass.
New England Center for Contemporary Art   105
Brooklyn, Conn.
Newport, R.I.   78
Norcross Wildlife Sanctuary   24
Wales, Mass.
Northfield Mountain Recreation Area   18
Northfield, Mass.
Ocean Sea Grill   134
Bridgeport, Conn.
Old Farm Inn   48
Rockport, Mass.
Old Lighthouse Museum   91
Stonington, Conn.
Old Lyme Inn   100
Old Lyme, Conn.
Old Putt Tavern   108
Brooklyn, Conn.
Old State House   113
Hartford, Conn.
Old Yarmouth Inn   69
Yarmouthport, Mass.
Orchard House   41
Concord, Mass.
Paper House   47
Rockport, Mass.
Picot's Place   26
Hampden, Mass.
The Pier   81
Newport, R.I.
The Pillar House   37
Newton Lower Falls, Mass.
Pippins   129
Hamden, Conn.
Pjura's   135
Bridgeport, Conn.

163

Poor Lads 127
New Haven, Conn.
Poor Richard's 94
Waterford, Conn.
Prescott Farm 78
Middletown, R.I.
The Promenade 115
Hartford, Conn.
The Publick House 32
Sturbridge, Mass.
The Puppet Theatre 120
Stony Creek, Conn.
Putnam and Thurston 32
Worcester, Mass.
Putnam Memorial State Park 144
Redding, Conn.
Ralph Waldo Emerson Memorial House 41
Concord, Mass.
The Reading Room 116
Farmington, Conn.
Ridgefield, Conn. 144
RISDE Museum of Art 73
Providence, R.I.
Rockport, Mass. 44
Roger Williams Park 73
Providence, R.I.
Roseland Cottage 102
Woodstock, Conn.
Roseland Park 105
Woodstock, Conn.
The Rudder 49
Gloucester, Mass.
Rue de l'Espoir 73
Providence, R.I.
Salem Cross Inn 24
West Brookfield, Mass.
Sandwich, Mass. 67
Sandy Bay Historical Society 47
Rockport, Mass.
Sandy's 94
Stonington, Conn.
Signature 113
Hartford, Conn.
1661 House 86
Block Island, R.I.
Slater Mill 70
Pawtucket, R.I.

Soups and Crepes Unltd. 81
Newport, R.I.
Stagecoach Hill Inn 11
Sheffield, Mass.
Stonehenge 144
Ridgefield, Conn.
Stonington, Conn. 91
Stony Brook Wildlife Sanctuary 35
Norfolk, Mass.
Sun-Inside Inn 13
Monterey, Mass.
Tanglewood 4
Lenox, Mass.
Tapping Reeve House & Law School 138
Litchfield, Conn.
Thimble Islands 117
Stony Creek, Conn.
Today's 141
Washington Depot, Conn.
Top of the Dock 123
Clinton, Conn.
Trailside Museum 59
Milton, Mass.
Under Mountain Inn 13
Salisbury, Conn.
U.S. Tobacco Museum 157
Greenwich, Conn.
The Victorian 30
Whitinsville, Mass.
Wadsworth Atheneum 113
Hartford, Conn.
Westwoods Trail System 120
Guilford, Conn.
Wheatleigh 7
Lenox, Mass.
Wheatsheaf 26
Wilbraham, Mass.
White Flower Farm 138
Morris, Conn.
White Hart Inn 13
Salisbury, Conn.
Whitfield House Museum 120
Guilford, Conn.
Whitlock Farm 124
Bethany, Conn.
Wolf Den State Park 105
Pomfret, Conn.

164

Woodman's 49
Essex, Mass.

Worcester Art Museum 30
Worcester, Mass.

Worcester Science Center 30
Worcester, Mass.

Yale Barn 13
East Canaan, Conn.

Yale University Art Gallery 127
New Haven, Conn.

Yale University Walking Tours 126
New Haven, Conn.

Yesteryears Museum 63
Sandwich, Mass.

About the Authors

Betsy Wittemann, a former daily newspaper reporter, writes regular features for the *West Hartford* (Conn.) *News*. This book is an outgrowth of her "Day Away" column featuring unusual or special places to visit within a day's time. A native of Bridgeport, Conn., the author has lived in Athens, Greece, and San Juan, Puerto Rico, and now resides with her husband and two children in Glastonbury, Conn. An intrepid traveler, she prefers places which offer a new perspective on life and living. Her travel articles have appeared in newspapers in the Northeast, including the *Boston Globe* and the *Christian Science Monitor*.

Nancy Webster started her gourmet dining experiences in her native Montreal and as a student waitress at summer resorts across Canada. Now married to an American newspaper editor, she resides with her husband and two sons in West Hartford, Conn., where she has written her "Roaming the Restaurants" column for six years for the *West Hartford News*. She has lived in London, England, and has travelled extensively in Europe and in this country, collecting memorable dining experiences as well as interesting cookbooks along the way. In this book she describes many of her favorite dining spots in Southern New England.